Praise for *America's New Map*

"*America's New Map* offers a dazzling collection of ideas and arguments united by compelling storytelling and Barnett's thoughtful approach to the impact of past upon future. The book is nutrient-rich and a pleasure to read."

—Ian Bremmer, founder and president of Eurasia Group

"Looking at the great currents shaping our world, Barnett provides unique insights. At once wise and provocative, *America's New Map* forces us to open our eyes and think."

—Honorable William "Mac" Thornberry, former Chair
of the House Armed Services Committee

"Barnett is a strategic thinker who sees around corners. Here he draws on his inter-disciplinary strengths to paint a convincing picture of the world to come—and how America remains a pivotal superpower."

—Dr. Parag Khanna, author of *Connectography* and *MOVE*

"Barnett has done it again. *America's New Map* is a creative and thought-provoking exploration of a world in accelerating transition—but with a clear strategic vision. Like a graphic novel for futurists, it will make you think of things you hadn't thought about before."

—Allison Stanger, Leng Professor of International
Politics and Economics at Middlebury College

"*America's New Map* is a remarkable piece of work—an inspirational and grounded manifesto for the next American Century. In simple but powerful language, every chapter overflows with provocative ideas for dealing with globalization's successes and failures. Barnett describes the pathways to a future where our nation can both heal and prosper."

—Chris Bellavita, academic programs director of the
Center for Homeland Defense and Security

"Barnett's analysis of our geopolitical present and future is startling, innovative, and persuasive. As always, he presents much that is commonly unknown and rearranges 'well known' things into patterns no other writer can create. Students of history and strategy will find a depth of thinking and understanding that provides insight and motivates brainstorming. Regardless of the reader's prior experience, I recommend *America's New Map* as a rare, fantastic blend of history, strategy, and creativity in one cogent work."

—Carmi Zlotnik, president of television at Legendary Entertainment

"A brilliant, highly readable, and timely guide to what makes America great. Barnett presents a compelling path to healing our nation with a challenge bigger than ourselves. The best way to predict the future is to create it, and *America's New Map* does both."

—Bruce McIndoe, founder and CEO of McIndoe Risk Advisory

"*America's New Map* is another tour de force by Barnett. This wide-ranging and provocative book analyzes the myriad challenges facing the US with breathtaking originality and insight. His strategic prescriptions are brilliantly pragmatic and promising. As the world enters an uncertain era of technological revolution and geopolitical rivalry, we should all read this book for guidance and hope."

—Minxin Pei, professor at Claremont McKenna College and opinion columnist for Bloomberg

"*America's New Map* is an essential book for our world's young leaders. Barnett offers fresh and provocative course-changes for America so it might steer the 21st century toward prosperity and peace."

—Jerry MacArthur Hultin, chair of New York Academy of Sciences and former under secretary of the Navy

"In boldly arguing for North-South integration, *America's New Map* upends decades of conventional thinking on West-vs-East power struggles. Barnett makes a compelling case for how America can prevail against rising great-power autocracies in a world experiencing rapid climate change. This fascinating book deserves a lot of attention from across the political spectrum."

—Laurence C. Smith, professor at Brown University and author of *The World in 2050*

"Once again, Barnett incisively maps the world we thought we knew. At a time when so much of what passes for strategic analysis offers little more than elaborate stylings on coarse conventional wisdoms, *America's New Map* stands apart. A wholly original diagnosis of globalization, an unsparing prognosis of where we're headed, and a challenging prescription for a new American grand strategy worthy of its superpower brand. The book follows the logic of its analyses to some iconoclastic places, but from them Barnett reveals a hopeful perspective on the seemingly intractable problems of the 21st century. No one understands the tectonics of global affairs better than Barnett."

—Steven Grundman, program manager of National Security Studies at Syracuse University

"*America's New Map* offers the first coherent, post–Cold War US grand strategy for the global commons. Barnett masterfully knits together themes that appear disparate but are in fact inexorably interconnected. This book compels younger Americans to imagine a world worth creating."

—Capt. Rich Suttie, USN (ret.) and former assistant dean at the U.S. Naval War College

"Barnett dissects history like very few analysts can. In a world rapidly reaching a painful turning point, his responsible analysis paves the way for intelligent solutions. *America's New Map* should be obligatory reading for any US policymaker."
—Gennaro Buonocore, chair of Maitland Primrose Group and US Navy Reserve foreign area officer

"A geostrategic cartographer of uncommon skill, Barnett eviscerates conventional wisdom on globalization's past, present, and future. *America's New Map* is a roadmap all Americans would be smart to follow."
—Mark Thompson, national security analyst for the Project on Government Oversight

"Dr. Barnett's geopolitical analysis is always spot-on and drives tremendous clarity in strategic thinking. As a corporate strategic planner in the commercial vehicle industry, I regularly refer to Barnett's publications. His ability to blend panoramic views of history and the future—coupled with granular insights rooted in economic, social, and geographical realities—makes his geopolitical prognostications highly effective and useful. I recommend *America's New Map* to anyone who cares about humanity and our planet."
—Sandeep Kar, chief strategy officer at Noregon Systems

"Barnett clearly lays out the interwoven threads of globalization's DNA across provocative essays that culminate in a decidedly hopeful view of our shared future. *America's New Map* details our Union's vital—yet evolving—leadership role in driving peace, prosperity, and stability in an era of heightened superpower competition. This is a must-read for anyone seeking to realistically address climate change's unfolding."
—Stephen F. DeAngelis, president and CEO of Enterra Solutions, LLC and Massive Dynamics, LLC

"A remarkable feat of clear, easy-to-read writing and striking imagery that spans the globe. Barnett illuminates a North-South pathway to a bright future for America within globalization. Forward-thinking policymakers and business leaders will relish this book, as it showcases how America can lead in the decades ahead."
—Daniel P. Forrester, founder of THRUUE, Inc. and author of *Consider*

"There is no more important book you can read to understand how America should confront climate change amidst great-power competition. Far from doom and gloom, Barnett's grand strategy plots a more prosperous future for America and the world."
—Mark Sharpe, president of Hogback Ventures, Inc.

"*America's New Map* offers a new set of tools for visualizing the challenges US policymakers face over the next several decades. Rising above the fray of today's culture wars, Barnett alerts us to the long-term challenges to US global leadership."
—Robert Farley, senior lecturer at the Patterson School of Diplomacy and International Commerce at University of Kentucky

"Barnett analyzes the throughlines of an inevitable future already bearing down on us. This lucid and nuanced book empowers Americans to craft their own desired storylines for this century. Every US policymaker should be paying attention to *America's New Map*."

—Daveed Gartenstein-Ross, founder and CEO of Valens Global and author of *Enemies Near and Far*

"Barnett's ability to provide critical insight into America's pacing security threats, as affected by demographics, climate change, political polarization, and more is superb. No one ties these threads together better than him."

—Brigadier General Mark Kalin, land component commander of the Massachusetts Army National Guard

"Building on *Pentagon's New Map* and its sequels, Barnett greatly expands our understanding of global dynamics in *America's New Map*. His clarion call for EU-style integration of the Americas in the face of five-headed superpower competition and climate-fueled migration pulls America out of its nostalgic doldrums and into a future it deserves. Barnett convincingly urges America to burnish its brand and manifest its destiny."

—Jeffrey Itell, former senior analyst for Special Inspector General for Afghanistan Reconstruction

"As a worldwide operator in the security space, Dr. Barnett's concepts are highly relatable to my everyday experience. Far more than an academic discussion, *America's New Map* packs a realism and practicality that security practitioners in the field will immediately recognize and put to good use."

—Scott Massey, organizational operations executive

AMERICA'S
NEW MAP

Also by Thomas P.M. Barnett

Romanian and East German Policies in the Third World:
Comparing the Policies of Ceausescu and Honecker

The Pentagon's New Map:
War and Peace in the Twenty-First Century

Blueprint for Action:
A Future Worth Creating

Great Powers:
America and the World After Bush

AMERICA'S NEW MAP

Restoring Our Global Leadership in an Era of Climate Change and Demographic Collapse

THOMAS P.M. BARNETT

Foreword by Scott Williams

Illustrations by Jim Nuttle with Sara Nuttle

Data Visualizations by Juraj Mihalik and Tom Zorc

BenBella Books, Inc.
Dallas, TX

BenBella Books, Inc.
10440 N. Central Expressway
Suite 800
Dallas, TX 75231
benbellabooks.com
Send feedback to feedback@benbellabooks.com

BenBella is a federally registered trademark.

Printed in the United States of America
10 9 8 7 6 5 4 3 2 1

Library of Congress Control Number: 2023004597
ISBN 9781637744291 (hardcover)
ISBN 9781637744307 (electronic)

Editing by Glenn Yeffeth and Rachel Phares
Copyediting by Judy Gelman Myers
Proofreading by Lisa Story and Michael Fedison
Indexing by Amy Murphy
Text design and composition by PerfecType, Nashville, TN
Illustrations and data visualizations © Throughline Inc.
Cover design by Julia Tylor
Cover image © iStock / -slav-
Printed by Lake Book Manufacturing

TO MOM

THE CLOSEST I WILL EVER COME TO KNOWING GOD

Lord, make me an instrument of your peace:
where there is hatred, let me sow love;
where there is injury, pardon;
where there is doubt, faith;
where there is despair, hope;
where there is darkness, light;
where there is sadness, joy.

O divine Master, grant that I may not so much seek
to be consoled as to console,
to be understood as to understand,
to be loved as to love.
For it is in giving that we receive,
it is in pardoning that we are pardoned,
and it is in dying that we are born to eternal life.
Amen.

—Prayer of Saint Francis

CONTENTS

THROUGHLINE SEVEN

The Americanist Manifesto: Summoning the Vision and Courage to Remap Our Hemisphere's Indivisible Future   **279**

CODA

An Americas-First Grand Strategy: Crowdsourcing the Right Story, Choosing the Right Paths   305

FOREWORD

When the US Navy sent me to a seminar at the University of Virginia's Darden School twenty-three years ago, I had no idea how it would change my life. Three Toms spoke in succession: *New York Times* columnist Thomas Friedman; business author Tom Peters; and Thomas P.M. Barnett, a military geostrategist who was teaching at Naval War College. Friedman and Peters provoked us, of course, to see the world in new ways. But Barnett challenged us to rethink the rule sets defining America's national security. Using a form of sophisticated visual storytelling that I hadn't seen before, his material pushed us to recognize America's role within the world in a whole new way. Like many others in the US defense establishment, I began closely following Barnett's work.

Then 9/11 occurred. Life and operations at NAVAIR (Naval Air Systems Command), where I worked, shifted into a new paradigm. Thomas was immediately reassigned to the Pentagon's Office of Force Transformation—a special strategy unit created by Secretary Donald Rumsfeld within the Office of the Secretary of Defense. Like the Pentagon, everyone at NAVAIR was trying to make sense of our new reality and our VUCA (as in, volatile, uncertain, chaotic, and ambiguous) world. Thomas's thinking and framework—summarized in his well-circulated brief, a viral *Esquire* article called "The Pentagon's New Map," and later in a book with the same title—served as klieg lights for reframing the global landscape of conflict. It inspired me and many of my Navy teammates to realize that the new frameworks we sought for transforming US national security were within our reach—if we were willing to embrace this new mindset and where it took us.

Fast-forward a few years: I left the Navy and started a Washington, DC–based company, Throughline, dedicated to (a) visualizing leaders' strategies as they navigate complex realities, and (b) empowering them with innovative and efficient tools to spread their vision. Over the years, our firm has proven just how powerful a good map can be in propagating new thinking, obtaining new funding, and then seeding these new ideas and approaches throughout an enterprise as rapidly as possible. We also believe in the power of brands and have brought brand strategy to many nontraditional organizations. Thomas has long been a voice for reflecting on brand USA and the offer it represents across our world, exploring the kinds of affiliations our Union expertly sustains and those it has trouble accessing. In many ways, it was only natural that Throughline eventually linked up with Thomas: what we've been doing for organizations over the years, Thomas has continued to do for decision makers the world over.

Humanity needs a new vision if we are to survive the looming catastrophes generated by climate change and demographic collapse. Leaders everywhere must peer into our ambiguous-but-collective future, assess the broader landscape, and determine a way forward—with firm intention. Even so, choosing a path isn't nearly enough. Leaders can't actualize vision on their own; they must enlist others into understanding their worldview and feeling the same inspiration for action.

To me and my colleagues, a *throughline* is the core, believable, fundamental truth running through an organization and its efforts—essentially the narrative it writes for itself. A good throughline moves people from intent to impact, with authentic momentum. It inspires creativity, creates agency, and raises the spirit of the entire enterprise.

What spoke to me post-9/11 was Thomas's ability to look beyond the military—to financial predictors, environmental stressors, demographics transitions, technology shifts—to predict where future conflicts would arise or wane. His unique form of executive education stuck with me from that moment on, causing me to reach out to him during America's recent withdrawal from Afghanistan. He's just someone to whom I naturally turn when seeking to make sense out of our VUCA-infused era.

That's why Throughline is so proud to have partnered with Thomas in visualizing his ideas and bringing this innovative book to fruition. Our aim here is to present a series of geopolitical throughlines that will fuel the intentions of current and future leaders, motivating them to genuinely constructive action on the part of our nation and our species. Our world's current challenges demand new approaches, courageous ideas, and bold leaders. In this book, we hope you find a throughline or two that resonate with you. If they do, let us offer—in advance—our gratitude for your work in applying them to these collective tasks.

Suffice it to say, we're excited to join the conversations that ensue and stand ready to support the agendas they generate.

—Scott Williams, founder of Throughline, Inc.

PREFACE

Globalization's Throughlines:
Restoring US Global Leadership in a Turbulent Era

I could say that America is at a turning point, but that would disguise a darker truth—namely, that we are at a turning-back point. Too many of us choose to resist the future and escape the present by retreating into the past. This hardly makes us unique. Many economic powers facing decline reject reinvention, instead embracing the fantasy of recapturing lost greatness by scapegoating "evil" internal forces deemed responsible for this "treasonous" outcome. And if democracy is hollowed out by this viciousness? That just tees up the authoritarian reboot.

The politically inexpedient truth is this: America has spent the last seven decades systematically promoting a liberal international trade order whose cross-border flows of goods, services, technologies, investment, migrants, information, and entertainment have methodically integrated the world's major economies, creating profound levels of interdependence among nations, peoples, and cultures—what we now call globalization (**Throughline One**). Our goal was simple: preventing world wars through increasingly inclusive economic advance. America was fantastically successful in this world-shaping grand strategy, globally creating more wealth and reducing more poverty across those seven decades than had occurred in the previous five centuries.

With the fall of the Berlin Wall in 1989, a new world order emerged with America as sole superpower, a situation that naturally invited Washington's overreach on its unilateral policing of regional crises. Our nation wisely remedied that imbalance by encouraging the peaceful rise of other great powers—most notably China. In the meantime, Washington vigorously wielded its unmatched power, toppling nefarious dictators, disrupting transnational terror networks, and radically speeding up globalization's advance. When the Great Recession hit in 2008, our citizenry correctly perceived that America's success in encouraging the rise of numerous economic powers had significantly diminished our ability to steer global developments. At this point, China and other rising economies helped sustain globalization's transformation into an increasingly digitalized phenomenon defined less by the flow of goods than by services and content, giving lie to simplistic notions of de-globalization.

Even in the post–Cold War era, America's grand strategy remained phenomenally successful, enabling the emergence of a majority global middle class long thought impossible. Now, because the bulk of humanity spends a growing share of its income on things beyond the bare necessities, the world enters an age of superabundance matched by super-consumption. That unprecedented achievement has turbocharged three global dynamics that, in their daunting combination, caused Americans to recoil from our glorious creation (globalization) and demonize it as the cause of all our problems.

There is no denying globalization's role in spiking these global crises, but we must reject the hindsight that their emergence invalidates America's strategy of encouraging globalization's poverty-eradicating advance. We made the world an infinitely better place that now faces new challenges. Who can argue that humanity's economic betterment should have been denied—despite these costs?

The first of these tectonic forces set into motion by skyrocketing global consumption is accelerating climate change (**Throughline Two**), which, like globalization, began reshaping the planet soon after America took it upon itself to steer the world's development following two world wars. Climate change now remaps the planet, tragically rendering much of Middle Earth—my term for the lower latitudes extending 30 degrees north and south of the equator—systematically unable to sustain, without outside assistance, their exploding populations, national economies, and ultimately their political systems. Climate change is also creating enormous new areas of economic opportunity across the North. Accommodating this vast poleward transfer of natural wealth—to include all manner of species and peoples—will test humanity's ingenuity and empathy like no global dynamic before it.

The second force is the global demographic transition (**Throughline Three**) stunningly accelerated by globalization's rapid integration of Asia, home to over half of humanity. Our species will collectively age across this century in a manner totally at odds with both nature and human history: the old surpassing the young in nation after nation. That demographic transformation will factor heavily in the superpower struggles now unfolding. Youth-bulging powers tend to be warlike and unstable (recall America's violent 1960s), while elderly societies retreat into nostalgia and social rigidity (see Japan and Italy today). Even nations achieving a large middle class succumb to virulent bursts of nationalism (China and India already). The good news? There are ways to avoid extreme aging, and America is supremely endowed with such capacity. We just need a bigger Union and a new map to that destination.

The third of these global forces arises in how the first two dynamics—climate change and demographic transformation—will collide across this century (**Throughline Four**). That collision will dramatically redefine Middle Earth's economic needs and political priorities, and the superpowers (US, European Union [EU], China, India, Russia) that most effectively meet those needs and address those priorities will see their global influence radically expand. In responding to Middle Earth's increasingly dire plight, these five powers will invariably compete in propagating new models of North-South security, economic, and political integration. Russia's Vladimir Putin and China's Xi Jinping have openly voiced such ambitions, imagining their own new maps. India's minister of external affairs has declared his nation's duty to serve as champion of the Global South on climate change and economic development. Washington, swept up in its political infighting, seems dimly aware of a competition already begun.

America's economic future is on the line here: Much of the world's consumer growth will be concentrated across Middle Earth, meaning the race to integrate North and South will simultaneously constitute a superpower brand war—an avowedly ideological competition to prove which economic model of trade and development best preserves and expands the global middle class amidst climate change's destabilizing impact. Capturing the political allegiance of that ascendant middle class will determine which superpower's definition of global stability reigns supreme in the decades ahead. If America wants to possess both power and influence in this remapped future, it cannot sit out this contest obsessively guarding its borders.

We have long framed superpower competition as which side (East or West) captures more of the other side's players. In the future, we will define it as which Northern power most comprehensively integrates its respective South—ameliorating its climate-induced decay and preventing its virtual absorption by competitors. This new superpower competition will define our era, either seeding a second American Century or launching some other (Chinese? Indian?).

No matter which superpowers prevail, regional and hemispheric integration will flourish (**Throughline Five**). This tightening of supply chains represents less a de-globalization than an optimization of material trade befitting the rise of multiple competing consumer blocs across the global economy. A generation ago, Asia manufactured goods for the rest of the world. Now, it manufactures largely for itself. On its own, this positive development has triggered a remapping of global value chains—an absolute good generating regional trade efficiencies. In this next iteration of globalization, those superpowers accumulating the most demand power will rule global consumer tastes in a way America once did—and now faces losing.

In this century, superpowers will prevail not according to the millions they field as lethal soldiers but the billions they attract as loyal subscribers. Size matters in this struggle to shape globalization's future, which means America will be disadvantaged compared to far more populous China and India. *These* United States will be greatly incentivized to grow their ranks—as they have long done—by integrating hemispheric neighbors. By scaling its demand power, a once-again expanding American Union can constitute an economic center of gravity of equal or superior attractiveness to the global middle class whose brand loyalty we seek.

Rest assured, come midcentury, we will all be living in *somebody's* world. I simply prefer our map over China's for reasons I will make eminently clear.

To our great good fortune, America's position as the dominant economic power of the Western Hemisphere clearly advantages us for the North-South integration to come (**Throughline Six**). Our true West enjoys several natural resource advantages over the far more crowded, diverse, and historically conflicted Eastern Hemisphere. The Americas also share culture and civilization worth defending on their own merits. By capitalizing on these advantages, America stands to benefit environmentally by managing climate change's harsh equatorial impact, as well as economically by adding Latin America's middle-class consumer power to that of North America. That larger union, however achieved, will then be able to extend its rule-setting power to significant portions of the Eastern Hemisphere, merging with regions not wholly lost to China's or India's economic orbits. For now, consider the entire board in play.

I understand why any call for hemispheric integration feels like an inconceivable reach from where we stand domestically today, but our current bout of nativism and xenophobia highlights the powerful pull of this very path (**Throughline Seven**). In other words, what we now fear most is that which we sense is inevitable. Like comedy (tragedy plus distance), conceivability emerges with enough pain and time. With Central America's environmental refugees already stressing our southern border, America is just beginning to feel Latin America's pain on climate change.

I likewise understand the instinct to wish away the problem of climate refugees by insisting that technological solutions can spare us this path, but this book purposefully focuses on adaptation versus any such direct responses, which I stipulate will be made and will succeed to some extent—just not fast enough to forestall the global dynamics explored here.

Thankfully, we do not start from scratch. After all, America started out as a baker's dozen of independent colonies. Today, hemispheric integration is likewise achievable through mechanisms and approaches already employed by both the EU in the political realm and China in the economic realm. Both carefully crafted integration schemes ultimately target security integration—the ability of superpowers to defend and optimally police their chosen spheres of influence. Meanwhile, America, lost to its intergenerational culture wars, satisfies itself with limp efforts to revitalize and extend military alliances focused on containing Chinese expansionism—a defensive and reactionary strategy more appropriate to retrograde Russia than the forward-leaning, world-shaping superpower we have long been.

Americans are modern globalization's original networkers, wiring the world in our wake. By nature, we are a revolutionary force offering nations increased connectivity to all manner of economic opportunity and disruptive content. China and Russia, by comparison, offer control—namely, a model and means for national governments to surveil their growing middle-class ranks, restrict their access to disruptive content, and aggressively thwart their inconvenient tendency toward democracy.

This is where our national infighting becomes self-destructive: the world is watching how America navigates a future where our leadership is not a given, nor our ideals naturally preeminent. We witness Americans increasingly resenting—even as we increasingly resemble—a globalization originally made in our image but now no longer with our likeness. We ran this show for decades, but our success in creating this world cost us control over it—by design. Now, with climate change fueling the poleward movement of all life, globalization's churning of races, species, and microbes lies beyond anyone's control.

That intimidating reality transforms America's global leadership while reaffirming its enduring source. Our nation has been—and always will be—a petri dish of globalization's evolution. These United States remain the world's source code for both integration (our immigrant nation's fabled melting-pot dynamic) and disintegration (our institutional racism and chronic culture wars). We are globalization-in-miniature—its de facto proof of concept. America does not take its political cues from the likes of Hungary.

Americans do not endure history; we make it. This is our true superpower: reliably resetting our internal rules in response to history's punishing waves of change, and then spreading those new and better rules across the world. American grand strategy does not merely confront rivals but shapes a global environment that tames their—and our—worst impulses. We are the best thing to ever happen to our world.

Russia and China aggressively market their competing rulesets, exploiting vulnerable trade partners who distrust and dislike them. Yet both regimes, as internally brittle as they are, currently outpace America's half-hearted attempts at global leadership. How is this so? It is because the stories we now tell of globalization do not envision a happy ending, much less a way ahead. No surprise there: when creators abandon their creation, monsters abound.

My task here is to propose that happy ending, one avowedly cast from an American perspective. Your task, as reader, is to maintain an open mind as to its feasibility and desirability. If, as our politicians love to proclaim, America's best days lie ahead, then we citizens cannot merely await that future but must craft its story lines—both foreign and domestic. Given our truly revolutionary achievements, we must not allow our currently flat trajectory to determine the upper bounds of our ingenuity and ambition, both of which the world desperately needs now.

As such, this book is all about unearthing globalization's throughlines and their constituent threads, operationalizing—through storytelling—that navigational knowledge across America's political leadership, business community, and citizenry. Throughlines are those persistent national and global drivers that Americans will confront, balance, and trade off as we manage the national and global challenges laid out here. Think of them as history's guardrails forcing us down a plausible range of pathways—certain *inevitabilities* that compel us to consider some version of the *inconceivables* we must in years ahead embrace. As for the connecting threads parsed within each throughline, consider them our protagonist's inner dialogue about the fork-in-the-road decisions lying before us. Now, more than ever, the world needs America to stay in character—my overriding purpose in writing this book.

Let our storytelling begin, for therein we discover the contours of America's new map.

Frankenstein's Monster: Coming to Grips with Our Most Powerful Creation

THROUGHLINE ONE

Globalization is America's gift to the world and our greatest strategic success, yet Americans now fear and loathe it for the profound challenges it imposes on our nation.

M odern globalization arose from the ashes of World War II. America's purposeful creation, it was forged as a permanent solution to the Eurasian continent's stunningly destructive conflagrations of the preceding decades. In our triumph, we projected our continental model of political and economic integration onto those European and Asian powers still free of communism's grasp. Unlike the collapsing colonial model it replaced, American-style integration promised equal standing in a democratic alliance that achieved mutual improvement through radical interdependency. That is how we built the Free World: getting longtime enemies to choose mutually assured dependence over mutually assured destruction.

By the early 1980s, our strategy's success was plain for all the world to see: a mere quarter of the world's population, the advanced capitalist economies we helped resurrect, was generating two-thirds of global economic activity. Once Deng Xiaoping took the bait and marketized China's economic system, the Soviet threat faded into irrelevance and the global economy was born.

Admittedly, US-style globalization offers a Faustian bargain: harmonize your nation's rules with the world's and, in doing so, sacrifice control for connectivity. Why? Because that connectivity, governed by those rules, powers production chains, enables digital flows, and fuels popular consumption. Any individual's pursuit of happiness increasingly depends on their government's effective balancing of that control/connectivity equation—national confidence being a function of consumer confidence. Conversely, any regime's stability increasingly depends on improving its populace's standard of living while somehow addressing—or dissuading—democratic impulses triggered by rising incomes.

The alternative to this bargain, known as economic nationalism, disastrously applies zero-sum thinking to globalization's non-zero-sum dynamics. Did California grow wealthy at New York's expense? Of course not. Nor will Florida outperform Georgia by adopting a made-in-the-Sunshine-State mandate. Ensuring our standard of living does not require other countries' permanent poverty—just the opposite. Their growing consumption is our opportunity.

Indeed, how the rest of the world leaves poverty behind will determine, in concert with climate change, our children's standard of living in the decades ahead. The North will need to salvage and integrate as much as it can of Middle Earth to preserve, and profit from, those regions' expanding middle classes.

Where does that leave America? We must accept the reality that, despite being our creation, globalization now shapes our nation more than we shape it in return.

Plenty of Americans rightfully sense a literal reversal of fortune in this history-bending development: we feel relatively poorer than preceding generations while the rest of the world clearly got richer. Without a doubt, it was far easier for early–Cold War America to retain dominance in a global economy long divided into "haves" and "have-nots" because we lacked strong competition on production and our large consumer pool ruled global markets.

In such a lopsided—and clearly unjust—situation, entire generations of Americans came to expect a middle-class lifestyle based on a high school diploma and lifetime employment in manufacturing. That golden age, lasting from the end of World War II through the 1960s and fondly remembered as *when America was great*, could not possibly have been sustained while Washington justly supported de-colonialization around the world. It was also completely at odds with our vision of fixing a world subject to increasingly destructive great-power wars. To champion democracy is to champion economic freedom, accepting the competitive pressures the latter creates. We either stay true to our principles or we can no longer claim them.

To our eternal credit and at the very height of our power, America chose not to hoard its economic greatness. Instead, we methodically extended such opportunity around the world through the international rules and institutions that we established, maintained, and defended. That liberal international trade order, based on how we knitted together these United States into the most powerful economic union on the planet, was source code for modern globalization—the single greatest achievement of any nation in human history. Be proud of that.

Except now many Americans view globalization as an existential threat to our way of life, something so dangerous as to warrant our departure from democracy to save us from *globalists committed to our destruction!*

Sound frighteningly familiar? Humanity has met this moment before.

Modern political science began with the question, Why did Germany's Weimar Republic fail in the 1920s, ultimately fueling both Nazi fascism and the Second World War? How did such a sophisticated political design succumb so completely to dark forces suddenly beyond its control? Recall that Adolf Hitler pegged an imagined global cabal of Jewish financiers as determined to enslave and ultimately destroy the German people and their way of life.

Future historians may well ask similar questions about America—as in, Why did the world's most successful and robust democracy fail in the 2020s? How did modern globalization's progenitor and longtime defender suddenly succumb so completely to such anti-democratic impulses? Why did this nation choose to demonize and sabotage its wildly successful creation?

To avoid such political collapse, America must relearn how to thrive within globalization. We need to account for its skyrocketing complexity and restructure our capitalism—as we have done in the past—to address challenges both old (e.g., class inequity, institutional racism) and new (demographic aging, climate change).

In the post–Cold War era, world leaders cooperatively responded to such system-perturbing shocks as the 9/11 terrorist strikes and the 2008 financial meltdown. When global institutions originally built to prevent a rerun of the Great Depression and WWII proved outdated and unwieldy, these leaders updated and reinvented them (e.g., expanding the Group of Seven [G7] into the G20), allowing globalization to march on in its wealth-creating whirlwind.

But something emerged in the Great Recession to arrest that momentum. Our world's stabilizing pillar, its now-majority middle class, started fearing for their existence. Their keen suspicion of being hollowed while the rich became grotesquely wealthier drained our collective optimism. In America, this triggered a tsunami of angry voters flooding the "swamp" with change elections every two years.

Who runs for public office under such conditions? Primarily demagogues whose boundless narcissism and existential fearmongering fuel their self-image as celebrity saviors combatting inhuman opponents. As a result, America presently endures its worst cohort of political leaders since its late-nineteenth-century Gilded Age, or at least last century's Roaring Twenties.

Both periods witnessed technological and economic advances arriving far faster than security and political adaptations, resulting in the widespread sense of events spinning out of control. In both instances, society's greatest talent flocked to the private sector, while public service was popularly disparaged. Both tumultuous eras eventually triggered lengthy bouts of progressive reforms by which rigged economic landscapes were aggressively regraded into less uneven playing fields, in turn replenishing America's social optimism and political stability. Finally, each national correction was spearheaded by a New York blue blood from the same extended family—first Theodore and then Franklin Roosevelt. Both presidents successfully recast public service as a noble pursuit.

Today's angry America has reached the same historical tipping point.

Our nation needs a new type of political leadership based on a new political science, one that decodes globalization by leveraging interdisciplinary knowledge, data analytics, and human cognition–augmenting artificial intelligence (AI). We need to apply to socioeconomic and political issues the same sort of big data effort that our natural and data scientists now apply to a host of medical and environmental challenges. We have the technology; we just need to stop vilifying science and scientists.

That new political science must begin with the question, How does today's America surmount the wickedly complex problems triggered by globalization's success?

These challenges are not insurmountable. Considering how far humanity has advanced these past seven decades, they are our best problems yet.

1

The Empty Throne: Globalization Comes with Rules but No Ruler

> As an operating system, globalization is the global economy's open-source software: easy to apply, hard to quit, with no single authority, and subject to revisions from all participants.

There have been several pre-American world orders, but there will never be a post-American world system. Our model of globalization is too successful and transformational to suffer complete displacement. When European imperial powers took turns dominating global trade, none brought prosperity or freedom to anybody but themselves. Their cynical legacy of fake states marred by arbitrary borders haunts us still. What all thieving empires fail to do is radically increase—much less equitably distribute—global trade; they merely hoard it.

A good measure of globalization's advance is found in "trade openness," or the value of world exports and imports as a combined percentage of gross world product. Pre-nineteenth-century globalization was driven primarily by Europe's murderous colonization of weaker nations around the world, allowing those powers to pillage local resources and transfer that wealth back home. As a result, trade openness never exceeded 10 percent. The subsequent century of British world domination, extending to World War I, was defined by an explosion of intra-European trade, boosting the index to 30 percent before that conflict and the Great Depression sent it plunging. Once America stepped up to forge a truly globe-spanning system, the world's trade openness steadily increased to its 2008 peak of 60 percent, retreating to the mid-50s since.

Despite the flatlining of the global goods trade following the onset of the Great Recession, in 2018 there were still 125 nations (out of 173 reporting to the World Bank) enjoying trade-openness indices of 100 percent or more in relation to their national gross domestic product (GDP). This demonstrates just how widely internalized our global trade ruleset has become among smaller and midsized economies now left highly dependent on globalization's post-COVID survival—unlike big-market superpowers. A quintessentially American achievement, we fostered a world system within which those lacking military power could nonetheless thrive economically.

In that sense, America remains globalization's downstream ideal: a political union of minor military powers (fifty states with their own "national guards") enjoying off-the-charts interstate trade and investment flows under the protection of an all-powerful Leviathan—the US military. If we were to calculate the trade openness of individual US states—not just in relation to the wider world but among themselves (like the EU still records trade between Germany and France), we would discover within our ranks any number of "trading states" on par with Hong Kong, Luxembourg, and Singapore. Point being we remain the furthest along in this grand human experiment of deepening economic interdependence. It is illogical for Americans to fear globalization when we are—by far—its most experienced and accomplished practitioners.

That post-WWII, US-led global free trade system, along with the technological advances in transportation and communications that it pervasively spread, birthed modern globalization, where the cross-border flow of exports is forty times larger than its pre–World War I peak. America made the global trading system fairer, freer, more transparent, and far more inclusive. In doing so, we led a twelvefold explosion in global GDP (1950–2015), growing the global economy by $100 trillion in constant 1991 dollars—an absolute increase twelve times that generated across four centuries (1550–1950) of European imperial rule ($8.5T). Even adding in the profound global population growth since 1950, the increase in per capita global GDP is equally impressive: a fivefold increase in those 65 years versus a threefold increase over the preceding 130 years (1820–1950)—the heyday of Britain's world-spanning colonial empire. No matter how you measure it, US-style globalization has created far more wealth around the world at a far faster velocity than Europe's colonial empires ever could, all while radically reducing extreme poverty worldwide from more than half of humanity in 1950 to a mere one-tenth of the global population today.

America recast world trade by creating, propagating, and defending a global body of rules. Compared to the rapid establishment of the World Bank and International Monetary Fund (IMF) at a single 1944 international conference (Bretton Woods), the 1947 General Agreement on Trade and Tariffs

(GATT) was merely a provisional arrangement (not a treaty) that did not result in a permanent international organization. It took half a century and numerous negotiating rounds to grow that initial 23-nation agreement into today's 164-member World Trade Organization (WTO). Headquartered in Geneva, Switzerland—unlike the Washington, DC–based World Bank and IMF—the WTO oversees and administers rules spanning 98 percent of global trade, in addition to serving as a forum for trade negotiations and dispute resolution.

As opposed to the World Bank and IMF, the WTO cannot create and impose global rules on its own. New rules can only be negotiated by consensus among its ranks. That is typically easier to achieve on a regional level. Such Regional Trade Agreements (RTAs) are often viewed as WTO competitors at best and WTO failures at worst, but, in truth, they are WTO fellow travelers reflecting the reality that global rules accumulate "upward" from nations and regions. Moreover, these preferential agreements often reference WTO rules, simply copying that language into their texts. After first appearing in the 1950s, there are now 355 RTAs in force worldwide. More importantly, most of these agreements are now being concluded among developing economies.

Connectivity and rules naturally go together. The least externally rule-bound regime in the world (say, North Korea) is the one that least interacts with other nations, whereas the most rule-defined governments (for example, Singapore) are those with the highest degree of external connectivity.

The more you want to connect, the more rules you must accept, and the wider your economic playing field becomes. When we add up all possible state-on-state combinations (dyads) in the world in 1950, four-fifths of them featured no direct trade. Today, three-quarters of all dyads feature direct trade of some sort. That is a revolution in human affairs made possible by US-style globalization.

Key to that revolution is the expansion of trade outside of advanced capitalist economies. Trade among rich countries accounted for two-thirds of the global total in 1945, the rest involving less-developed countries. Today those proportions are reversed, meaning US-led trade liberalization efforts democratized global economic connectivity—another hugely positive legacy.

Abundant historical data proves that the more your nation trades, the faster your economy grows due to heightened competition, economies of scale, and more exposure to, and adaptation of, advanced technologies created elsewhere.

The WTO aptly expresses US-style globalization by distributing power across states versus concentrating it among great powers, as in the case of the UN Security Council or Group of 20. Like our invention of the internet, where the US government voluntarily relinquished control over domains to a private, nonprofit organization dedicated to addressing global needs (Internet Corporation for Assigned Names and Numbers, or ICANN), America morphed GATT into an international organization (WTO) beyond our control—all for the greater good.

The true danger that globalization now faces is a hard partitioning of its operating system on a bloc-by-bloc basis, replicating Cold War divisions. Here is the tricky thing to keep in mind: after globalization's stunningly rapid expansion across the planet (1990s–2000s), the Great Recession naturally triggered a stabilizing re-regionalization or consolidation of those gains (e.g., the rise of new global demand centers like China). That many-steps-forward-and-one-step-back development is both natural and good. Every transformational process needs to take a breather now and then. The underlying danger today, as in all things political, would be in allowing that process to snowball into something destructively extreme (e.g., some new "iron curtain" dividing the Eurasian landmass between autocracies and democracies). Whenever humans are involved, nothing succeeds like excess.

In the Cold War era, two great blocs competed over which state-level operating system was superior: communism or capitalism. It was no contest. This time, the struggle will be over which model of multinational integration is superior, the question being which scheme offers (a) just enough security and certainty for that ascendant global middle class to feel comfortable amidst the turbulence generated by climate change and demographic transition, and (b) just enough freedom for that empowered group to politically rule itself—its natural, prideful inclination.

If the United States embraces this new superpower competition with genuine vigor and ingenuity, we will prevail. Despite our clear flaws, America possesses the most tested and proven ruleset as the world's oldest multinational republic—now fifty members strong.

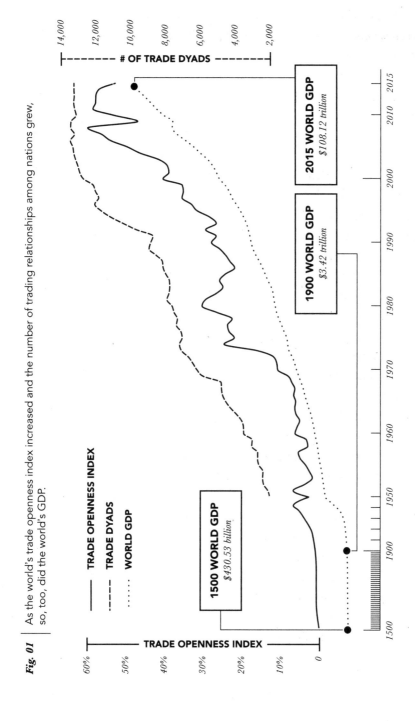

Fig. 01 As the world's trade openness index increased and the number of trading relationships among nations grew, so, too, did the world's GDP.

OF TRADE DYADS

14,000
12,000
10,000
8,000
6,000
4,000
2,000

TRADE OPENNESS INDEX

60%
50%
40%
30%
20%
10%
0

TRADE OPENNESS INDEX
TRADE DYADS
WORLD GDP

1500 WORLD GDP
$430.53 billion

1900 WORLD GDP
$3.42 trillion

2015 WORLD GDP
$108.12 trillion

1500   1900   1950   1960   1970   1980   1990   2000   2010   2015

2

The Eye-of-the-Storm Fallacy: Americans' Poor Understanding of Globalization

> US consumption has long shaped global consumption. That economic self-centeredness makes it hard for Americans to understand globalization's liberating and disorienting impact.

Outside of the radical Islamist response, most Americans remain unaware of how the spread of US-style globalization around the world challenges traditional societies. Globalization's state-integrating dynamics so mirror our American Union's long-standing practices for meshing our member states that we struggle to view them as anything but entirely normal. However, the basic freedoms that fuel US economic activity remain challenging concepts across much of the world.

Take unrestricted movement: the idea that you can be born in one state (for me, Wisconsin), go to graduate school in another (Massachusetts), let your career move you around (Maryland, Virginia, Rhode Island, Indiana, Ohio), and then retire somewhere else (Minnesota?) is something Americans take entirely for granted. Surprisingly few people in this world can claim similar rights. The EU only achieved "freedom of movement" across its member states in its 1992 Treaty of Maastricht. In China, movement is restricted according to the *hukou* (house registration) system that regulates migration between rural and urban areas.

Americans' self-directed mobility incentivizes our member states to make themselves as attractive as possible to workers—a powerfully integrating force enabling a singular labor market spanning a vast array of distinct legal environments. The trick? Your government must trust its own people.

Would most people welcome America's version of interstate mobility? Absolutely. But without all the necessary rules and systems in place? That would easily destabilize most countries or regions. US-style globalization has spread such revolutionary aspirations: people have seen the future and want it now. As for the most ambitious? They vote with their feet, increasingly moving north-ward to the great hubs of legal free movement—North America and the EU.

There is also a generational factor that makes it unusually difficult for Americans to recognize, much less own up to, the profound impact that our brand of globalization has had around the world. Starting with our Boomer generation (1945–1964), America served as the undisputed center of global demand. For decades, that meant the global economy revolved more around our tastes and desires than those of any other region. While Americans consti-tute 5 percent of the world's population, our share of global consumption has long been a multiple of that (four to five times). It is not just that Boomers have long dominated the US market; by extension, they have long exerted outsized influence throughout the global economy.

So yes, when the preeminent power of your consumer demand, along with your rule-setting role, places you at the calm eye of the globalization storm, you really do have a tough time comprehending the transformational power you have unleashed along its vast front. You may even be completely oblivious to it.

That is . . . until the terrorist strikes of 9/11 remind you that there are bad actors who will wage unspeakable war to prevent your ways from overwhelm-ing their own. Or 2008 reveals Wall Street's latest risky debt instrument just collapsed the US housing market, in turn imploding global financial centers and markedly slowing growth among emerging economies whose most vulner-able populations then feel forced to emigrate. Then it gets easier to recognize and comprehend.

But what really makes that influence clear is when you discover you no longer possess it, which is what has happened over the last couple of decades, thanks to China's stunning rise. Remember when, in the 1990s, cable business network analysts were always saying that as long as US consumer spending remained strong, the global economy would be fine? Nobody says that any-more. Now, economists speak of Chinese consumers with such reverence. A good example: Hollywood self-censoring its films to avoid offending China's vast audience.

That is a big part of explaining America's recent loss of self-confidence, along with growing fears of globalization itself. The future just does not look like us anymore. That can be particularly unnerving for older Americans who, looking around their country today, no longer see "the America I grew up in."

The good news? Our younger generations (Millennial, 1981–95; Gen Z, 1996–2010; and Gen Alpha, 2011–25) have already experienced our shared demographic future, growing up in an America that far more approximates the world's diversity. As such, their concerns for the future are eminently more practical, while their deepest fears center on climate change—as they should.

The bad news? The Boomers are still largely in charge of our political system (we have yet to elect a post-Boomer president) and seem stubbornly reluctant to cede authority to succeeding generations.

Why that matters: Boomers, those inveterate weaponizers of nostalgia, are inherently attracted to the notion of resurrecting America's golden age— namely, their childhood and youth. Cold War Boomers also have a tough time detaching themselves from that era's enemy archetypes—Russia and China. While we clearly face genuine threats from each power, the Boomers' tendency to view both competitions in entirely existential terms only pushes Beijing and Moscow into confrontational stances with America and—worse— each other's arms.

This is especially unhelpful as China steps into its role as globalization's demand center in so many domains. Just as we Americans had a hard time owning up to the global footprint of our inordinate consumption, so now the Chinese struggle with such responsibility, seeing themselves, after their "century of humiliation" at the hands of colonial powers, as a perpetual underdog at worst and an avenging superpower at best. To the extent that America's political leadership continues defaulting to cold-school demonization of communist China, we can expect Beijing's stability-obsessed leadership to avoid global responsibilities they might otherwise embrace. While Washington hard-liners would welcome that outcome, it would be to the world's detriment. America's global leadership is no longer feasibly unilateral in execution.

The clock is ticking. For now, the world blames America for globalization's defects and damage. Over time, that fierce anger will shift overwhelmingly to China.

3

The World at War:
Our Successful Downsizing of
Conflict Over the Years

> We are a world overwhelmingly at peace—more so on a per capita basis than at any other time in history. That allows us to focus on looming security challenges posed by climate change.

H umans today live more safely—and longer—than ever. Yes, we still live under the threat of nuclear war, yet that widely accepted scenario has, since those weapons' invention in 1945, effectively killed direct wars among nuclear powers. As proven yet again in Ukraine, superpowers can wage whatever forms of conventional (i.e., non-nuclear) war they want, while opposing nuclear powers similarly limit their responses to non-strategic means. A bloody fate for Ukraine, but an incredibly positive ruleset for the world.

So why are Americans so easily convinced that we live in a world at war? It stems partly from increased media coverage of distant conflicts. Then there is America's long record of military interventions around the world. Researchers have also downsized the definition of war to conflicts generating one thousand deaths per year (three deaths per day). To put that in perspective, World War II averaged twenty thousand deaths per day for most of a decade (1937–1945)— truly a world at war. It is, of course, a very good thing that we are now far more aware of such smaller-scale conflict and suffering around the world, but it does exaggerate our perceptions of crisis by blowing things out of proportion and blinding us to globalization's ultimately pacifying impact. In truth, the world system today suffers very little "chaos," despite experts' frequent use of such hyperbolic terminology when analyzing events—a great method for their getting booked on cable news networks.

An effective way to disaggregate warfare is found in US political scientist Kenneth Waltz's 1959 classic of international relations theory, *Man, the State, and War*. Waltz tackled the age-old question of why wars occur, organizing his answers along three levels of analysis: (1) individuals (human nature in general, leaders specifically); (2) states (democracies versus dictatorships); and (3) the international system (pervasively warlike due to the absence of an all-powerful hegemon). In reverse order, I shorthand Waltz's images as system, state, and subnational, allowing us to categorize warfare by scale and scope.

System-level wars are world wars, superpower wars, and nuclear or strategic wars. The world has suffered none of these since the invention of nuclear weapons. These terrifying devices provide us a genuine crystal ball when it comes to strategic warfare, forcing us to recognize its logical endpoint—if we are not careful. There are distinct rules to this existential game, which is why Russia's invasion of Ukraine in 2022 does not trigger global nuclear war—even if Moscow were to use a tactical nuclear weapon. In that sense, the world is governed by a true global hegemon in the form of Mutually Assured Destruction (MAD)—the foreknowledge that direct war between nuclear powers would ultimately turn cataclysmic.

State-level wars are either non-superpower state-on-state wars—now increasingly rare—or conflicts in which a superpower wages war on a non-nuclear state to (a) flat-out conquer and capture (Russia-v-Ukraine), or (b) effect a regime change (US-v-[INSERT REGIME HERE]). Neither type is going away during globalization's consolidation along regional lines. They are also not particularly frequent, as superpowers tend to take turns on this activity.

Last is subnational strife (e.g., government-v-rebels or terrorists, civil war) that sometimes attracts interventions by great powers. Whenever America gets involved, it is, by definition, a "war" until we pull out. After that, it goes back to being just a "conflict."

History is clear: since the United States assumed world leadership and began propagating its style of globalization, our planet has seen mass violence downshift from the system level, through the state level, to the subnational level, reflecting the enduring reality that globalization's advance destabilizes world order primarily along subnational and transnational lines—just like climate change. As such, progressively redirecting US national security planning and activities toward both of these system-shaping dynamics is entirely warranted and does not constitute "taking our eyes off the ball" that is China or Russia.

4

Cold Wars as Comfort Food: The Pentagon's Need for a Near-Peer Competitor

During the Cold War, the Pentagon had a peer enemy against which to plan—the Soviet Union. Since then, it has struggled over how best to build, organize, and employ its force.

In the late 1990s, when I was working as a US Naval War College professor, I ran across a satirical personal ad taped to a wall in the Pentagon. It read:

Mature North American Superpower seeks hostile partner for arms racing, Third World conflicts, and general antagonism. Must be sufficiently menacing to convince Congress of military financial requirement. Nuclear capability is preferred; however, non-nuclear candidates possessing significant biochemical warfare resources will be considered. Send note with pictures of fleet and air squadrons to: CHAIRMAN JOINT CHIEFS OF STAFF, THE PENTAGON.

During the Cold War, the Defense Department had a singular, unifying strategic vision. But in the 1990s, it was stuck babysitting a messy world demanding all sorts of missions: some it was comfortable conducting (regime toppling) and many it was extremely uncomfortable performing (postwar reconstruction, stability operations, nation-building, counterinsurgency, etc.).

The Cold War taught the Pentagon how to buy a big-war force designed to fight another superpower, but the post–Cold War's demand signal was full of small wars and stability operations short of war. As such, the Pentagon was guilty of buying one type of force while operating another. Sound awkward for troops on the ground? It was like using a hammer to sink screws.

Once 9/11 hit, the Pentagon was compelled to comprehensively embrace that small-wars reality. Without a doubt, much of the defense community, particularly the big defense firms, disliked this downshifting from global war to so-called stability operations. Global war requires supremely expensive platforms (e.g., aircraft, ships, tanks), while suppressing civil strife, insurgencies, and terrorist networks requires a lot of personnel, equipment, and contractors. Defense firms did just fine adapting their wares to the Global War on Terror (GWOT), but nothing compares to lengthy contracts to build hundred-million-dollar aircraft or multibillion-dollar naval vessels.

When Americans grew weary of expensive postwar occupations in Iraq and Afghanistan, the Pentagon's planning pendulum swung from those small wars, which burned out our—by uniform color—Green forces (Army, Marines, Special Operations), back to the more familiar big wars, triggering a rebuilding of our neglected Blue forces (Navy, Air Force). This logic dovetailed with Barack Obama's strategic "pivot" to Asia to confront China's military buildup and later Donald Trump's decision to ramp up military spending. Toss in Putin's invasion of Ukraine, shoot down a spy balloon or two, and our resurrection of Cold War planning paradigms is complete: with globalization declared dead, we return to preparing for the drone/robot-centric Third World War. The best example of this turnabout are the Marines, which are being recast as a China-centric force in an incredibly narrow strategic bet.

Just as globalization enters its next, ever-more-complicated evolution, our senior leaders are instinctively eager to declare new cold wars with both Russia and China in what can be described as strategic reboots of beloved franchises within the Boomer Cold-War Universe (BCU). Every generation succumbs to a strategic Alzheimer's in response to a world spinning incomprehensibly faster. They instinctively cling to their fondest memories: a simpler time when you could tell the players without a scorecard. As policymaking goes, though, this is a tragic retreat from reality.

The world is at a frighteningly uncertain inflection point in its history. Globalization is being pervasively—and invasively—digitalized just as it suffers a democratic recession, clearing pathways for surveillance-state models right out of George Orwell. Meanwhile, a vast, overpopulated portion of the planet becomes increasingly uninhabitable, setting in motion the largest planet-spanning migration of life-forms in human history. Stuck between that rock and a hard place is an increasingly nervous global middle class desperate for assurances that they will never be forced back to the chronic poverty they thought they left behind. What all these trends speak to is security—not defense. There are no military solutions to these wickedly interdependent challenges.

America must manage more than one global security crisis at a time without resorting to Cold War defense paradigms. Foreign policy "realists" deem such thinking naïve, sticking with their balance-of-power models. They will always find firm validation in any Russian move against former vassal states, just as any China-Taiwan scenario is reflexively cast as a world-system breaker. Like a broken face clock, these pessimists are correct twice each day.

When trying to balance climate change with the fate of the global middle class, such "realism" can feel like reshuffling deck chairs on the *Titanic*. While it is tempting to fight one doomsday argument with another, understanding globalization's trajectory yields more accurate strategies.

When all you have is a hammer, all you see are nails. The United States needs a bigger tool kit for globalization's next phase. As far as much of the world is concerned, America's narrow national offering—far too reliant on military aid—is rapidly losing its appeal. See our hemispheric "War on Drugs" for the worst examples.

Defense is all about saying no (*We can't let you do that*), while security is more about saying yes (*We can make that happen*). Right now, America is all about telling the world no, while China is all about saying yes to that ascendant global middle class. In a bit of strategic misdirection, Beijing has Washington so concerned about Taiwan's military defense that we fail to appreciate just how successfully China sells its model of middle-class security around the world—including our so-called backyard of Latin America. The prime example: national flagship telecom company Huawei's marketing of its Safe City solutions, a comprehensive and pervasive urban surveillance system already installed in dozens of countries but particularly those pairing non-liberal governments with expanding middle-class populations. China's public sales pitch is crime prevention, when in truth Beijing is selling its expertise in suppressing middle-class aspirations for political freedom.

Our defense establishment, so long uncomfortable executing low-end security missions versus acquiring high-end defense platforms, now eagerly embraces China as a near-peer military competitor. The problem is, as far as globalization is concerned, we are stuck playing the player, while China plays the board. Over time, that will relegate America to China's near-peer competitor on global security.

5 *Nuclear Clubbing:* America's Obsession with Preventing Proliferation

Experts have long predicted a recklessly rapid expansion of nuclear powers. The exact opposite has happened, reflecting an underappreciated success of US foreign policy.

F ollowing the first and only uses of nuclear weapons by the United States in 1945, six additional nuclear powers (the Union of Soviet Socialist Republics [USSR], United Kingdom [UK], France, China, Israel, and India) came into being over the next three decades. Since India joined the so-called nuclear club in 1974, there have been two new members reluctantly admitted: Pakistan (1990) and North Korea (2006). That record describes a profound slowing of nuclear proliferation over eight decades—from one power every four years to one every twenty. Despite those persistently scary predictions, we remain stuck in the single digits at nine club members.

It is not hard to see how experts generate their predictions of "dozens" of new nuclear powers. The North Atlantic Treaty Organization (NATO)'s sharing of nuclear weapons (i.e., stationing of US nuclear weapons within allies' territory) presently involves five states (Belgium, Germany, Italy, Netherlands, and Turkey). Then there are the dozen-and-a-half states that have given up their nuclear weapons and/or programs—shared or not. Finally, there are those states whose nascent nuclear capacities were destroyed by Israel in preemptive attacks (Iraq, Syria, and someday possibly Iran). Add that all up and you have three dozen states with some nuclear weapons history. However, for every state that joined the nuclear club, three walked, or were escorted, away.

What does that anything-but-uncontrollable dynamic tell us?

Nuclear arsenals only make sense for certain great powers—namely, those in antagonistic rivalries with other great powers capable of large-scale conventional and nuclear warfare. So, once America invented nukes, the Soviet Union needed them in reply. That pushed France and the UK to counter the USSR within Europe. China needed nukes against both the United States and the Soviets. Israel needed them to protect itself against the combined forces of the Arab world. India needed them against both China and its archenemy, Pakistan. Pakistan followed suit vis-à-vis India. Finally, North Korea made the reach out of fear of US-backed South Korea's significant military capability—and our nuclear arsenal.

There is your history of "out of control" proliferation, which has resulted in zero strategic wars among that constellation of powers once their individual nuclear status was achieved and recognized by the rest. In the meantime, both the Soviet Bloc and the USSR collapsed without nuclear war, China rose peacefully, and India now does the same. Europe has had two wars (Balkans, Russia-v-Ukraine), but neither went nuclear. India and Pakistan still spar to no effect. In the Middle East, a nuclear Iran likely someday faces off against Israel and a suddenly nuclear Saudi Arabia in a dangerous but familiar strategic standoff. Or the nascent Saudi-Israeli-Emirati alliance will succeed in permanently postponing that scenario.

There will always remain the danger that one nuclear power will, in a moment of desperation or confusion, press the nuclear button. But the world's superpowers have managed that reality for decades now through all manner of proxy wars, standoffs, and the like. It is not a foolproof system by any means, yet the total lack of all-out, direct conventional or strategic warfare among nuclear powers for almost eight decades is an amazingly stable record—so much so that it is hard to imagine having achieved that situation *without* nuclear weapons. As Faustian bargains go, this one is totally worth it.

There will also always remain the danger of a non-state actor gaining access to weapons of mass destruction (WMD) for the purpose of a terrorist strike. If Osama bin Laden could have placed WMD on those hijacked jets on 9/11, we all know full well that he would have. Fortunately, nuclear powers are anything but lax in controlling their strategic arsenals, as any such "leakage" would inevitably be traced back to the source.

In both scenarios (direct or proxy use), nuclear powers are existentially incentivized to stick with the fundamental strategic ruleset that says these weapons are for *having* and not *using*. Once employed in a "first strike" (even as a tactical demonstration), the deterrent value of nuclear weapons evaporates. One seeks membership in the nuclear club to rule out strategic warfare, not trigger it. Nuclear weapons are the ultimate get-out-of-jail card regarding superpower military interventions in smaller states, Russia invading Ukraine being just the latest example.

Nuclear weapons thus establish mutually recognized boundaries for any conflict involving nuclear powers, which is an exceptionally good thing and a key pillar of the US-created international order now defined by globalization.

At the Cold War peak of 1986, there were 64,000 nuclear warheads. Today there are fewer than 10,000—an 85 percent drop signaling both their excessive cost and the recognition that strategic deterrence can be suitably achieved with far smaller numbers. In short, MAD still works.

Within superpower military establishments, there will always be factions pushing for a reconsideration of smaller (tactical) nuclear weapons, just as there is persistent pressure to plan, build, and train for all-out strategic warfare. China's military continues to suffer such strategically myopic vision, as evidenced by its pointless ramping up of the nation's nuclear missile stockpile to modestly narrow the gap with those held by Russia and the United States.

Most debate on nuclear proliferation focuses on its horizontal expression—an increase in the number of nuclear powers. It is the vertical form—nuclear powers increasing their arsenals—that dangerously blurs the non-nuclear/nuclear boundary by insinuating that limited nuclear warfare can be successfully waged in a regional conflict without escalating to world-decimating strategic nuclear missile exchanges. That could well become the most dangerous legacy of Russia's war with Ukraine, which once hosted Soviet nuclear missiles only to surrender them to Moscow following the USSR's collapse.

Expect more US allies to seek such missile-hosting privileges (both nuclear and non-nuclear) in the years ahead, meaning there remains plenty of work—largely self-disciplinary—for US diplomats on the proliferation issue.

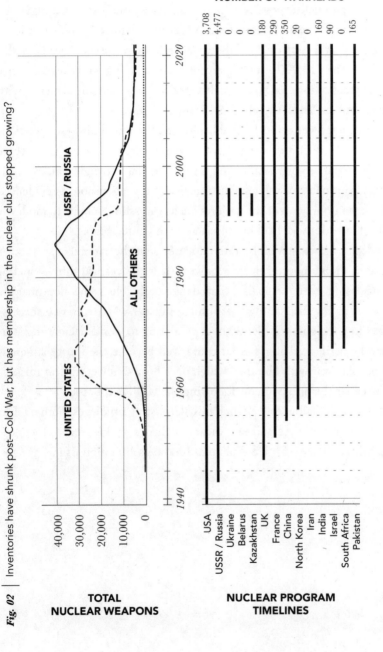

Fig. 02 | Inventories have shrunk post–Cold War, but has membership in the nuclear club stopped growing?

TOTAL NUCLEAR WEAPONS

USSR / RUSSIA

UNITED STATES

ALL OTHERS

40,000

30,000

20,000

10,000

0

1940   1960   1980   2000   2020

ESTIMATED CURRENT NUMBER OF WARHEADS

USA	3,708
USSR / Russia	4,477
Ukraine	0
Belarus	0
Kazakhstan	0
UK	180
France	290
China	350
North Korea	20
Iran	0
India	160
Israel	90
South Africa	0
Pakistan	165

NUCLEAR PROGRAM TIMELINES

6

State-on-State War in the Post–Cold War Era: How America's New Rules Come Back to Haunt Us

America's exploitation of globalization's unipolar period saw us promulgate controversial new rules on policing smaller powers, leading great powers to emulate our unilateralism.

I n historical terms, people think of war as State A versus State B, or two national armies going at it over territory. During the Cold War (1946–1991), the world averaged two state-on-state wars each year. Once globalization eclipsed the superpower standoff (1992–2020), that frequency dropped to one per year. Meanwhile, the world's total number of nation-states doubled over the same seventy-five years, meaning we should have expected a sharp increase in such bilateral wars.

Instead, the rising number of nation-states translated into more warfare within states, with civil conflicts quadrupling from the low teens in the late 1940s to a peak of fifty-one in 1991—the year the USSR dissolved. During the Cold War, these civil conflicts infrequently attracted military interventions by outside powers (consider, for example, the Vietnam War), as only one out of every twelve were internationalized. We tend to remember the Cold War as this endless string of Soviet-v-US proxy wars, but both superpowers were judicious in picking fights that might unduly escalate.

The year 1991 was crucial for another reason: the United States took it upon itself to function as "global policeman," ejecting Iraq from Kuwait following its Putin-like invasion. America's fear was that Saddam Hussein's unaddressed aggression would initiate a post–Cold War free-for-all. President George H. W. Bush's "line in the sand" thus signaled new rules for state-on-state conflict—his self-declared New World Order.

As for the 50 percent decline in state-on-state war that followed, some of that reflected a deterrent effect from the Gulf War. The frequency of civil strife also dropped by more than one-third from 1992 to 2010. Those decades constituted peak US global policing as measured by the frequency and length of US military operations during the Bill Clinton and George W. Bush administrations.

The economic determinist in me says globalization's full blossoming over the same two decades is the bigger reason civil strife declined so dramatically. Still, US policing kept things unusually calm despite globalization's revolutionary reformatting of the planet. Compared to today, those were optimistic times.

What changed next was everything: the Great Recession sent the global economy spinning, while decades of US foreign policy activism came to a sudden end with the elections of Barack Obama (2008, 2012) and Donald Trump (2016), both of whom campaigned on promises of ending America's "forever wars" and rebuilding our nation. While Trump criticized Obama's "lead from behind" approach to Middle East conflicts, he later outdid his predecessor's strategic retreat by outsourcing US national security policy in that region to the Israelis, Saudis, and Emiratis—in effect blessing their unprecedented anti-Iran alliance.

Unsurprisingly, the combination of economic tumult and a retreating United States ushered in a period of rising conflicts, as the total number of civil and state-based conflicts increased by 80 percent across the 2010s. The year 2020 featured the most state-based conflicts since World War II, with 95 percent of them involving governments fighting their own citizens. Reflecting a rudderless world, foreign interventions in civil conflicts tripled across the 2010s. On one hand, you could call this a good thing: with America in strategic retreat, other regional powers were stepping up. On the other hand, you could describe this as a negative development—a great-power ruleset run wild.

America's two decades of post–Cold War policing established the superpower ruleset that says, if you consider Regime X to constitute a profound national security threat to your nation, then you are within your rights to preemptively replace that regime—even to the point of a lengthy military occupation. That was the fundamental ruleset change imposed on the system by the George W. Bush administration through its Global War on Terror (GWOT) and the extended military interventions it undertook in Afghanistan and Iraq.

Make no mistake: Russia and China were paying attention, as were several great powers across the Middle East (consider, for example, the Saudi Arabia-v-Iran proxy war inside Yemen). In effect, Vladimir Putin proved Russia's freedom to behave similarly vis-à-vis both Georgia (2008) and Ukraine

(2014)—two smash-and-land-grabs—prior to his would-be knockout punch of Ukraine in 2022. Everything Putin said and did prior to Russia's full-scale invasion revealed his belief that he was well within his superpower rights to declare an existential threat that left him "no other choice" but to engage in a "forced measure"—however brutal.

Putin clearly expected some international respect for his checking-all-the-boxes approach to explaining his invasion—despite the far-fetched lies. He also bet everything on his belief that Russia's energy-supply power would protect his economy from any combined effort by the world's opposing great powers to de-globalize it in retaliation (e.g., drastically curtailing Russia's access to global financial markets and their services). As he stated in a public meeting with Russian business leaders shortly after the invasion began: "We are not going to damage the system of the global economy that we are in—to the extent that we are in it. So, I think our partners should understand this and should not try to force us from this system."

Putin's empty threat of "damage" showed he did not understand how vulnerable a supply-rich-but-demand-poor Russia was to a disconnection campaign. The 97 percent of the world economy that is not Russia does not depend on that state's small consumer market. Given sufficient cause, Europe decided to radically reduce its energy dependence on Russia—no matter the short-term pain—thus shattering the illusion that it needed Russia more than the other way around. Instead of reclaiming greatness, Putin merely accelerated Russia's reduction to China's economic vassal, the best example being the heavily discounted price Beijing now pays for Moscow's oil. Putin's miscalculation dramatically boosted the institutional appeal of both NATO and the EU while puncturing the myth of Russia's military and cyber prowess. These are all wins as far as America is concerned—at the bargain price of supplying Ukraine's military.

In leading the Western economies' response to Russia's invasion of Ukraine, the United States once again revised the rules of acceptable state-on-state war, this time elevating the penalty of economic sanctions—once applied to Iraq—to the systematic de-globalization of a nuclear superpower. As this new penalty exacts a tremendous toll on Russia, it suggests that such superpower rule-breaking can result in a jettisoning of that national economy from a globalization still led by the United States.

Will China's leadership, eyeing their "Taiwan province," respect this proposed new rule? Would such a de-globalization threat even be possible with the vastly more integrated China?

Rest assured that Beijing took notice and now feels far more justified in partitioning globalization to mitigate that strategic risk. America's attempted taming of Russia only encourages China to spread its own ruleset more aggressively. Such is the nature of globalization today.

Fig. 03 | As conflicts between states have grown more rare, civil conflicts define the international landscape.

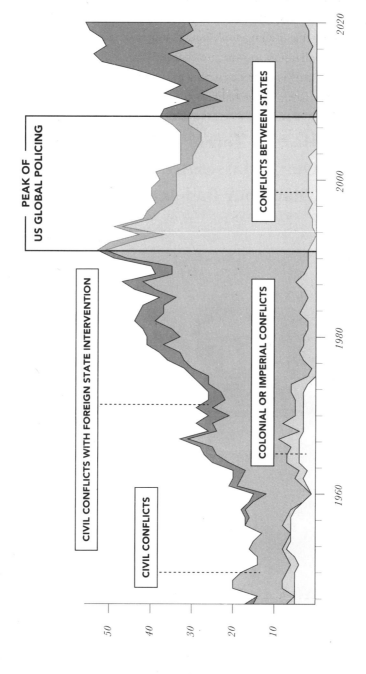

Symmetrizing the Global War on Terror (GWOT): Our Badasses Are Better Than Your Bad Actors

7

After 9/11, America deployed a big-war force to combat a small-wars opponent. Obama rightsized our GWOT effort while embracing targeted killings, creating risky new rules.

I nside the US national security community across the early decades of the Cold War, there arose the following tagline to explain how America kept ahead of the Soviets on arms and space racing: "Our Germans are better than their Germans." That toss-off statement expressed the judgment that the United States had bested the USSR in snatching up Nazi Germany's top scientific talent at the end of World War II. True or not (and it was mostly true), the key concept here is the wisdom of symmetry when assembling national assets for employment in a competition or conflict. In other words, show up with the appropriate weapon.

Sounds sensible, but it is quite hard when you are a democracy acting as the world's policeman. First, you must cover the whole strategic nuclear war challenge. Then you must field a conventional force capable of taking on all comers anywhere in the world. Finally, you must cover the *everything else* out there: terrorism, insurgencies, disasters, piracy, postwar reconstructions, training local forces—in all, a daunting spread of required capabilities.

During the Cold War, the Pentagon's answer to this coverage issue was to focus on big-war scenarios—namely, fighting the Soviet Red Army. The assumption was, if we could do that well, then we could cover all those smaller missions, collectively known in the post–Cold War era as Military Operations Other Than War (MOOTW).

Unfortunately, history has repeatedly proven that notion to be wrong. In the 1960s, America took its big-war force to Vietnam's civil war and found we could win every large-scale battle with the North Vietnamese army but could not prevail in an insurgent-led conflict within South Vietnam. By the time our forces made progress on the latter front, the US public wanted out. We would repeat this entire process in Somalia in the 1990s (consider, for example, the film *Black Hawk Down*), and both Iraq and Afghanistan in the 2000s. In each instance, we employed our big-war force in small-war situations and failed to adjust fast enough to that asymmetry. For those of us making such arguments within the Department of Defense during the George W. Bush administration, that was a tough sell, but one mostly realized with the publication of an Army–Marine Corps Counterinsurgency Manual and the 2007 Iraq "surge" of additional US troops. Then Barack Obama was elected president in 2008, reflecting America's exhaustion with the entire GWOT.

What happened next was both more of the same (e.g., an Afghanistan surge in 2010) and something different. Obama wanted out of both GWOT wars. Understanding the futility of fighting asymmetrically (i.e., our big-war force fighting insurgents and terrorists), he symmetrized the GWOT, turning it into a fight between our scariest and most capable badasses (Special Operations Forces) and their bad actors. By doing so, the Pentagon re-embraced the our-Germans-are-better-than-your-Germans ethos and stopped stubbornly trying to make the enemy fit our force.

Kudos to Obama on that. However, that strategic shift came with a catch: now the argument arose that the big-war Blue forces needed their own special buildup after years of watching small-war Green forces gobble up so much of the Pentagon's budget. To justify America's withdrawal from Iraq and years later Afghanistan, the Obama administration required a new strategic target— hence, the proclaimed "pivot" to Asia. To attract congressional funding, the Pentagon needed a new force-sizing opponent for the foreseeable future—the long-anticipated Chinese military threat. Our Leviathan needs a near-peer challenger, and, thanks to Putin, we now have two to plan against. The Pentagon strongly prefers a foreseeable future.

An awkward legacy of Obama's GWOT makeover was his vigorous embrace of select killings of high-value targets—those enemies our government most wants dead. By doing so, America established precedents that competing great powers now readily exploit. Consider Putin's targeted killings of Russian émigrés and defectors, Israel's assassinations of senior Iranian government officials, and Saudi Arabia's murdering of regime critics such as the journalist Jamal Khashoggi. China's maximally preemptive targeting of its restive Muslim Uighurs elevates this approach to an industrial scale, to include forced abortions and sterilizations (per *Terminator* logic, there is no need to assassinate the rebel leader never born).

True to our era, great powers primarily wage war on individuals, but with a frighteningly preemptive, "pre-crime" logic fundamentally codified by US actions and policies across the GWOT. See Steven Spielberg's 2002 *Minority Report* for a compelling projection of that dystopian future.

Israel's stubborn GWOT-era strategy across its Palestinian territories, known as "mowing the lawn," involves regularly decimating bad-actor groups through military strikes that often cause significant collateral damage. To critics, that approach cruelly symmetrizes means (punitive destruction) and ends (terrorized population). While the United States often condemns Israel's cutthroat variant, our GWOT approach uncomfortably resembles it and, by doing so, intrinsically justifies it. Donald Trump correctly noted that the GWOT turned many world leaders into "killers."

History will record America's GWOT wars as superpower-scale examples of "mowing the lawn." In their self-serving justifications, the same can be said of China's brutal policies in its western provinces and Putin's punitive campaigns against former Soviet republics: superpowers trying to prevent populations from defecting to forces they view as existential threats. In its zero-sum thinking, this approach is the opposite of the voluntary affiliation that increasingly defines digitalized globalization, wherein individuals maintain a portfolio of self-selected identities, loyalties, and allegiances across a panoply of both real and virtual communities worldwide.

As such, the United States must supersede such sticks by developing and prioritizing new carrots. To prevail in the superpower brand wars, ours must be a different path. Our world craves security far more than defense, and no state is more experienced or talented at exporting the former around our planet than America.

8

America's New Map:
Climate Change as Globalization's
Next Ordering Principle

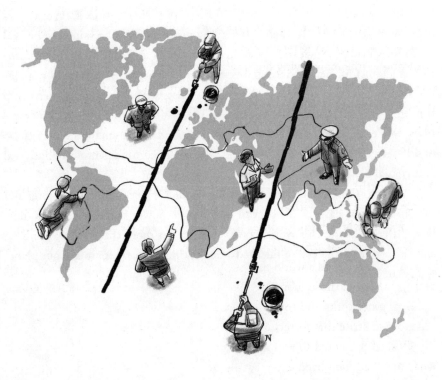

During the post–Cold War era, globalization's least connected states generated the most salient threats. Climate change further "verticalizes" global instabilities, forcing consolidation along North-South lines.

Two decades ago, I was tasked by my superiors in the Office of the Secretary of Defense to explain how 9/11 had redrawn our military's geostrategic outlook. My book *The Pentagon's New Map*, which began as a PowerPoint briefing delivered throughout the US government and overseas, subsequently morphed into a viral *Esquire* article and landed on the *New York Times* bestseller list. Over the years, its iconic image of the world has been replicated in military strategy documents around the world, often without attribution—the map having outgrown its maker.

To populate this new map, I plotted where US military forces had been deployed around the world since the Cold War's end in response to conflicts, crises, and disasters. I then simply drew a line encompassing virtually all of them, resulting in an equatorially centric shape falling overwhelmingly within a latitudinal band stretching 30 degrees north and south (rechristened here as Middle Earth). Upon further research, it became clear that my map comprised all the mass violence within the global system, concentrated in less-developed nations narrowly or weakly connected to the global economy—hence my mantra, *Disconnectedness defines danger.*

My map revealed a world that the US military had been tasked with reluctantly managing: those "non-integrated gap" regions that lacked globalization's stabilizing networks and the rules that come with them, leaving them susceptible to civil strife that fosters terrorism and other transnational instabilities.

What I presented to admirals and generals in briefings merely confirmed what they had long been experiencing, which is why they embraced that perspective in the years that followed. But to many Americans, this was a decidedly new map, one that suggested that most of what they would understand as threats, instabilities, dangers, and bad actors would flow from our globe's middle regions and toward the poles—just as scientists were already tracking the spreading impact of climate change.

In evangelizing this strategic vision, I was under no illusion that great powers would abandon their rivalries. Their growing mutual integration only incentivizes the most ambitious within their ranks to revise globalization's recognized rulesets in their favor—a dynamic on full display in Ukraine. Proxy wars would continue, driven more often by great powers other than the United States (e.g., Russia working its "near abroad," China recompiling its Middle Kingdom). Globalization's rapid advance was putting all sorts of regions in play, as far as the world's superpowers were concerned. Where some saw only burden, others spotted opportunity.

In my worldview, globalization is a stabilizing, pacifying force that nonetheless initially triggers significant social unrest, political instability, and mass violence as it penetrates far-less-connected regions. In quickly leveling the economic playing field by directly connecting individuals to global markets through technologies like smartphones, globalization disproportionately empowers those historically disadvantaged in the political realm—particularly women. That transformation fosters grassroots pressure for increased political freedom, directly challenging authority figures in traditional societies, along with regional hegemons fearful of losing their spheres of influence (see Russia on Ukraine). I described this geostrategic landscape as the *Pentagon's* new map for a reason: such revolutionary dynamics are inherently destabilizing, which is why civil unrest tends to be most concentrated in countries embracing globalization at higher velocities. So yes, globalization remains a clear long-term good; it just comes with some terrifically stressing near-term consequences— insurgencies and terrorism chief among them. With such tectonic forces at work, significant friction is guaranteed.

In the last book of my "Pentagon's New Map" trilogy, 2009's *Great Powers*, I predicted that America's Global War on Terror would inevitably succumb to a new national-security ordering principle: the next preeminent and—for too many—existential threat of climate change. In sensing that inevitable shift, I was less prescient than realistic. Once America got good enough at suppressing transnational terrorism, Americans would instinctively gravitate toward a bigger, more compelling crisis.

That time has arrived—as has America's new map.

Many experts say we need to heal our nation before addressing such external dynamics. I tell you that taking on these global challenges is exactly how we heal America.

Climate Changes Everything:
A Horizontal World
Made Vertical

THROUGHLINE TWO

Beginning in 1950, globalization sent every measure of human activity sky-rocketing, in turn greatly accelerating climate change. Now, climate change remaps globalization in reply.

F lat maps deeply influence how we see our world, establishing—and often distorting—our spatial understanding of where we stand relative to everyone else. Those global projections most familiar to us present America in the upper left-hand corner, confirming several cultural biases: Being on top is good and powerful. Being on the far left marks us as the truest Westerners. As many of us originated in Europe, that region naturally sits smack dab in the center. Since we read left to right, America begins the map in the narrative lead. Finally, with the dominant, north-biased Mercator projection, our fifty states visually equate to the entirety of South America, when—in truth—we occupy half its landmass.

Three-dimensional globes represent our spherical world with genuine accuracy, albeit with one huge bias. Nothing in this universe mandates that magnetic north is up while south is down, which is why plenty of ancient maps looked "up" to the east or even the south. Ptolemy, the second-century Greek cartographer who first applied the grid methodology of latitudes and longitudes, decided—for reasons lost to history—that north was on top. If he had chosen differently, America could have ended up where Australia is relegated today: the strategic cul-de-sac that is the lower right-hand corner. Imagine the ignominy!

Then there are our cognitive maps, or the way our minds organize and remember spaces once explored. For the longest time, our forebearers came (or were forcibly brought) here from continents to the east. Having landed on our East Coast, they settled ever westward as our nation expanded. To us, the East is old, yesterday, and crowded, while the West is forever new, tomorrow, and limitless. We apply no such distinctions to North or South—just colder or warmer.

All those geographic biases are challenged by a globalization that recently elevated Asia and now empowers the South. Climate change adds injury to that insult, turning our world upside down by centering itself in the Global South and unleashing its most destabilizing dynamics northward. In short, those Northern powers that long ruled this world now feel themselves on the receiving end of its turbulent waves of change—a truly humbling experience that nonetheless reflects humanity's stunning capacity to redefine our planet.

When the United States set in motion what would eventually become globalization, no one involved in propagating that economic ruleset had any idea they were initiating a new geological era. But in making the world ultimately safe enough for a global middle class to emerge, American-style globalization did just that: transforming so much of our environment as to elevate humanity to Earth's prime geological force. For example, human activity, measured in species and habitat loss, has altered 97 percent of lands outside of Antarctica and each year moves ten times more rock and sediment than Mother Nature. We have altered the atmosphere far more, suffusing it with one trillion tons of carbon, which, according to *New York Times* science journalist David Wallace-Wells, "weighs more than absolutely everything that humans have ever built on this planet and still standing on Earth today."

In recognition of humanity's extraordinary influence over Earth, the scientific community debates changing the name of our planet's current geological age from Holocene (meaning "entirely new epoch" following the last Ice Age) to the controversial Anthropocene ("human epoch"). Some scientists designate the Anthropocene's start date as 1945, or when humans started detonating nuclear bombs. Given the nuclear age's role in enabling modern globalization, that seems logical.

As to the larger implication of this name change, it is not reductionist to blame climate change on humans. In seeding and spreading a world economic system, American-style globalization sent consumption skyrocketing across numerous resources (e.g., energy, water, fisheries, wood, fertilizer), in turn radically expanding numerous industries (mining, manufacturing, construction, agriculture, transportation, telecommunications, tourism) and triggering an explosion of pollution (carbon dioxide, methane, nitrous oxide, chlorofluorocarbons, heavy metals, "forever" chemicals). All this economic activity results in vast environmental damage (forest loss, biosphere degradation, ocean acidification, species extinction) and—yes—rising surface temperatures. When climate change deniers reduce that vast equation to *humans = warmer planet*, it does seem ludicrous. Thus, it is crucial that we all understand the true breadth of globalization's environmental impact.

If America deserves the lion's share of credit for globalization's successes, then we must accept similar blame for climate change. The two dynamics cannot be separated, which is probably why America leads the world in climate change denialism. Already stressed by globalization's competitive pressures, many of us cannot imagine simultaneously leading the world's response to climate change. The size of the task is simply too intimidating.

Yet there is no escaping this historical moment. As Gaia Vince details in *Nomad Century: How Climate Migration Will Reshape Our World*, we are on course for as much as a 4°C (7°F) rise in average global temperature by century's end, a development that will "render the planet unrecognizable from anything that humans have ever experienced." Humanity now enters an era of environmental turbulence that will last decades and recast our species' future. Yes, our ongoing technological efforts to mitigate climate change are likely to dampen its effects across the second half of this century, but that begs the question of how much geopolitical stress and destruction the world system will have to endure between now and then.

No government or multinational union can be certain of its survival in this unprecedented journey: neither vulnerable Southern nations suffering radical depopulation nor brittle Northern ones facing waves of environmental refugees. All we can be sure of is (1) the most innovative and radically adaptable nation-states will do better than those choosing inaction or rigidity, and (2) those superpowers offering the most attractive North-South integration schemes will end up not just running their "vertical" slice of the planet but dramatically influencing, by the power of their example, how other slices come together. This competition begins now.

We can hope, per Vince, for an eventual "species-wide approach." We also see one coming together *ever so slowly* in the United Nations Framework

Convention on Climate Change (UNFCCC) and its highly publicized annual Conference of the Parties (COP 27 being the latest in 2022). But if history is any guide, the biggest breakthroughs will emerge out of a fiercely competitive contest among the most capable and ambitious powers that craft—and subsequently leverage—regionalized North-South schemes for their own political, economic, and ideological gain. In other words, the geopolitical marketplace decides. America can choose to embrace this inescapable competition as an opportunity to both improve and expand our Union's standing and influence in the world, or we can choose to hunker down, erect walls, and content ourselves with watching the world's other superpowers take the lead—China first and foremost.

Vince describes the "four horsemen of the Anthropocene" as fire, heat, drought, and flood—all requiring enormous state resources to combat. America witnesses their arrival throughout our Union, along with the pressures they generate among citizens to seek safer ground, often with government aid.

Vince points out that over half the world's population is concentrated along the 27th parallel north in a belt that "has traditionally been the latitude of most comfortable climate and fertile land." That band, lying within my definition of Middle Earth, sits just below the US southern border. With that sweet zone shifting tectonically northward every year, how can Americans believe a thirty-foot wall will block that global dynamic? As Vince declares, there will be two types of people in this future: those put on the move by climate change and those receiving them.

Nomad Century notes that "mass migrations this century will be dominated by people from the poor, climate-ravaged world moving to the richer world, countries whose wealth has largely been enabled by changing the climate." In Vince's judgment, this looming reality compels us to rethink the nature of the nation-state, elevating it beyond creed, race, and ancestry.

Agreed.

These United States have spent well over two centuries working on exactly such a model. Far from perfect but always perfecting, America is the world's most successful exercise in suppressing—for good and ill—the primordial mindset that humans, in Vince's words, "belong to a particular land and that it belongs to us." Many Americans left such sacred lands to come here and build something entirely new: states united merely by shared rights and pooled sovereignty.

Now Americans are tasked by history to take that vast experience and apply it to uniting states in the common cause of navigating our hemisphere through these tumultuous waters and landing us safely on history's far shore, our shared civilization intact and our collective citizenry beholden to no external powers.

A product of globalization, climate change presents America with this new map. There can be no greater challenge, nor any greater generation to meet it.

9

When Wide Beat Tall:
Why Humans See an
East-West World

Across history, geography and environment determined which continents ruled and which were ruled. With climate change cresting, they do so again along an entirely different vector.

Humans have historically viewed Earth primarily along an East-West axis because, with national power so consistently concentrated in the North, that is where the most significant action has unfolded—longitudinally. Today, all five superpowers (US, EU, Russia, India, and China) are spread west to east across the Northern Hemisphere. That has been the case throughout history, as there has never been any great tropical or Southern power. The North is where all the East-v-West system-reshaping wars were centered, while the tropics and South remain overwhelmingly the lands of small wars and insurgencies. Most notably throughout modern history, the North colonized and the rest were colonized. There has never been a compelling reason to recognize a North-South world—until now.

Climate change tilts our planet's strategic axis from West-East to South-North in what is the biggest and most rapid environmental transformation that humanity has ever experienced. You can challenge that judgment by noting how pervasively humanity has conquered the environment over time, so why assume the planet still possesses the capacity to detour human history so thoroughly? The answer is, the Earth has done so repeatedly to humanity in the past.

Earth's last Ice Age ended twelve thousand years ago. At that point, humans were hunter-gatherers dispersed across the world. Since then, humans, self-organizing into civilizations, have experienced what geographer Jared Diamond labeled "lopsided outcomes" in his 1997 classic, *Guns, Germs, and Steel*. Diamond asked why Eurasian imperial powers so readily conquered and colonized the rest of the world. In his analysis, the reason Eurasians had more advanced militaries (guns), stronger immune systems (germs), and better technologies (steel) did not stem from differences in race but from differences in geography and environment. Where you lived determined whether you were conqueror or conquered.

Diamond detailed how Eurasia's development raced ahead of other continents due to an underlying environmental advantage—the horizontal (longitudinal) width of its landmass relative to its vertical (latitudinal) height. Eurasia is twice as wide (13,000 km) as it is tall (7,000 km). In contrast, Africa is proportionally taller (8,000 km tall and averaging 5,000 km in width), while the Americas are Eurasia's opposite at 15,000 km tall versus 5,000 km at their widest—and 50 km at their thinnest.

Eurasia's primary developmental advantage was thus its environmental *sameness*—that 13,000-km band stretching from Ireland to Japan. Anything (viruses, crops, animals, technologies, social advances, etc.) that thrived anywhere along that vast swath found easy transmission and spread throughout the rest simply because adaptation was only minimally required.

In tall parts of the world like the Americas, that environmental sameness was limited to much thinner bands. When traversing latitudes (heading north or south), humans encountered profound environmental differences that naturally limited such developmental diffusion. What might work at one latitude typically could not find similar purchase in significantly higher or lower climes, where the environment was too different in temperature and seasonal profiles.

Per Diamond's telling, nature rewarded Eurasia's wide environmental sameness with a uniquely broad array of species suitable for domestication as crops and livestock. That led to the earlier and more rapid development of farming, which enabled a sedentary life that, in turn, encouraged the concentration of people in cities. All those domesticated animals transmitted, through zoonosis, their viruses to humans, bolstering the latter's immune systems, which, in turn, strengthened their biological capacity to live more densely in cities. The rise of cities led to the stratification and specialization of economic roles, which triggered technological advances that expanded and accelerated all the above-mentioned developments.

These positive feedback loops propelled Eurasian civilizations to heights such that, when the Age of Exploration brought them to other continents, those adventurers were supremely advantaged for conquest. The world's tall regions never had a chance. Because of its continental width, Eurasia ruled the world.

Through Diamond's analysis, we understand the power of one geographically expressed axis (East-West) over another (North-South). Once we accept that, we can imagine that power relationship being reversed through superior environmental forces. If previous, imperial iterations of globalization were fundamentally predetermined by our planet's environmental makeup, then we can posit that US-style globalization, having so reshaped Earth's environment as to earn its own geologic era, now determines humanity's future path.

Moreover, Diamond's analysis permits our agnosticism about the relative merits of one racially defined civilization over another. Such tolerance has been a crucial driver of US-style globalization these past seven decades. Drawing upon the examples of the English and, before them, the Dutch, the American commercial mindset is one of being willing to conduct business with anyone.

Finally, Diamond's work reestablishes the primacy of our planet in enabling and shaping human development—an environmental determinism to rival our embrace of economic determinism. Both capitalism and Marxism have too long suffered the mentality that humans find primary fulfillment in reshaping the world in their own image—no matter the cost. We saw where that took the Communist Bloc, and we now realize where capitalism has taken the planet. In that sense, climate change is the Industrial Revolution's karma finding full expression.

Does this new North-South axis portend colonialism's return? Just the opposite. Demographics, as we shall see (**Throughline Three**), work against that outcome. An aging North needs a youthful, consumer-confident South for its economic health. As such, a truly multipolar North will naturally compete to see which superpower can win, from across that South-centric global middle class, the most subscribers to their respective network offerings. Over time, this superpower competition will create a new international economic order (NIEO) of the sort long sought by the non-aligned South, in that sense repairing some portion of the developmental destruction wrought by the long colonial era.

10 *Middle Earth Is Doomed!*
North Integrates South or
Faces Its Disintegration!

Climate change renders Earth's lower latitudes increasingly unsuitable for nation-states as we have known them. The North addresses this harsh reality or faces something far worse.

Two inevitabilities arise from the scientific community's increasingly firm projections of climate change: First, higher latitudes (closer to poles) will experience significantly greater weather volatility—temperate zones made intemperate. Second, lower latitudes (closer to equator) will experience a harshening of their climes with increasingly frequent and extreme droughts accompanied by unlivable temperature ranges. In sum, the North's climate grows frighteningly erratic while the South's grows depressingly predictable.

Scientists have long warned of catastrophic outcomes if the world warmed merely 1.5°C (2.7°F) above preindustrial levels. Earth will hit that mark by 2040, with worldwide sea levels rising by one foot a decade later. For advanced Northern countries, we can anticipate monumental public expenditures and all manner of political controversy over how best to raise those funds. As for the South's most vulnerable states, it is not hyperbole to state that many of them should anticipate the end of life as they have long known it.

The South, except for South America, is far less urbanized than the North, reflecting a reliance on farming for jobs. With droughts, floods, fire, and heat making agriculture that much harder to conduct, rural masses will head for cities typically lacking both the infrastructure and opportunities to sustain them economically. Once there, these internal migrants are often trapped within the informal economy (black markets), rendering them both a burden to the state and prey to exploitation by criminal networks. Sufficiently oppressed, this displaced population is ripe for radicalization leading to extreme political paths.

Among the most ambitious or abused populations (take your pick), emigration becomes the next best option—no matter the dangers encountered. This is why environmental refugees risk dying on the high seas or in deserts in their attempts to access Northern states: they spot better odds in endangering their families than in toughing it out in their increasingly stressed-out homelands.

By midcentury, both the wider world and those peoples located along Earth's middle band will recognize that, in many instances, it no longer makes sense—politically or economically—to sustain independent nation-states there. I am not stating that it cannot be done, only that, in many cases, it will not be practicable. The North, with its rapidly aging populations, will not readily pay for it. Meanwhile, fragile Southern governments will find it hard to afford amidst persistent weather disasters and depopulation triggered by departing environmental refugees.

Development experts increasingly link state failure in the South to climate change, which reduces economic activity, forcing domestic factions to fight ever more fiercely over diminishing natural resources. According to the UN High Commissioner for Refugees (UNHCR), "ninety percent of refugees under UNHCR's mandate, and 70 percent of people displaced within their home countries by conflict and violence, come from countries on the front lines of the climate emergency." Today, we measure that distressed population in the tens of millions. Later this century, we will count them in the billions. Left to its own modest devices, much of the South will crater politically.

Today, less than 1 percent of the world's land surface consistently endures temperatures above 30°C (86°F)—life in today's sparsely populated Sahara Desert. By 2070, one-fifth of Earth's lands—and one-third of humans—will suffer such extremity on a continuous basis. Already across Middle Earth, laborers forced to endure high temperatures are proving to be highly vulnerable to organ damage, for example triggering epidemics of chronic kidney disease. Rich Persian Gulf monarchies may be willing to finance such a rarefied existence for their citizens—perhaps even critical workforces—but they will be the exception. We should instead anticipate that many of those three billion souls will be forced to leave their homelands.

Most will choose internal displacement in their home country or emigrate to a neighboring state. Even so, the North could face a billion environmental refugees heading their way this century. From today's perspective, this seems inconceivable. But let us factor in just how much livable land will be revealed in the North by climate change (twice the size of Australia) and then calculate just how empty Canada, Russia, Greenland, and Alaska are in relative population density (a mere fraction of the world average). Taking both into account, it seems implausible that Northern states would expend great blood and treasure solely to keep that mass of humanity suffering in place when clear alternatives (e.g., Russia's depopulation) present themselves. As Gaia Vince argues in *Nomad Century*, "The conversation about migration has been stuck on what ought to be allowed, rather than planning for what will occur." That will soon change.

This growth in South-to-North migration will mirror the uneven impact climate change has on crop yields throughout the world. Canada, America, and Europe will enjoy a slight improvement through 2050 (1 to 2 percent), while Russia and Central Asia will welcome a 7 percent gain. Meanwhile, other highly populated regions face double-digit declines (East Asia, South Asia, Africa, and the Middle East).

Climate-driven water and food insecurity already fuels the northward migration of environmental refugees. Sub-Saharan Africa and Central America, for example, currently suffer devastating, record-breaking droughts. As a result, the Institute for Economics & Peace estimates that upwards of half of the world's population—overwhelmingly concentrated in that Middle Earth band—"will reside in countries with high and extreme ecological threats." Today, our estimates of likely northbound environmental refugees are based on the historical experience of ecological disasters occurring on a national or regional basis. To be realistic, we should expect that the simultaneity of world-spanning disasters associated with climate change will redefine our sense of how much pain populations can endure before they emigrate. In most cases, the traditional response of moving within the country or to a neighboring one will not be sufficient, meaning we should expect the unexpected when it comes to the poleward migration of Middle Earthers who feel they have no other choice when it comes to their long-term survival.

For some time now, America has experienced a seemingly permanent surge in asylum seekers from the Northern Triangle region of Guatemala, Honduras, and El Salvador. While the US anti-immigration movement accuses them of gaming our system, most are genuine environmental refugees whose journey was triggered by successive crop failures and destructive hurricanes. Across that region's infamous Dry Corridor, the World Food Programme estimates that "two out of every three people are in urgent need of food assistance due to years of drought." Washington attempts to address local government corruption stemming from the drug trade and gang activities, but that does not address the underlying causality, which grows far worse with time. Come midcentury, climate change will trim Latin America's GDP by 4 percent each year—more than triple the US impact.

Some small portion of those northward-flowing refugees will be radicalized by the fate they and their peoples suffer. A grim scenario is today seen in Africa's Saharan and Trans-Sahel regions, where growing water shortages trigger civil strife among fishers, farmers, and herders. We can label these struggles a "clash of civilizations" pitting Muslims versus Christians, but that confuses correlation with causality. Skyrocketing environmental stress drives radicalization, with religious extremists exploiting the resulting conflicts.

The North, in its continuing efforts to wall itself off from the South's violent extremist and transnational criminal organizations, can try to geographically contain those negative dynamics. In extremis, we can even attempt to go full *Escape from New York* on those typically far weaker states—much like Donald Trump's southwestern wall scheme supposedly protected Americans from Mexico's criminal elements. But unless we are prepared to accept some sort of *Mad Max* dystopia in these godforsaken regions, we must imagine a better path.

The United States currently pursues a strategy of limited regret with Middle Earth's slate of failed/fragile states. We send foreign aid. When that is not enough, we send military personnel to train security forces. And when that fails, we send in Special Forces to kill their bad actors. This narrow approach will not suffice in coming decades because it makes it far too easy for China and even Russia to outperform us by peddling Orwellian social-control technologies and techniques.

America needs to ramp up its game by innovating new forms of state affiliation for connecting South to North. These must broker more viable forms of statehood in the former while modulating the flow of climate refugees to the latter, the goal being to keep the South's most resilient populations in place. Ultimately, the North must develop new bilateral and multilateral schemes that allow for the pooling of political sovereignty among stronger Northern states and their more vulnerable Southern counterparts. These unions will stabilize the latter by offering varying degrees of economic protection from their increasingly dire local circumstances—bringing them in from the heat, so to speak.

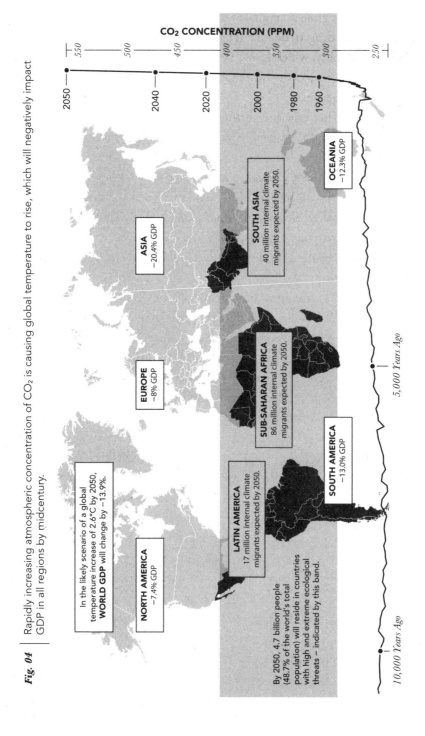

Fig. 04 | Rapidly increasing atmospheric concentration of CO_2 is causing global temperature to rise, which will negatively impact GDP in all regions by midcentury.

CO₂ CONCENTRATION (PPM)

550 | 500 | 450 | 400 | 350 | 300 | 250

2050
2040
2020
2000
1980
1960

In the likely scenario of a global temperature increase of 2.6°C by 2050, **WORLD GDP** will change by −13.9%.

NORTH AMERICA
−7.4% GDP

LATIN AMERICA
17 million internal climate migrants expected by 2050.

By 2050, 4.7 billion people (48.7% of the world's total population) will reside in countries with high and extreme ecological threats – indicated by this band.

EUROPE
−8% GDP

SUB-SAHARAN AFRICA
86 million internal climate migrants expected by 2050.

SOUTH AMERICA
−13.0% GDP

ASIA
−20.4% GDP

SOUTH ASIA
40 million internal climate migrants expected by 2050.

OCEANIA
−12.3% GDP

5,000 Years Ago

10,000 Years Ago

11

Poleward Bound (I Wish I Were . . .): Climate Change Puts Every Species on the Move

Climate change forces every life-form to adapt, move, or die. Moving pole-ward is the only realistic path for most, resulting in the greatest wealth transfer in human history.

A s a child growing up in Wisconsin, I was dazzled by rainbows, as they were rare. After living several decades out east, I moved back to the Dairy State and was stunned to see more rainbows in one summer than I had encountered across my youth. That frequency is hardly unprece-dented; spend any time in Hawaii, the Rainbow State, and you will routinely spot them. But in Wisconsin, those rainbows really knocked me for a loop, as though my home state had imported some other state's weather.

It turns out that is exactly what is going on.

Thanks to climate change, global cloud patterns and dynamics have migrated poleward. What used to be midlatitude storm tracks are now found at significantly higher latitudes, in large part because subtropical dry zones, saddled with mega-droughts, have expanded, pushing higher-altitude clouds poleward. At higher latitudes, this crowding effect stacks cloud formations, rendering them thicker and taller and thus turbocharging their precipitation. All this makes Middle Earth far hotter and drier and the North tumultuously wetter—hence more Wisconsin rainbows.

Pragmatically speaking, climate change is most easily grasped like real estate, where the three most important rules are *location, location, location*. Climate change transforms our planet location *by* location, taking things long associated with one region and moving them somewhere different. *What* is hap-pening may not seem unprecedented to you, but *where* it is happening should.

Humans consider land to be the most elemental form of wealth. Climate change relocates that wealth, whether we like it or not—much less believe in the science. We should be stunned by what we are seeing around the world today, because we are witnessing the greatest transfer of wealth in human history. In terms of reshaping the global order, nothing compares to climate change right now or for the foreseeable future—*nothing*.

People already migrate poleward in search of basic food security because that is where they will ultimately find new arable land. Scientists project that humanity's farm belts will shift well over 1,000 km poleward this century, with the biggest gains obviously for Canada and Russia. However, any such windfall in the North will be offset and negated by losses in the South. No money changes hands in these climate-driven real estate transfers: winners take all, while losers are left high and very dry. Recall America's Dust Bowl era of the 1930s and the westward migration it triggered, and understand this is how terrorist movements, insurgencies, and revolutions arise throughout history: peasants forced off the land.

In response to such profound environmental change, any species has three essential choices: adapt, move, or die. We will see plenty of each this century.

Like evolution on steroids, climate change demands that all species—including us—adapt to environmental shifts that used to unfold over hundreds of thousands of years but now proceed in mere decades. Asking animals and plants to speed up their evolution ten thousand times is a nonstarter for most. That means a stunning number of species are disappearing across Earth's current and sixth mass extinction era—due to human activity.

Thousands of studies indicate that most species, while furiously adapting, still fall behind the climate change curve. Shifting the timing of key biological processes (e.g., salmon showing up earlier to spawn) is one thing, while changing morphology (body characteristics) or diet is far more difficult. In general, species smaller in size, with shorter life spans and higher-frequency procreation, adapt better than larger, longer-lived species.

That means climate change is an evolutionary boon for parasites and pathogens—vectors of human disease. Invasive species can quickly devastate a local environment, rendering what once made it desirable into something dreadful. As a rule, parasites and pathogens stay put, but introduced to a new latitude, they opportunistically adapt to new hosts—the worst sort of evolution. Think about a recent local news story about some nasty species showing up in your backyard.

Even scarier is humans' increased exposure to all manner of viruses that, until climate change unearthed them, remained buried deep in the Amazon rain forest or Siberia's permafrost. Add wildfires to the former and rapid melting to the latter and humans can expect many "first contacts" with novel viruses like SARS-CoV-2, the virus that causes COVID-19.

For many species, migration is the only answer. For decades, species have been moving toward the poles at an annual rate of two kilometers. They also annually shift one meter to higher elevations. To us house dwellers, that seems minor. For nature, these rates are three times the normal pace. As with all things climate changed, developments advance imperceptibly until suddenly achieving system-threatening impact—the boiled frog parable.

Over the next decades, humanity faces several accelerating feedback loops that will trigger no-turning-back points in regions such as the Arctic/Antarctic (ice melt, loss of solar reflection); Amazon (carbon-sink loss); and Siberia (methane release). Once tipping points are reached, the resulting climate dynamics leap beyond human causality and become self-perpetuating.

Humans rule Earth because we are supremely adaptive and resilient. Unlike other species struggling to adapt at ten thousand times normal evolutionary speed, we can achieve that tempo through technological advance. What is missing right now are the political and economic relationships and mechanisms necessary to mount such a multilateral effort at adaptation while ensuring universal access to its innovations. In effect, climate change can reestablish a divide between haves and have-nots that humanity essentially erased through the ascendancy of US-style globalization and the global middle class it birthed. America's single greatest achievement is thus put entirely at risk by climate change.

Per the location mantra, America needs to start constructing those North-South relationships and mechanisms here in our hemisphere. If we cannot achieve such synergy with our neighbors, it will not matter if we can generate it elsewhere.

Multination-building should begin at home.

Fig. 05 | As global temperatures rise, climate zones around the planet are shifting.

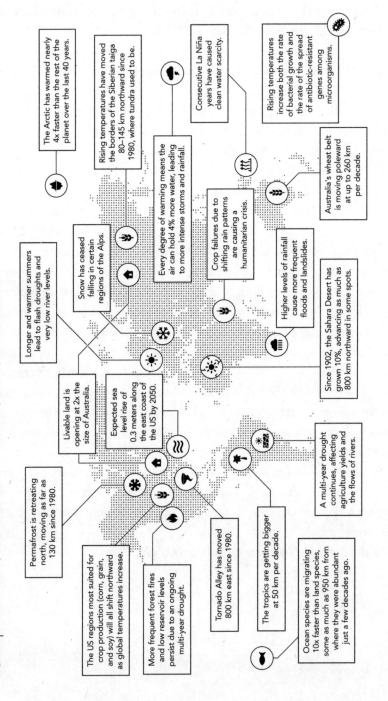

The Arctic has warmed nearly 4x faster than the rest of the planet over the last 40 years.

Rising temperatures have moved the borders of the Siberian taiga 80–145 km northward since 1980, where tundra used to be.

Consecutive La Niña years have caused clean water scarcity.

Rising temperatures increase both the rate of bacterial growth and the rate of the spread of antibiotic-resistant genes among microorganisms.

Longer and warmer summers lead to flash droughts and very low river levels.

Snow has ceased falling in certain regions of the Alps.

Every degree of warming means the air can hold 4% more water, leading to more intense storms and rainfall.

Crop failures due to shifting rain patterns are causing a humanitarian crisis.

Australia's wheat belt is moving poleward at up to 260 km per decade.

Higher levels of rainfall cause more frequent floods and landslides.

Livable land is opening at 2x the size of Australia.

Expected sea level rise of 0.3 meters along the east coast of the US by 2050.

Since 1902, the Sahara Desert has grown 10%, advancing as much as 800 km northward in some spots.

Permafrost is retreating north, moving as far as 130 km since 1980.

The US regions most suited for crop production (corn, grain, and soy) will all shift northward as global temperatures increase.

A multi-year drought continues, affecting agriculture yields and the flows of rivers.

More frequent forest fires and low reservoir levels persist due to an ongoing multi-year drought.

Tornado Alley has moved 800 km east since 1980.

The tropics are getting bigger at 50 km per decade.

Ocean species are migrating 10x faster than land species, some as much as 950 km from where they were abundant just a few decades ago.

12 *Go North, Young Man!*
The Geopolitical Upside
of Climate Change

What the South loses in usable land, the North gains. With a handful of Northern powers in charge of the Arctic, expect mergers and acquisitions among powers looking to scale up.

N o part of our world will be more transformed by climate change than the northern quarter of the planet, home to the vast circumpolar biome known as the taiga—a thick boreal forest resting on rapidly melting permafrost. Framed by the treeless tundra to the north and grasslands to the south, the taiga's northward *climate velocity*—the rate and direction that climate shifts across Earth's surface—is three kilometers per year. As this biome shift reveals arable land in its southern wake, it will render livable a band of Northern territory twice the size of Australia (14 million km²).

Gaining that 10 percent of the world's landmass will offset a similar loss of livable territory along its middle quarter. Humanity swaps one environmental collapse (equatorial) for another (Arctic), accepting in compensation what geographer Laurence C. Smith dubs "the New North." There, a new civilization appears destined to arrive—or not, depending on which rulesets prevail. Toward the too-hot South, Northern states must develop strategies and institutions that manage first economic distress and then political collapse, while to the warming North, they must first generate civic structures and then economic development—all amidst an unstoppable poleward migration of humans.

It may strike you as implausible that Latin Americans will somehow show up in Canada's New North as immigrant farmers, but it should not. Recall Abraham Lincoln's wartime scheme (the 1863 Homestead Act) to lure European immigrant farmers to the American West with the promise of 160 free acres. Who migrates to a country during its civil war? Well, Lincoln needed to keep up wartime food production. If Canada once populated its west with a similar offering to European immigrants, then why not its North with Latinos? In recent years, some of the fastest-growing US counties for Latinos sit just below Canada's southern border in states like North Dakota. Just give it some time.

The good news: except for Russia, the Northern states in charge of the Arctic's future are among the best-run and most progressively globalizing governments in the world—namely, the United States, Canada, Denmark (representing its autonomous territory of Greenland), Iceland, Norway, Sweden, and Finland.

While many security experts forecast a tense race to militarize the Arctic, there are reasons to believe this frontier's eventual development will unfold without great-power conflict. Primary among them has been the agenda-setting success of the Arctic Council, established in 1996 by that octet of Northern states. While just a dialogue forum that generates guidelines—all strictly non-military in scope—the council has established nonbinding rules that nonetheless modulate members' competing ambitions. There are, for example, no serious land border disputes among members—fingers crossed post-Ukraine.

Meanwhile, the 1982 United Nations Convention on the Law of the Sea (UNCLOS), with its designation of each maritime nation's offshore 200-mile Exclusive Economic Zone (EEZ), has served as the Arctic's most workable, if nonspecific, international treaty, ratified by all council member states save America, which still abides by its rules. There are conflicting interpretations of which, if any, states control the two "Northern passages" now made available for cargo shipping during an increasingly longer ice-free summer each year: Moscow claims sovereignty over most of the Northern Sea Route running the length of Eurasia's Arctic shoreline, while Canada argues the North-West Passage comprises its interior waters. The United States considers all such waterways free and open to all international traffic.

All of these issues take a back seat to the anticipated exploitation of the Arctic's hydrocarbon deposits. Thirty percent of the world's conventional natural gas reserves are found there, enough to draw energy-fixated Beijing's determined attention. Granted observer status in 2013, China has significantly ramped up its diplomatic and investment activities across Greenland, Iceland, and Finland. Beijing finances Russia's segment of China's Polar Silk Road initiative linking naval stations, military outposts, and ports. Still, with most of those hydrocarbons (84 percent) located within members' EEZs, there are few disputes to be had.

In the end, the Arctic Council succeeds because it has no rulemaking rival. As far as the Arctic goes, it is the only game in town. That may change with time.

The big question going forward is whether Eurasia's East-West divide eventually splits the Arctic Council, which currently comprises five NATO members (United States, Canada, Iceland, Norway, and Denmark) and—post-Ukraine—two NATO partners suddenly seeking and inevitably receiving full membership (Sweden and Finland), leaving Russia out in the cold. The council suspended activities in 2022 following then-chair Russia's invasion of Ukraine.

As usual, the prime beneficiary of Russia's growing isolation is Beijing, which years ago formally declared its ambition to be a "polar great power." It is easy to imagine a special arrangement between cash-strapped Moscow and cash-flush Beijing resulting in China's purchase of Russia's Far East, earning it full membership in the Arctic Council. Recall China ruled Outer Manchuria until 1860. Remember, too, that America acquired its seat from the very same source under similar circumstances—otherwise known as the Alaska Purchase of 1867.

As for Smith's idea of a new Northern civilization in the making? It all comes down to competing rulesets. In North America, the United States and Canada have pioneered the ruleset of empowering their Northern Indigenous populations with substantial land ownership—in sharp contrast to how they disempowered First Nation peoples in southern Canada and America's Lower 48. Today, Native Alaska–owned regional corporations control one-ninth of that state's territory (forty million acres and their mineral rights), while various Canadian tribes similarly control more than one billion acres across that nation's vast northern territories.

In contrast, Europe and Russia remain committed to, in Smith's judgment, the "mummification" of Indigenous populations by encouraging their isolated maintenance of distinct cultures while denying them ownership of land sufficient to control their developmental destiny. Herein lies the lesson: If you seek political buy-in, first enable the economic buy-in among all involved.

Still, there is a tendency among Western experts to assert that Russia is far more likely to "win" climate change than Europe or North America. In terms of sheer size, there is no question that Russia brings far more to the table, but it is important to remember that such large-scale frontier development will require unprecedented migrations from the South.

Canada was built by immigration; Russia was not. Both face aging populations and must overcome domestic xenophobia, but the key differentiator here is political: Canada possesses one of the most competent and admired governments in the world, whereas Russia's is infamously corrupt, brutal in its authoritarianism, and widely despised. Finally, Canada is likely to attract Latin Americans, while Russia will pull in neighboring Muslims and Chinese. Given the respective histories of these civilizations, it seems a safe bet that Canada will dramatically outperform Russia in integrating large stocks of immigrants, if only because Canada does not have to change its political or social culture to do so, while Russia most certainly does—and drastically.

Considering just how strategically important the Arctic North will become, along with how much more climate change will reformat Canada than the United States, there are solid arguments for the two to seek genuine union. Canadian journalist Diane Francis, author of *Merger of the Century: Why Canada and America Should Become One Country*, argues for the inevitability of this political development:

> If the United States and Canada were corporations, or European states, they would have merged a long time ago. Each has what the other needs: The United States has capital, manpower, technology, and the world's strongest military; Canada has enormous reserves of undeveloped resources and ownership of a vast and strategically important Arctic region.

Canada plus America would be the perfect twenty-first-century superpower, securing control over, in Francis's words, "more oil, water, arable land and resources than any jurisdiction on Earth." Each would make the other that much more powerful while together fielding a supremely attractive global brand. The most plausible path? A straight-up business merger not unlike that of East and West Germany. In grand strategic terms, I cannot imagine a smarter US move this century—whatever the cost. I mean, Alaska worked out, did it not?

Both the United States and Canada, along with Northern powers worldwide, will need to engage in such radically pragmatic strategizing as climate change remaps our planet. Instead of viewing this global transformation as triggering imperial or "White man's" burdens, we need to recognize it as opportunity—as in, what can America get out of this? How do we collectively define "winning" and what will be required to achieve it? America will exit this tumultuous era either bigger and stronger or smaller and weaker. As homeostasis is unachievable in human affairs, there will most certainly be winners and losers. Presently, America is on track to lose—an outcome unacceptable to any who truly love our nation.

If we restrict our strategic goals to simply preserving "American civilization," we will most certainly lose it—if not to climate change, then to demographic aging, for the two are inextricably intertwined. Climate change will depopulate the world's most crowded and youngest regions while opening vast new frontiers of economic opportunity across the world's least densely populated and most rapidly aging regions. As they have throughout history, human civilizations will rise and fall amidst such cataclysms unfolding in the natural world. If we want American civilization to emerge on the far side of these dueling disasters in the best possible shape, then we need to play our demographic aging off against our climate's changing—and vice versa. Only by putting each to use in solving the other can we balance this wickedly complex strategic equation and restore America's global leadership.

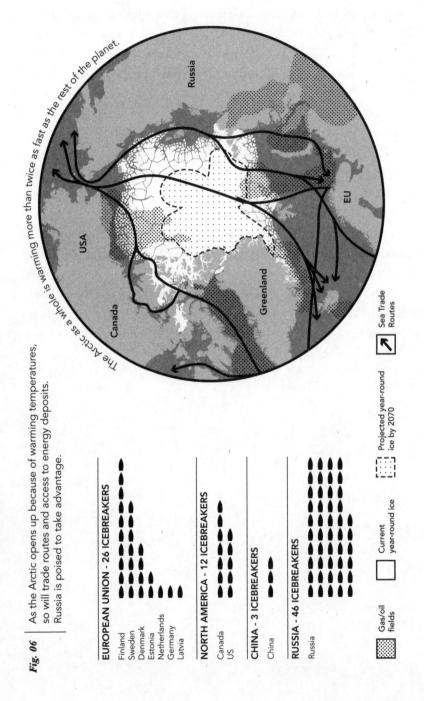

Fig. 06 | As the Arctic opens up because of warming temperatures, so will trade routes and access to energy deposits. Russia is poised to take advantage.

The Arctic as a whole is warming more than twice as fast as the rest of the planet.

EUROPEAN UNION - 26 ICEBREAKERS

Finland
Sweden
Denmark
Estonia
Netherlands
Germany
Latvia

NORTH AMERICA - 12 ICEBREAKERS

Canada
US

CHINA - 3 ICEBREAKERS

China

RUSSIA - 46 ICEBREAKERS

Russia

Gas/oil fields

Current year-round ice

Projected year-round ice by 2070

Sea Trade Routes

Destiny's Child:
How Demographics Determine
Globalization's Winners,
Losers, and Future

THROUGHLINE THREE

> Any nation's transition from a younger population to an older one creates opportunity for deep integration with the global economy. But even in such success, the social costs are daunting.

For most of human history, we adhered to the basic directive governing all species—maximum procreation. Numbers ensured survival, so we structured the foundations of our societies around that goal, in particular organized religion. Until very recently in history, this approach was entirely warranted. Preindustrial societies featured both high birth and death rates—a never-ending race to stay ahead of extinction's many enablers (e.g., disease, famine, pestilence, war).

But once industrialization takes root, it forever alters that primordial calculation. Improvements in farming drive laborers to cities, where advances in medicine—particularly vaccines—render early childhood less treacherous to navigate. Babies start making it to age five at far higher rates, dramatically extending life expectancy for society as a whole.

As the death rate declines, families follow suit on procreation. Once urbanized, it is no longer crucial to maximize the number of children, who shift from a family asset on the farm (more hands) to a family liability in town (more mouths). Women enter the workforce and gain access to reproductive controls, further depressing fertility. A new mindset emerges—family planning.

But it takes time for this new social understanding to spread. During that lag, a demographic transition is set in motion—one impossible to stop once it begins. Despite no longer needing to, people continue to procreate at the rural rate, triggering a natural increase in the form of a disproportionately large generation.

At first, this development is celebrated—a baby boom! Years later it engenders social fears of a youth bulge certain to trigger popular unrest, primarily in the form of crime but occasionally political revolution. If comprehensively employed by industry, that youth bulge morphs into an economic windfall—so many workers to provide for both young and old! This is the demographic dividend—the inflection point to a nation's economic rise. Celebrated at home, economic competitors will vilify its threat of *cheap labor!*

But here is the catch: Once the python has swallowed that pig, there is no turning back. The boom-turned-bulge-turned-dividend inevitably triggers an elder tsunami. With the birth rate permanently depressed by modern life (*Who can afford a big family nowadays?*), your society inexorably ages, in some instances (e.g., Japan, China) at a stunningly rapid rate.

Before you know it, your society is middle-aged and navigating a global economy driven primarily by youthful demands that strike you as trivial and greedy. You eventually become the elder sitting on globalization's porch, yelling at those *damn kids to get off my lawn!* That fear-driven sense of replacement can motivate your society toward cruel and hateful policies. As your body politic grows increasingly aged and infirm, you stop investing in a tomorrow you both fear and expect you will never see.

At that point, your nation faces a choice: open your economy to more youthful immigrants and accept how they alter your national identity, or indulge in xenophobia, shut yourself off from the world, achieve self-sufficiency no matter the economic cost, and somehow manage your aging from within (*How much for that robot in the window?*). In the latter strategy, your government might go to great lengths to encourage a natural increase (e.g., tax breaks, subsidized childcare, "hero mother" medals). You can add a stick to those carrots by outlawing abortion—even contraception, recasting pregnancy as legal jeopardy.

History says none of these will be enough. China recently rescinded its one-child policy that accompanied a demographic transition of breathtaking speed. But industrialization and urbanization have permanently stunted the average young Chinese's concept of family size. After thousands of years of exceptionally large families, most Chinese today cannot imagine risking a second child. That gives you a sense of the enormous power this demographic transition exerts over even the most traditional of civilizations.

Even so, the maxim "demography is destiny" is misleading because this transition, while all-powerful in its social impact, nonetheless contains a potential inflection point that can radically recast a nation's destiny. As that demographic dividend appears, nations can choose to seek foreign direct investment (FDI) and integration with global value chains, allowing them to turn their labor surplus into rapid economic development that improves standards of living. This choice is time limited: there are, at most, two to three decades of labor growth to exploit before succumbing to some combination of baby-bust and silver tsunami.

If you succeed, your economy's integration within globalization's production chains can eventually be reengineered to accommodate the explosion of domestic demand generated by your burgeoning middle class. If your economy is big enough, like China's, you become a new, gravity-altering demand center within globalization, which in turn begins to revolve around your mass consumption.

That journey, even when successful, is a wild ride requiring a cohesive society and a strong state. But there really is no good alternative to making that all-or-nothing effort. If your nation fails to grab this historically unique opportunity, any demographic boom you experience is like a tree falling in the forest—unheard, unexploited, unproductive.

The worst fate in our world is being destabilized by globalization's embrace while earning no long-term integration, for therein lies state failure. As climate change renders portions of Middle Earth unlivable, such failure is tantamount to state disintegration. At that point, what remains is absorbed—for good or ill—into some larger, more stable entity, or it is lost to some *Mad Max* hellscape.

The solution set is self-evident: there is some yet-to-be-determined optimal flow of the South's excess labor to the North that reduces Middle Earth's looming exposure to climate change while addressing the latter's rapid demographic aging. It is paramount for the North's superpowers to determine, on a region-by-region basis, this Goldilocks range—not so much that it destabilizes a depopulating North but just enough to demographically de-pressurize a climate-ravaged South.

It is precisely because immigration is already such a hot-button issue across the North today that such planning is anything but fanciful. This political conversation has already begun; we are just not being honest with ourselves over what is causing it and where such planning must ultimately take us.

13 *The Golden Ticket:* Cashing In a Demographic Dividend Is Hardly Guaranteed

Success breeds a middle class with unlimited expectations. Falling short risks joining the desperate ranks of failed states generating waves of northward-bound climate refugees.

D emographers speak of age pyramids because of the shape evoked in age-structure diagrams that vertically distribute population by age groups, with youth on the bottom and elders on top: traditional societies feature a broad base that narrows as you move up in age. A demographic dividend appears when that pyramid shape has been replaced by one resembling a diamond: narrower on the top and bottom and wider in the middle—a great economic situation but one impossible to sustain without significant immigration. Given enough demographic aging, what was once that stable pyramid morphs into a wobbly spinning top—an unprecedented and wholly unnatural age profile that Japan and South Korea are slated to achieve midcentury.

A demographic dividend becomes "cash-able" when the great bulk of your population lies between the working ages of fifteen and sixty-four, meaning your dependency ratio (youth plus elders relative to workers) is at its lowest. China is the classic example: in 1965 there were four Chinese dependents for every five workers (4:5), but by 2010 that burden was more than cut in half (<2:5). This radical transition fueled China's economic rise through a handful of complementary developments: an expanding supply of labor, particularly as women joined the workforce; rising GDP per capita because of that low dependency burden; a dramatic increase in the personal savings rate; and parents spending far more money on their children's education. Those reinforcing dynamics, married to export-driven growth that attracted foreign direct investment (FDI) flows, explain China's ascent, following the path trod by Japan and South Korea.

China's demographic dividend was triggered by a radical decline in fertility. It took America eight decades (1844–1926) to lower fertility from six children per woman to three. China did it in a decade (1967–1978). History attributes that decline to Beijing's infamous one-child policy, when, in truth, that edict only took effect in 1980, by which time China's fertility crash was well underway. Tellingly, China's fertility decline mirrored that of Taiwan across the same decades. Taipei had no such restrictive reproduction policy, suggesting that government policies mandating lower fertility are as ineffective as those promoting the opposite.

Fertility is primarily determined by what happens with girls and women when economic development takes root. If you want a demographic dividend, keep girls in school for as long as possible. It is as simple as that. Better-educated women have fewer kids, who in turn are themselves better educated—an economic win-win. Conversely, the easiest way to sabotage a dividend is to marry off young girls or mandate forced births. Capturing the full demographic dividend requires investment in human capital. Over the period of China's economic rise, Latin America enjoyed the same demographic opportunity, only to squander it through political corruption, minimal investment in education and health, and limited reproductive rights for women. While China's GDP increased sevenfold over those decades, Latin America merely doubled its output.

While a nation enjoys a demographic dividend, it needs to aggressively move up the global production ladder from low-end manufacturing and product assembly to higher-end manufacturing that leverages technology. Eventually, that superabundance of labor ages out, and, with lower fertility locked in, fewer young people entering the workforce invariably drives up wages. At that point, your nation joins the ranks of developed economies seeking cheap labor abroad for upstream portions of their global value chains. If you are wise, your economy starts investing in the next wave of demographically blessed economies.

Once that window closes, your nation is looking at a growing demographic tax as elders pile up and your mean age soars. The whole point of this drill is to get rich *before* growing old and eventually triggering depopulation dynamics—a decline China has already begun.

There are a great many things that can go wrong in this national endeavor. The rapid shift from a rural-centric population to an urban one is, per Karl Marx's theory of workers' revolutions, politically risky. Wealth can grow fantastically unequal—another political danger. It can be perilous to quickly open up your economy and culture to globalization's many liberating influences, fierce competition, and migrations. Such integration is revolutionary across the board, but especially in how it empowers women relative to men in traditional societies—a dynamic that fuels a lot of terrorism by fundamentalists unwilling to turn their cultural "clocks" ahead. Locally dominant religions feel challenged or even under siege (including in America). Fragile environmental landscapes are particularly at risk. But if you desire that demographic dividend, you either go all-in or lose out to more aggressive competitors for value-chain-building FDI.

Demographic transitions stall when the death rate decreases but the birth rate does not because the accompanying transformations prove too hard to manage—particularly in terms of adequate food production. This is the over-population danger first described by British scholar Thomas Malthus in his highly influential 1798 *Essay on the Principle of Population*, which upended traditional thinking on the value of a growing population for the next two centuries. The classic example of the so-called Malthusian trap is the mid-nineteenth-century Irish Potato Famine. Recent examples include Haiti (chronic) and Rwanda (consider, for example, the related outburst of genocide in the 1990s). Today, rapidly-growing-but-food-insecure populations are spread across Middle Earth, their fate to be determined by some combination of climate change and how their Northern neighbors choose to respond (reactively versus preventively) to the mass migrations already begun.

For the world, there is genuine uncertainty about whether humanity has conclusively left behind the threat of the Malthusian trap. Absent climate change, the answer may have been a decisive yes, as world fertility drops below the replacement rate well before this century's end while agricultural productivity inexorably rises. But with climate change so dramatically remapping the world's distribution of arable land, any such judgment remains literally up in the atmosphere. In high-concept Hollywood terms, think of it as *Soylent Green* meets *Children of Men* with the third act yet to be written.

Middle Earth still features a youth bulge of two billion souls—a number that will continue to expand through midcentury. Can South Asia, the Middle East, and Africa replicate East Asia's success? Has Latin America already blown its historic chance? Will this golden ticket simply lie beyond the reach of those regions experiencing the most damaging climate change?

The power and resources to solve this geostrategic equation lie overwhelmingly in the North, which, for now, remains far too obsessed with its East-West conflict dynamics (Ukraine, China's military rise) and appears entirely incapable of calmly exploring long-term approaches to managing climate migration. Eventually, the right combination of disasters and threat perceptions will arrive to pierce the North's strategic self-centeredness. Bank on it.

In many ways, Donald Trump's stunning rise, thanks to his political weaponization of such growing domestic fears, was a genuine harbinger of things to come (see his copycats throughout Europe and Latin America). Given America's weak, self-destructive political leadership right now, the public rightfully fears a future that seems unmanageable. Our democracy thus remains highly vulnerable to the rise of an authoritarian leader promising to fix everything by radically insulating America from a turbulent world characterized as shoving its human "trash" our way.

There are profound reasons why America's climate denialism and xenophobia go together: both seek to distance our nation from the world we created but now fearfully disavow.

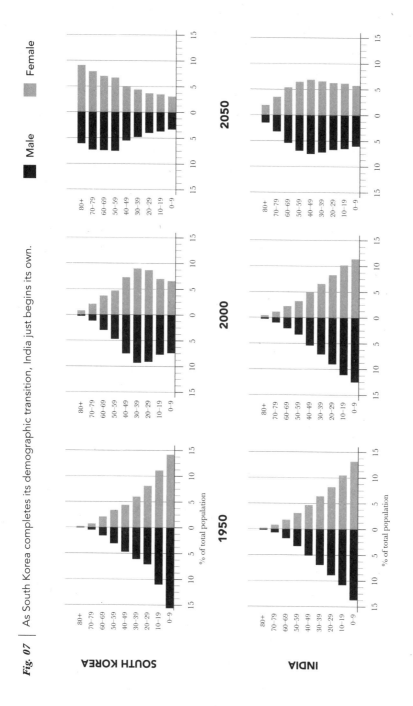

Fig. 07 | As South Korea completes its demographic transition, India just begins its own.

14

The Secret History of Globalization:
Follow the Demographic Dividend

We tend to view globalization's advance as resulting from the appearance of successive development models, when, in truth, the same demographic dynamic has driven each "rise."

The popular history of modern globalization unfolds as a series of world-conquering economic models. It begins in the 1950s and 1960s with America's big-firm capitalism and its unprecedented domination of global manufacturing, segues into Japan's stunning rise (1970s and 1980s) as a model of state-guided "industrial policy," and culminates with China's system-reshaping rise (since 1990) as an authoritarian, state-controlled economy. In each instance, the dominant economy's reign was predicted to last forever, while the dethroned loser was relegated to history's economic dustbin.

When American corporations suddenly seemed outmatched by Japan Inc., our nation fell into a declinist funk that has haunted us ever since—even during the best of economic times. The clearest proof is how our presidents (e.g., Reagan, Clinton, Trump) keep promising to *make America great again*. As for Japan, it never recovered from the collapse of its "bubble economy" and has ever since seemed complacent slipping into demographic retirement. Of course, China remains unprecedented and unique—until its rapidly declining labor pool proves it is neither. Be a bit patient and you will soon be deluged with global buzz surrounding India's world-beating—and uniquely Hindu—rise.

While it is tempting to view history as steadily steered by great powers and their great policies, those superstructures arise from an underlying base both technological and biological. All things being equal, bigger populations control more territory, create more powerful states, and field larger and better-equipped militaries. Nations enjoying population growth tend to be more youthful, vigorous, confident, ambitious, dynamic, and, well . . . fun. As a rule, the sixty-year-old is no match for the thirty-year-old, whether we refer to individuals or median-age countries.

In Marxian terms, our world's technological and biological base (e.g., technological singularity, climate change, global aging) shifts tectonically beneath our feet, inevitably shaking our political superstructures to their very cores. This explains why democracy is so much in doubt right now: we need better political, economic, and security constructs for what lies ahead, but we will not build them so long as we inhabit the wasteland of our past, Ozymandias-like, despairing of lost greatness.

My secret history of globalization acknowledges those great powers but deterministically describes their rise-and-fall dynamics from a demographic perspective. America escaped World War II demographically and industrially unharmed, only to immediately enjoy a baby boom that allowed it to capitalize on its supremely advantageous position as sole surviving economic superpower. America was indeed great but sought to share that greatness with others, engineering the economic resurrection of former enemies (Japan, Italy, Germany) and encouraging Western Europe's cloning of its integrating political union (the EU).

Taking advantage of America's largesse, Japan's three-decades-long postwar demographic boom fueled its amazing industrial rise while preordaining its rapid aging. Tokyo and its imitators, known as the Four Asian Tigers (South Korea, Singapore, Hong Kong, and Taiwan), were too successful for China to ignore, particularly as the Soviet Union's rapid dissolution confirmed the economic backwardness of state socialism.

China's own demographic dividend (1980–2010) followed closely on Japan's heels, only to peak during the Great Recession. Not only have factory wages risen ever since but now Beijing also faces a loss of 200 million workers by 2050.

Fortunately for China, globalization's next great pool of cheap labor emerged next door in Southeast Asia, to which Beijing is already directing its lower-end manufacturing assets and investments in increasing competition with Japan and India. But Southeast Asia's own rapid aging is well underway, compressing its demographic margins and marking it as mere placeholder for its far-larger successor: India, with its youth bulge of half a billion souls. India's demographic dividend will peak in the 2035–2040 time frame, subsequently yielding to similar dynamics in both the Middle East and Africa, which in combination will offer up a dividend approaching one billion workers.

By following this treasure map, one can track globalization's center of gravity as it moves over this century, to include its transforming instabilities, rapid urbanization and industrialization, emerging middle-class consumption, out-of-control environmental damage, and fitful democratization. It is also the easiest way to follow the money (foreign direct investment, or FDI).

A good example: in 1990, China attracted a mere $4 billion in FDI, then watched that total shoot up to $42 billion in 2000 and peak at $290 billion in 2013. China recently achieved the rare feat of serving as the world's biggest inbound target and outbound source of FDI—a double crown previously worn by America. Tellingly, India now repeats China's initial trajectory, jumping from $4 billion in received FDI in 2000 to $74 billion in 2021.

In 2020, amidst a global pandemic that halved FDI flows from advanced Western economies, developing Asian economies surpassed them as a source of outbound FDI—a passing of the torch or at least a preview of what is to come.

Globalization's shifting center of gravity is best represented by the auto industry. The *automobile*, a French word for the first practical vehicle powered by an internal combustion engine designed and built by the German Karl Benz in 1885, emerges in Europe at the height of its global economic domination. The fledgling industry jumps next to rising America, where our genius for mass production elevates the *car* (also of French origin) to middle-class status symbol. Our saturated auto market is then "invaded" by cheap Japanese and Korean *vehicles* (enough with the French!). Now, risen China's auto industry balloons to three times our size, putting Beijing in the driver's seat in an industry synonymous with American greatness. In 1960, the United States manufactured half the world's motor vehicles; we now produce one-tenth of a global market five times larger in size.

What does this history of globalization tell us about our world and its future?

First, Americans need to get over this tendency to view each new rising power (Japan, China, India) as somehow representing a condemnation of our current economic state, an existential threat to our long-term economic health, and a repudiation of our globalization scheme. In truth, their regular appearance only validates (a) US-style globalization's integrating advance; (b) our long-term military efforts to serve as Asia's strategic "glue" as local powers peacefully rose; and (c) the inherent power of demographics in timing any "new" economic model's apparent—if short-lived—global "supremacy."

Second, America must avoid the temptation to view any of these powers as somehow better representing—much less automatically steering—the future of the global economy. They represent nothing more than replications of our past development success and copycatting of our next wave of technological success (consider, for example, America's current AI race with China), thus telling us little to nothing about where we need to steer our economy next. Technological revolutions are not centrally planned. As such, Xi Jinping's growing authoritarianism threatens China's economic future—not ours.

Third, and as a direct result of our admitting the previous two points, America's capacity for global leadership remains. It has simply migrated to the next system-shaping dynamic, which is climate change. There we enjoy a uniquely advantageous strategic environment in the Western Hemisphere (**Throughline Six**), within which to forge a next-generation model of North-South integration that—true to our historical record—establishes the global standard.

Point being if we still desire global influence, it is there for the taking. The playing field has changed, so we need to change with it. Americans need not fear globalization's future because our Union remains best positioned to create it.

15 *Globalization's Prime Directive:* Accommodate Peacefully Rising Economic Pillars

US-style globalization enables rising powers, which naturally defend their rapidly expanding interests. That non-zero-sum dynamic grows the global economy to everyone's benefit.

I n the classic TV science fiction series *Star Trek*, the United Federation of Planets strictly adheres to a single rule when encountering "new life and new civilizations": the Prime Directive. This directive prohibits members from meddling in the natural development of alien worlds, thus allowing them to grow into candidate status based on their own choices. Since launching our model of globalization, America has struggled with that meddling instinct, consistently lapsing into fear-threat mode whenever our protégés insufficiently Americanize themselves. In our strategic impatience, we are too much Captain Kirk and not enough Mr. Spock.

Americans are often disappointed with our NATO/EU sidekick, consider Japan still far too Japanese, and feel utterly disillusioned and betrayed by Moscow's and Beijing's insistence on embracing their own superpower standing instead of obediently slotting themselves just under ours. We never feel enough gratitude for our efforts to boss everyone on how they should run their nations.

That my-way-or-the-highway mentality might have been justified by the Cold War's bipolar playing field, but our subsequent success in propagating globalization renders it painfully counterproductive today. We are not the only game in town, in part because that town has grown big enough for several superpower brands to compete. Moreover, the global economy's future health depends mightily on not losing any pillars of future growth and investment.

On that score, Russia and China do not compare: the former can be punished with isolation for acting out; the latter, only at the cost of globalization itself. America can outcompete China, but we cannot outlaw it. Our success in enabling Beijing's "peaceful rise" now forces us to live with its world-shaping demand power and its critical role as lead financier of globalization's next phase of integration. Put more bluntly: Ukraine is a pothole on globalization's pathway, while Taiwan would be a *Thelma and Louise* driving-off-the-cliff choice for all involved.

That may be a humbling definition of success, but understand that any attempt to sabotage China's natural ambition to steer globalization's future risks the world economy's hard partition, quite possibly leaving America with a stunningly small share. A generation ago, America outpaced China on trade with four-fifths of the world's economies; today, China out-trades the United States across two-thirds of those nations. During the long age of colonialization, trade most definitely followed the flag (i.e., naval power); in modern globalization, the flag follows trade. That is why China now deploys the world's largest naval fleet—challenging for the US but entirely logical.

China will never trust its future to US definitions of security and success, any more than we would in return. Our sole option is outperforming China as an integrating force while accepting its unmovable domination of East Asia. That is admittedly a daunting notion, given our current civil strife and reticence to lead, but America has emerged from such funks before when the right global crisis moved us—and we will again. As a disruptive global actor, we can trust climate change to regularly deliver crises—no motivation required.

America will not be able to just throw money at the problem as we often have in the past. Heavily indebted, the United States will not outspend China on global integration. Our leaders constantly propose Manhattan Projects and Marshall Plans, but this is complete fantasy. We do not have the money; China does. Indeed, our future economic well-being depends on Beijing intelligently spending down that accumulated treasure in a cashing-out strategy that allows China to become a financial and technology superpower not unlike America, the EU, and Japan before it. This is the core of Xi Jinping's plan of "national rejuvenation." China's success enables Southeast Asia to continue its rise, followed by India, the Arab world, and Africa as their respective demographic dividends play out. The alternative—China's economic downfall—almost certainly triggers more trouble than America would be comfortable managing from afar.

America was the security "glue" that once kept Asia peacefully rising, but that role will eventually shift to China—no matter how small or nervous that makes us feel. Today, China's petty bullying of its neighbors generates a certain security cohesiveness among them in a regional balancing dynamic that America is pleased to support for the foreseeable future with arms sales and expanded basing rights for our forces. But, over time, Beijing will most certainly displace Washington as East Asia's security guarantor—for good and ill. America can delay that outcome; we cannot prevent it.

If the Global War on Terror taught us anything, it is that regions disconnected from globalization collectively produce persistent instability, stubborn insurgency, and rage-filled violent extremism. America cannot compete with China—and later India—in integrating Central Asia and the Middle East. We can shape those integrating dynamics, but we will never command them. Africa remains a possibility, in our partnership with the EU, but it is hard to imagine America making that effort without first having succeeded similarly over here in the Western Hemisphere with a far more democratic, urbanized, and closer-in-age Latin America.

The same realism holds true in Europe's struggle with revanchist Russia, which most definitely can be flipped into the EU's camp post-Putin—if Europe offers Moscow a better integration path than the scheme currently imposed by opportunistic Beijing. Russia's Arctic superpower status only grows with climate change's advance, rendering it a forever-attractive acquisition—not unlike Canada. But there again, why would America attempt to lead such an integrating effort with Russia when a far better match sits on our Northern border—the longest and most peaceful in the world? Better to pick the lowest-hanging fruit.

To US defense hawks, such talk sounds like America simply leaving Eurasia to its own devices. After all, our rise as a global superpower saw us embrace exactly such geographic ambition across the second half of the twentieth century. However, considering that in our twenty-first-century global economy, this vast continent is home to four out of the five global superpowers (EU, Russia, India, and China), it seems far more fantastical to presume we can still play a dominant role in how all those dyad relationships (EU/Russia, EU/China, Russia/China, China/India, Russia/India, and India/EU) play out. Everybody wants to rule the world, but there must be some middle ground between that residual instinct and America's current bout of strategic reclusiveness and self-harming civil strife. I locate that middle ground to America's south, precisely because it encompasses our current divisions and fears over emigrants emanating there. When faced with competing emergencies, it is best to deal with the one on your doorstep before addressing the one on the other side of town.

For some time now, Washington has been growing alarmed at Beijing's Belt and Road Initiative (BRI), a global infrastructure development strategy begun a decade ago and designed to literally cement China's status as a world economic leader. Often compared to America's post-WWII Marshall Plan, China has already committed a trillion-plus US dollars in deals involving most of the world's nations. Nothing strange here: China has been the world's top saver for three decades and it needs to move up the production ladder and cash out its demographic dividend. For China's subsequent advancement, its BRI scheme must enable India's follow-on, dividend-fueled rise.

India's successful rise to global economic pillar will constitute a locking-in point for America's globalization grand strategy. When we successfully attracted China's emulation in the 1980s, we soon started speaking of a "global economy" and not just the "West." By fostering India's full integration—ideally with significant Chinese investment—America helps insulate that ancient rivalry from system-destructive conflict. Better still, India's rise will erase our current fears of globalization succumbing to authoritarian leadership—the dreaded Beijing-Moscow axis. Time for the world's largest democracy to notch our camp a win.

As soon as *rising* India grasps globalization's "baton" from *risen* China, New Delhi assumes the mantle as the economic development model of choice—a new consensus emphasizing political pluralism, cultural diversity, and an information technology/service-centric approach to cashing a demographic dividend. India is already moving down this path, as exemplified in its *AatmaNirbhar Bharat Abhiyan* (Self-Reliant India Movement), clearly signaling its intent to achieve—on its own terms—its integration within globalization as an accepted superpower and champion of the Global South. As always, nothing is guaranteed, and New Delhi has recently revealed plenty of anti-democratic impulses, but the country starts in a good place and should remain there with the right kind of help and advice from powers that have trod that path before it.

At the turn of the twentieth century, Britain made a choice to accommodate—even mentor—America throughout its inevitable rise. That was a difficult call but one that proved to be Europe's salvation across two world wars. America chose to do similarly with rising Japan and the Asian Tigers in the 1960s through the 1980s, in the process ultimately luring China down that stabilizing path with both America's and Japan's patient mentoring. Now it is up to China to extend some level of mentoring to rising India. It will be a difficult accommodation on both sides of this long-standing rivalry, but Washington must support its unfolding, however it complicates our own strategic relationship with New Delhi.

With Taiwan looming as the mother of all Cold War triggers, the temptation here will be for America to reflexively demonize China, pursue an unrealistic containment strategy that costs more than it gains, and enlist New Delhi in unrestrained rivalry with Beijing. Americans must resist this impulse for both its strategic shortsightedness and its capacity to trigger Pyrrhic victories beyond our imagination. We need to shelve our Cold War reflexes with forward-leaning China—no matter their residual utility with retrograde Russia.

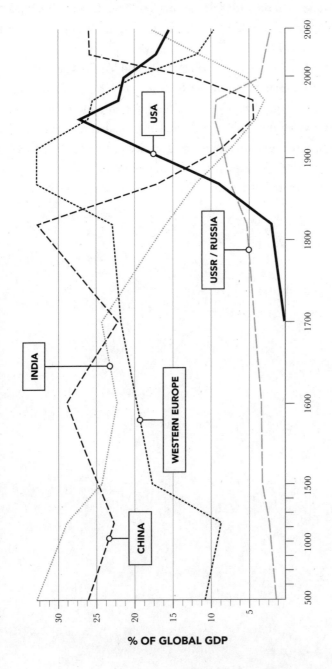

Fig. 08 | China's share of global GDP surges, as that of USA and Europe shrinks.

16

The Dorian Gray of Great Powers:
By Staying Young(ish), America Stays Relevant

The North's rapid aging arrives just as climate change collides with rising global middle-class demand—both next-generation issues. High immigration slows America's aging—at a price.

Humanity's lengthening life span is both entirely unnatural and our most complete victory yet over our environment. In 1900, global life expectancy at birth stood at the same level (low thirties) it had maintained since the Roman Empire. Despite the twentieth century's conflicts, human life expectancy doubled to seventy years by the year 2000. That stunning achievement was overwhelmingly enabled by the pervasive use of vaccines in early childhood. Talk about a buried headline.

The combination of lower fertility and heightened longevity is reconfiguring human society, aging it as never before in a process that—much like climate change—is already locked in. In terms of political and economic impact, this great replacement (i.e., elders replacing children) dwarfs any feared "mixing of the races." Frankly, it changes everything.

One of the many price tags associated with the worldwide spread of US-style globalization is the halving of the global fertility rate from five children per woman (1950) to two and a half today. There is no culture in this world strong enough to resist this development. By 2050, global fertility will drop to just over two kids per woman, balancing the death rate. Humanity's natural increase thus ends in this century. From here on out, population growth will be determined by human longevity.

The UN defines a rapidly aging society as featuring an elder share (sixty-five and older) of 7 to 13 percent. An aged society sits at 14 to 19 percent, while a super-aged society tops 20 percent. Until recently, virtually all societies featured an elder share below 5 percent. With a birth rate of 1.7—well below the replacement rate of 2.1—America will be super-aged by 2030, when the last Boomers (me included) reach retirement age. At that point, the elderly will outnumber children in America. Still, compared to other developed economies, we are doing well.

Between now and 2050, demographic aging will occur at faster rates throughout Europe (already significantly older than America) and East Asia (now aging at a rapidity never seen in human history). The United States took three-quarters of a century to shift from rapidly aging to aged; East Asia now accomplishes that in a quarter-century and achieves super-aged status just a few years after we do. In 2050, China's almost 500 million elders will outnumber America's entire population (400 million) and its elder dependency ratio (elders per working age population) will zoom past ours.

All this global aging puts humanity in uncharted territory. Like everyone else, America is getting older, but we are aging more slowly than our competition. Come midcentury, India will remain the youngest of our five superpowers with a median age of thirty-seven. Russia will keep its median age low at forty-two, but thanks primarily to its lower life expectancy (seventy years versus seventy-eight in the United States and China) and the population decline it suffers this century. At midcentury, America will be only forty-one, situating us far closer to the developing world than either China (forty-six) or the EU (forty-seven). That is a significant strategic advantage. Rapid aging means China's "century" will be far shorter than projected.

There are profound moral consequences of demographic aging. Elders need help more than they need things, so older societies naturally shift from manufacturing toward services. If you want "American made," then keep America as young as possible. The same holds true for "American owned," as an aged society naturally cedes ownership of assets to younger, faster-growing economies. Ditto for preserving civic organizations and the social capital they impart, because their decline tracks with that of family size. Then factor in declining innovation, because older societies invest less in research, dampening entrepreneurial spirit—not good during an era of technological revolutions, many of which humanity will need to mitigate climate change's ravaging effects.

As US demographers Richard Jackson and Neil Howe have noted, aged societies favor "consumption over investment, the past over the future, and the old over the young." History shows that diminishing demographic strength leads to lower economic growth and a risk-averse society where an elder-dominated electorate resists emerging priorities for public spending. There is a reason Fox News's audience skews so elderly and so many of our political leaders are twice as old (mid-seventies) as our nation's median age (thirty-eight). Fortune favors the bold—not the old.

There is a global-majority middle class out there eager to lock in their long-term status as consumers and successfully pass that lifestyle on to their children. That is the American Dream we so ably propagated around the world, and we are in danger of aging out of our ability to influence that global aspiration.

America's greatest soft-power asset is our unmatched worldwide cultural attraction. But as globalization's dynamism shifts to the developing South, that attraction diminishes with our relative aging. America looks more like the past than the future because Americans spend more time arguing about past "greatness" than anticipating future achievements, distorting our unique, forward-leaning patriotism so long and ardently admired by the world.

If history is any guide, the rise of a global-majority middle class inevitably ushers in a progressive period of political, economic, and social reform not unlike what Europe and America undertook when their middle-class populations ascended a century ago. Recall: America threaded that needle far better with its two Roosevelts (Republican Theodore, Democrat Franklin) than Europe did with its murderous dictators, genocidal ideologies, and world wars.

America cannot hope to globally champion our middle-class-centric approach to progressive reform if we ourselves are lost to generational conflict between old and young—particularly over our response (or lack thereof) to climate change. The danger we face, per Jackson and Howe, is that Americans are "no longer regarded as progressive advocates for the future of all peoples, but rather as mere elder defenders of their own privileged hegemony."

The vast bulk of America's recent and future population growth arrives in the form of immigrants not only younger (thirty-one years old) than our nation's median age (thirty-eight) but who exhibit a higher fertility rate at just over two children per woman.

While hardly a fountain of youth, America's relatively high rate of immigration offsets our declining birth rate. The United States will age only three years (thirty-eight to forty-one) by 2050 as measured by our rising median age. Europe (+five years), China (+eight), and India (+ten) will all age faster, with only India remaining younger than America. As Russia depopulates (144 million to 136 million) and Russians' lives stay relatively shortened, it will lower its median age—the hard way—from a peak of forty-four in 2035 to forty-two in 2050.

America remains demographically blessed because we are still more fertile than almost all our competitors, while our capacity to absorb immigrants is second to none. We therefore age less rapidly than the rest of this century's superpowers, marking America as the Dorian Gray of great powers. Like that fictional English character who cheated aging by selling his soul, America sacrifices its long-established racial identity (European origin) to stave off the rapid aging that now afflicts virtually every other advanced economy.

As a result, when America looks at its own portrait, there is a growing gap between a privileged White image long maintained and a multicultural reality that can no longer be denied.

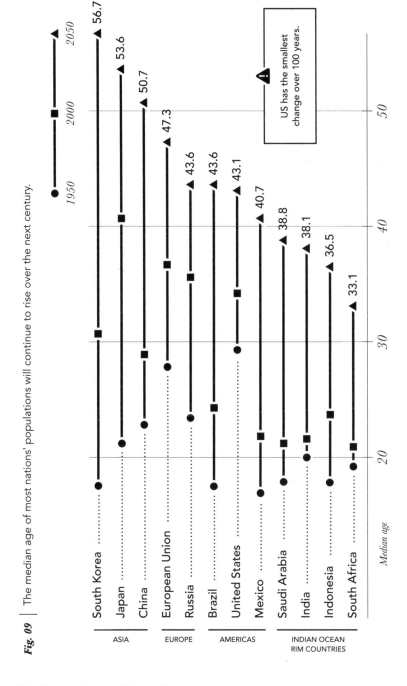

Fig. 09 | The median age of most nations' populations will continue to rise over the next century.

South Korea ▲ 56.7
Japan ▲ 53.6
China ▲ 50.7
European Union ▲ 47.3
Russia ▲ 43.6
Brazil ▲ 43.6
United States ▲ 43.1
Mexico ▲ 40.7
Saudi Arabia ▲ 38.8
India ▲ 38.1
Indonesia ▲ 36.5
South Africa ▲ 33.1

ASIA
EUROPE
AMERICAS
INDIAN OCEAN
RIM COUNTRIES

Median age

1950   *2000*   *2050*

US has the smallest change over 100 years.

17 *America's 50/50/50 Journey:* From 1950 to 2050, Whites Fall to Less Than 50 Percent of Population

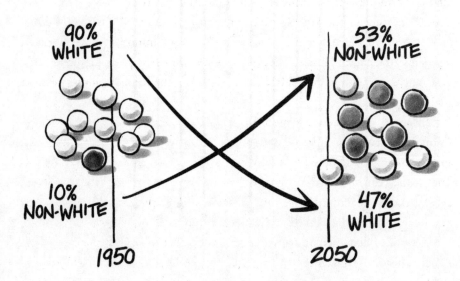

90%
WHITE

53%
NON-WHITE

10%
NON-WHITE

47%
WHITE

1950

2050

No great power has survived its dominant racial group declining so precipitously. How America navigates this new reality determines its global standing.

A 1970 book by Soviet dissident Andrei Amalrik posed the then-inconceivable question, "Will the Soviet Union survive until 1984?" Amalrik doubted the multinational USSR could handle a future in which that empire's non-Slavs challenged the dominance of Russians and their militarized nationalism, which, "although it may prove temporarily useful to the regime, is very dangerous for a country in which those of Russian nationality constitute less than half the total population." Russians were never more than 59 percent of the USSR's total population, but by 1970 they had fallen to just over 50 percent while remaining a distinct minority in all fourteen republics attached to Russia. The coup de grâce was Amalrik's prediction of a destructive war with Communist China triggering the Russian empire's violent "deimperialization."

Swap in an America where (a) minorities already outnumber Whites through age twenty; and (b) our military identifies China as its number-one threat, and one is tempted to ask, Will the United States survive until 2044? That is the year by which Whites, currently 59 percent of the US population, are slated to lapse into majority-minority status across the nation, meaning they are the largest racial group but collectively a minority—like the rest.

American documentarian Ken Burns notes that "race is at the core of the American story." Until recently, that story was told in a one-sided fashion befitting a country populated overwhelmingly by Whites. America was 81 percent White in our first national census (1790) and that share crept steadily upward until peaking at 90 percent at the middle of the twentieth century.

As America began exporting its model of globalization-through-integration following World War II, the White share of its population began its slow decline to just under 60 percent. What had been a pre–World War II immigrant flow dominated by Europeans eventually morphed into one dominated by Latinos and Asians. In 2050, Whites will comprise 47 percent of our population—just over half that 1950 high point. That steep demographic journey is unprecedented among the world's great powers. It has never been attempted—much less self-engineered.

As globalization's pioneering force, America must not only survive this demographic transition but also demonstrate how a predominantly multiracial union can thrive across its unfolding. Doing so will not only restore but define America's global leadership this century by providing the biggest, boldest answer to the greatest political challenge ever faced by humanity.

Northern states must learn how to create and sustain larger political unions that will over time extend themselves southward toward those states most vulnerable to climate change's ravages. We either spread Middle Earth's rising risk across a wider subscriber pool—just like in health insurance—or we are looking at widespread state failure there, resulting in all manner of "emergency room" treatments (i.e., US military crisis responses) that end up being a day late and many dollars long. Such a passive-aggressive approach invariably results in an uncontrollable northward migration of desperate climate refugees, so add that figure to our cost calculations.

For the United States to extend such political networks southward is, by definition, to rethink the geographic limits of our Union—although not by much, given the distant, non-contiguous states of Hawaii and Alaska. Right now, America demands that its Southern neighbors do everything possible to stem emigration. Imagine how differently those governments would be incentivized if controlling that flow determined their advancement in an accession process promising eventual US statehood.

However inconceivable that may seem from today's perspective, understand that the alternative is to undergo the same racial transformation but in an entirely internalized fashion. America's current path of immigrant-led population growth reformats our racial makeup along much the same lines as would any hemispheric expansion of our Union. Point being America heads down this path either way. The question is, do we face better odds—and outcomes—attempting this demographic journey strictly within our current borders? Or would it be a far less pressurized path to methodically extend our borders to encompass new member states where Whites are typically in the minority? Put another way, based on how Texas is behaving today, do you think the Lone Star State would welcome the opportunity to be taken off the immigration front line?

America already has in-house examples of political entities successfully living as White majority-minority states (Hawaii, California, Nevada, New Mexico, Texas, Maryland). The same is true of our nation's major metropolises. We are not walking into this situation uninformed or unexperienced. Then again, tipping points are called that for a reason: everything seems to suddenly change when they are reached.

White America must choose between preserving its privilege and preserving our democracy. There are ways to forestall the loss of White power, and America is well versed in all of them: stacking courts, gerrymandering legislative districts, suppressing non-White votes in the name of "election integrity," mass incarceration of non-Whites, and so on. None of these tactics staves off the inevitable, which is why the US alt-right speaks ambitiously of accelerating racial strife to the point of triggering civil war—a concept no longer held to be inconceivable among half of polled Americans.

America's failure in navigating this unprecedented domestic path would derail the world system and our privileged position within it—exemplified by the international community's consistent willingness to purchase our sovereign debt out of a firm belief in our long-term future. At this point in our shared history, the American lifestyle cannot survive without globalization.

Just as importantly, the American Dream cannot again be reduced to a Whites-only proposition, as its global drawing power is based on the possibility of anyone achieving it. US-style globalization is no different: we either prove that a White minority can thrive in its original multinational model (United States) or the looming economic dominance of the majority non-White global middle class will trigger similar self-destructiveness on a wider scale.

To understand White existential fears about America's multicultural present and future, we turn to the Great Replacement Theory (GRT) animating today's North American and European alt-right and Christian nationalism movements, both of which oppose racial, religious, sexual orientation, and gender equality. Most Americans first encountered this viral conspiracy theory via news reports of the violent Unite the Right rally held in Charlottesville,

Virginia, in 2017, specifically protestors' chants of "You will not replace us" and "Jews will not replace us." A fellow traveler of the 1990s American neo-Nazi concept of "White genocide," GRT tones down the former's fixation on "puppet-master" Jews in favor of more generic but equally profiteering "replacist elites" (often still Jews).

Primary authorship of the GRT belongs to a French intellectual, Renaud Camus. In his 2017 book, *Le Grand Remplacement*, Camus argues that globalization has rendered all humans economically interchangeable and thus subject to summary displacement within their native cultures. Camus cites the Middle East and Africa as primary sources of this reverse colonization of Europe ("Islamo-substitution") directed from above.

While a host at Fox News, the leading GRT champion was Tucker Carlson, known to tee up his alt-right arguments with the dog whistle lead-in "In the America most of us grew up in . . ." The television personality deftly framed GRT in electoral terms: accusing Democrats of importing "more obedient voters from the Third World" (read, non-White) "to replace the current electorate" (majority White). Carlson's frequent punching bag, Jewish American financier George Soros, is held in alt-right circles as the ultimate architect of globalization's replacist dynamics. The related QAnon theory, which Carlson frequently defended, covers much the same ground while narrowing its alleged criminality to a global child sex-trafficking ring led by anti-Trump Democratic "satanists."

It may seem like America is suffering some golden age of conspiratorial lunacy, when, in truth, our nation has always exhibited this perverse tendency, which now includes climate-change denialism. Still, when these conspiracy theories balloon into activist movements successfully fielding candidates for public office, they mainstream the politics of paranoia. This broad reach was demonstrated by the January 6th Insurrection, whose supporters, when polled, cited fear of replacement as the root of their collective rage. GRT is likewise cited by terrorism experts as "the master narrative for a vast number of far-right attacks" around the world (e.g., mass shootings, bombings).

In a world deluged with information, conspiracies offer a decoder ring enabling adherents to instantly parse all conflicting data into truth versus lies. They likewise feed millenarian narratives of the coming Judgment Day preceded by a "great awakening" during which the world's guilty are duly punished. Such insider knowledge is supremely empowering for those feeling powerless before globalization's tectonic shifts. Swallowing the red pill, outsiders are immediately admitted to the ranks of "true Americans"—no matter their race, creed, or origin.

This is where shared concerns for the preservation of identity collide: inside America, diversity means relatively fewer Whites, thus diminishing White privilege. Outside America, globalization means the rise of the non-White East and South, thus diminishing Western/White power. For decades, globalization reflected the unstoppable spread of Westernization, but now it connotes its retreat in the face of the same *them* relegating "true Americans" to minority status.

All this fearmongering prevents Americans from reasonably discussing what is going on. Latino migrants continue to flock to our border. Many of them are climate refugees, and their numbers will only grow significantly with time. If America does nothing to manage this dynamic at the source, our country will be incredibly stressed by this desperate northward migration. Like any species confronted by climate change, America can move (*Hello Canada!*), adapt (ideally by growing our Union southward and northward), or die (hollowing our democracy to the point of autocracy).

Faced with those limited options, I choose adaptation and believe most Americans will do the same when such decisions are suitably contextualized.

In the year 2050, our Boomer leadership will be long gone (then 86 to 105 years old), and Gen X will mostly be retired (70 to 85). Millennials (55 to 69) and Gen Zs (40 to 54) will be in charge. These two cohorts are indigenous to the future America here described—the undiscovered country that present leadership generations find so disturbingly alien. Millennials and Gen Zs are "digital natives"—having come of age amidst, or been born after, the internet's rise. They are likewise globalization natives, climate change natives, and post-White-majority natives. They have lived their entire lives within this looming reality and will do what they must to adapt America for success in a future shaped by their values.

Sometimes the best thing a leadership generation can do is simply get out of the way of history. This is one of those times.

18

Making America Great Again:
**Drunk on Nostalgia, We're
on a Road to Nowhere**

In yearning for an irretrievable past, nostalgia is a lie concocted by our younger minds and sold to our present selves. An internal dialogue of grief, it is the death of strategic vision.

When politically weaponized, nostalgia ruins our appreciation of the present and deadens our anticipation of the future. It reduces leadership to steering by the rearview mirror. As an animating ideology, nostalgia is a rallying point for culture warriors determined to roll back time—the knee-jerk response of religious fundamentalists across the world to globalization's liberating dynamics.

In economic terms, nostalgia often profiteers on prejudice by idealizing yesterday's less-equal society. It narrows ambition and suffocates innovation by idealizing a simpler—but always more patriarchal and constricted—past to which return is impossible without re-subjugating those who have since achieved agency, thus disparaging their contributions (*What have they ever done?*) while discounting their consumer demand (*Why must I serve those people?*).

Worst, in its rosy memorializing of the "good old days," nostalgia is social escapism bordering on emotional disorder. It is unhealthy and un-American.

The US political scientist Minxin Pei distinguishes between old-school nationalism, which is inherently backward-looking and grievance-based, and American patriotism, which is unusually forward-looking and achievement-based. As the immigrant Pei observes, America exhibits a willfully short collective memory that, when coupled with our missionary spirit, means Americans instinctively "look forward to even better times ahead, not just at home but also abroad." We believe in the future and aim to create it ourselves.

American-style nationalism embraces "universalistic ideals and institutions," meaning our identity is not constrained by ethnicity, religion, language, or geography. Pei notes that the American spirit is triumphalist (victory-defined) in contrast to those negatively defined by "national humiliations and defeats" (see China, Russia, etc.). As such, the American identity is not burdened with history's strictures, much less confined by its borders. In pursuing happiness, our collective definition of *American* sums up what we individually seek to become. This open-ended mindset is what makes culture-fusing America the most revolutionary force on the planet: refugees from the past, we fight for the future.

There is nothing shocking about America's current bout of nostalgia; it is the product of (a) our success in growing globalization beyond our control, and (b) America's journey toward White majority-minority status. While Democrats, at 40 percent non-White, mirror America's present demographics, Republicans, still more than 80 percent White, date back to our early 1980s racial profile.

That four-decade gap explains the GOP's weaponization of nostalgia for *the America I grew up in*, as well as Donald Trump's successful reboot of Ronald Reagan's 1980 presidential slogan, "Let's make America great again" (MAGA). While Reagan resold America's post-WWII golden age, Trump repackaged the Gipper's boom times (e.g., tax cuts, defense buildup, culture wars).

The Republicans' decades-long lag in demographic fidelity also captures why so many on the Left interpreted Trump's MAGA mantra as code for *Make America White again*. Trump only fueled this suspicion with his incendiary language about non-White immigrants from "shithole countries" and his use of alt-right dog whistles at mass rallies.

In his populist attacks on global elites, Trump conflated the threat from "open borders" with the perceived loss of American greatness. In his inaugural pledge to end "this American carnage," he promised to stop trade partners from "stealing our companies and destroying our jobs." This rhetorical stance reflected his administration's ideological commitment to radically decoupling the US economy from the international liberal trade order that Trump's predecessors spent decades constructing. In its place, Trump sought a far more bilaterally constructed, avowedly mercantilist trade regime in which America would "win" every transaction while avoiding cultural dilution—White Christian economic nationalism in a nutshell.

The Trump administration cratered America's global reputation as a trustworthy superpower, in addition to crippling it internally by nostalgia-fueled culture wars. The irony here is unmistakable: in attempting to reestablish

American greatness by disavowing US-style globalization, Trump only proved that world system's resilience. For, as America increasingly sidelined itself from trying to run the world, competing superpowers stepped up their efforts to replace us—but not the system. Alarmed US observers decry this as the "end of globalization," when it is nothing more than the end of America's singular ability to steer its advance.

Internally, America's increasingly fierce culture wars similarly distract, forestalling the inevitable loss of White privilege throughout our society. The 2020 US census revealed a demographic tipping point: for the first time in American history, population growth through immigration surpassed the "natural increase" of domestic births. The Right's focus on the (White) family reflects this startling trend: thirty-five US states (70 percent) saw White population decline across the 2010s, with that percentage rising to 80 percent among US counties.

The US political scientist Robert A. Pape examined the demography of the 377 Americans arrested following the January 6th Insurrection. Besides being 95 percent White and significantly older than your typical protestor, the group displayed a strikingly similar background: "Counties with the most significant declines in the non-Hispanic White population are the most likely to produce insurrectionists." This is nostalgia weaponized per the logic of the Great Replacement Theory.

British prime minister Winston Churchill opined that "if we open a quarrel between the past and the present, we shall find that we have lost the future." America cannot restore its global leadership so long as this quarrel predominates.

Superpower Brand Wars:
The Global Middle Seeks
Protection from the Future

THROUGHLINE FOUR

Middle Earth, facing climate change's worst ravages, is also home to the South's burgeoning middle class. Winning that global middle defines superpower competition this century.

Any just society—and the world for that matter—wants its population concentrated in the middle economic ranks, minimizing the special interests of both poor and rich. The poor naturally seek protection from their circumstances, while the rich want protection from the poor (e.g., crime, tax burden). The middle class, however, wants something far more complicated and difficult to deliver—namely, protection from the future. The middle class, having achieved or long enjoyed a good life, wants to pass it along intact to their children, meaning their kids start adulthood with better prospects and earning potential than they had. Mess with the middle class on that score and you put your nation—and most certainly any democracy—at serious risk of sliding into intolerance, cruelty, xenophobia, isolationism, and even civil strife.

Globalization, with its fiercely competitive forces, is particularly challenging for the middle class. It forces companies to increasingly pawn off risk to their workers (e.g., killing pension systems, eroding healthcare coverage), furthering the impression that the average person is on their own whenever things get tough. Technology kills one person's job but makes another rich. A pandemic like COVID-19 extinguishes certain businesses, yet others thrive as never before. Everybody is working harder and longer, but only a tiny fraction of us seem to be doing any better. All these dynamics prey on the middle-class mind, making us feel vulnerable and exposed to a future beset with even more complexity and uncertainty.

We live in millenarian times, with people spotting end-of-the-world dynamics in all manner of complex phenomena. Ours is likewise an age of conspiracy theories purporting to explain confusing developments as the work of powerful, sinister, hidden elites. Combine these bad habits during uncertain economic times and you unleash powerful political forces motivated by fear and loathing.

Politics, both domestic and international, naturally become a competition to see which models of governance most effectively reduce that uncertainty and the fear it generates. The easier answer, in terms of explanation and execution, is to build walls and insulate your populace from globalization's harsh vagaries and villainous scum. Typically, that only requires citizens to put their absolute faith in the "one great person" capable of "preserving our way of life." The harder answer is attempting to decode all that complexity and manage it head-on—the domain of experts whom many of us now blame for our predicaments. There is little doubt along which path democracy survives.

These are not new struggles; the North experienced them all when its majority middle class emerged at the turn of the twentieth century, when the price humanity ultimately paid for its poor choices included two world wars. This time around, thanks to nuclear weapons, the world's superpowers must compete on a more granular level for the hearts and minds—or stomachs and wallets—of that global middle class, proving which integration scheme best addresses their fears of the future. In this competition, the cyber realm is a primary theater of conflict.

The supremely complicating factor here is an irony most cruel: just as the South's middle class comes into its own, that blossoming desire for a more comfortable, secure, and predictable life gets T-boned by the red-light-running, North-triggered disaster of climate change. And when many Americans disavow any responsibility? That adds insult to injury.

This history-bending collision thrusts our world into an unprecedented and increasingly mad South-North scramble for new rules, mechanisms, and institutions. In reply, the North's quintet of superpowers (US, EU, China, India, and Russia) will be both tempted and—in many cases—forced to "vertically" integrate with Southern and Northern neighbors in new and unprecedented social, economic, and political configurations.

Already crowded nations (China, India) are likely to seek northward integration of their own—as seen in Beijing's ambition to be a polar superpower or

India's rising interests in Central Asia. Relatively underp[ ] Securi
sia, the United States, and Canada, will be forced into sou[ ] survei
only to modulate and control that tide of climate migrants. 1[ ] (anal
a target of integration for climate-stressed India and China[ ] this
slip into this integrationist mode relatively smoothly, given[ ] mon
colonial ties and its successful record of integrating post-Soviet[ ] you

The fundamental question is, Which superpowers will be n[ ] to
ing, and able to meet this immense geopolitical challenge? And[ ] dy
derailed along the way by internal strife, costly wars, or just too[ ] d
disasters? Because, when it comes to flags, stars will be added o[ ]
decades ahead.

There is both opportunity and danger along this path. The glob[ ]
class will not be satisfied with defense, as they fear interstate war less t[ ]
strife. Commensurate with risk shifting to the individual, the global midd[ ]
desires and values security as a permanent condition within which the asse[ ]
define wealth accumulation (e.g., cars, houses, land, education, savings) ca[ ]
protected and preserved while appreciating in value. In coming decades, th[ ]
political allegiance to the quintet of competing Northern superpowers will [ ]
determined on this fundamental point: Who supplies superior security?

Defense (or sheer military power) gets America into that game, but it will be
our ability to export security (via technologies, platforms, services, and expertise), in competition with the four other superpowers, that determines which
states' loyal subscriptions are won or lost. A glimpse of this future: America's
National Geospatial-Intelligence Agency (NGA)—a Department of Defense
combat support element—increasingly fielding requests from the Federal Emergency Management Agency (FEMA) to divert their powerful satellite-based
reconnaissance systems from monitoring, for example, North Korean nuclear
sites to locating hurricane victims. That repurposing of defense assets to security purposes will become commonplace as climate change's system-shaping
impact supersedes the dynamics of superpower military rivalries. In the end,
defense is necessary but insufficient to winning this global competition for affiliation, the outcome of which will be measured in member states accrued—the
geopolitics of belonging.

The danger here is that George Orwell's predicted dystopia of fascism
growing into a surveillance state—or vice versa—seems timelier than ever.

ty is increasingly achieved within and across borders through the state's
llance (observing behaviors and communication) and "dataveillance"
ysis of database records). According to noted security expert Kim Taipale,
post-9/11 global phenomenon gives rise to "omniveillance," or the constant
itoring of all human activity by both public authorities and—per the "know
r customer" ruleset—the private sector, which is already highly incentivized
do so solely for push-marketing purposes. It is within this omniveillance
namic that we spot the fusion of global middle-class consumer and political
sires for stability. The merger of these "confidence" requirements cannot be
met solely by the North's traditional military alliances.

As this era's globalization is vertically consolidated along South-North
lines, security increasingly displaces defense. Security leverages surveillance,
and effective surveillance depends on access and sensors, the most important of
which is a smartphone—the modern data chokepoint blending consumer activity with personal security. Those who own the sensors determine the access.
That is the nature of the security competition now underway among our five
superpowers, where Apple versus Huawei is a more compelling throughline
than US Navy carriers versus China's carrier-killer missiles.

These superpower brand wars are well underway. Vladimir Putin and
Xi Jinping disparage democracies to damage our brand. Russia and China
aggressively market their authoritarian models of economic security in a world
depicted as "chaotic." They do not offer belonging so much as refuge from the
storm, and that is their weakness: their sale is primarily about fear.

But there is also a flaw in America's current passive-aggressive posture: we
assume our superpower brand is so attractive that, even when we withhold our
affections, we remain more desirable than competitors. That is no longer true
in all things.

America's historic strength is its brand recognition and sheer likability,
which are currently weakened and damaged by our all-consuming demographic journey to White majority-minority status. The Western Hemisphere,
as we will discover (**Throughline Six**), is best situated when it comes to South-
North integration, but America's devolution into political apartheid threatens
to destroy those unique capabilities.

The EU's strength is its superb model of member integration, while its
weakness is that model's inability to process Muslim states (e.g., Turkey). Its

primary risk lies to its Muslim South, so that deficit is either addressed or proves to be the EU's dead end. Europe, as noted earlier, faces the real opportunity to flip a post-Putin Russia into its ranks, but any such ambition is threatened by the EU's growing North-South divide over climate-driven migrant crises.

China's strength is its economic success in building and maintaining its middle class, for which the South evinces enormous respect. Its brand weakness is the non-replicability of that growth model and its blatant authoritarianism. Thanks to Ukraine, Beijing can capture Russia and its natural resources virtually whole, but not if Taiwan proves the overriding near-term goal. That temptation threatens China's entire future by logically eliciting another deglobalization campaign by the West—however mutually destructive.

India presents the next-generation model of how to rise as a service-centric economy that conscientiously decarbonizes its energy profile. The immense opportunity afforded by its unfolding demographic dividend is threatened by climate change, which strikes at its Achilles' heel—an agricultural sector still employing 45 percent of its national workforce.

Its strength defined in natural resources, Russia nonetheless plays the weakest hand. Given its vast Arctic holdings, climate change remains more economic opportunity than threat. But Russia's depopulation bodes poorly for its ability to absorb large flows of immigrants without a nationalistic backlash. Having been de-globalized over Ukraine, Russia is more prey than predator so long as Putin rules. Post-Putin, a Russian regime seeking global reentry would be wise to play the EU, India, and China off one another to avoid becoming too captured by any one suitor. In the event of state failure, Russia's climate opportunity conceivably results in its partition into successor states crafted and captured by those intervening superpowers.

After decades of East-West competition, conflict, and cooperation, there exist plenty of international institutions, rulesets, and negotiating venues to manage inter-superpower relations. What is missing is similar transnational tissue connecting North and South, just as the latter's economic emergence is subject to sabotage by climate change's expanding impact. Our five superpowers, whether they realize it or not, are already engaged in a competition to invent, propagate, and secure those North-South lines of social networking, security cooperation, economic integration, and political consolidation.

To the victors go the spoils.

19

It's Not Personal,
It's Strictly Business:
Superpowers Compete to
Revise Global Rules

After World War II, America had the opportunity to create most of what became modern globalization's ruleset. Today's competing superpowers naturally seek to revise those rules.

An international system is made up of structure and norms. Organizations like the WTO, IMF, and World Bank constitute structure, as do military alliances. Norms are most easily identified in the rules propagated and sustained by those organizations. After World War II, America chose to simultaneously transform both elements with its vigorous, visionary leadership. We did not have to do this.

The Cold War obscured this stunning feat. That decades-long struggle featured various military wins, losses, and draws that—in the grand scheme of things—changed virtually nothing. America was simply waiting for the Soviet version of mini globalization to collapse in the face of our version's immense success. When it did, our version of globalization went truly global, birthing the first majority global middle class—*game, set, match* alright, but not the "end of history."

America's challenge now is dealing with the success of this grand strategy, particularly the rise of competing powers. All five of our superpowers face their own particular trials this century: America struggling with its ongoing racial makeover; Europe contending with the Kremlin's resurgent revanchism and, within its own ranks, incipient anti-immigrant fascism; de-globalized Russia being pulled into Beijing's economic orbit as a vassal state; China scrambling to lock in its global holdings before succumbing to old age; and India hurtling toward a hard collision of demographics (its huge labor dividend) with climate change (stressing its agriculture-heavy workforce).

With all that going on, it is logical and reasonable to expect each competitor to seek a revision of global rules in its favor. After all, is that not what Donald Trump sought as president—however clumsily? These superpowers' efforts to rewrite the rulebook constitute neither an immediate nor direct threat to our current international structure. America has pointedly kept that system easy to join and hard to quit, which is why none of those four match our roster of allies.

Of the four, China harbors the greatest ambition to remake the world in its own image and to its own advantage. A good example is China's championing of the so-called Beijing Consensus as replacement for the once-dominant Washington Consensus. The latter had its heyday in the 1990s as a set of policies to be applied in any international rescue of a state experiencing the national equivalent of personal bankruptcy. The IMF's loan conditions constituted a standard reform package designed to stabilize, liberalize, and privatize the recipient's economy. Governments on the receiving end often viewed these reforms as a premature and unduly cruel "shock therapy." They were usually correct.

The Beijing Consensus rejects the Washington Consensus's strict free-market principles. Instead, it allows for a Hamiltonian mix of protectionism (high tariffs), heavy state presence in the economy, and ambitious infrastructure development. If you are a national leader on the receiving end of the IMF's conditionality demands, Beijing's fewer reform requirements are highly attractive, as is its generous offer to invest in public infrastructure that both China and the local economy can exploit.

It is fashionable today among international relations experts to compare China's strategic motivations to pre-WWI Imperial Germany. This historical analogy argues that China, late to the globalization game as Germany was to European colonial empire building, must necessarily take on #1 America, just as Kaiser Germany warred with Imperial Britain. Per a dynamic chronicled as far back as the ancient Peloponnesian War between Sparta and Greece, the so-called Thucydides Trap compels a Rising #2 to militarily challenge an Established #1.

Speaking as a strategist who spent years mentoring a Chinese security think tank on exactly these strategic concepts, I would argue that China is far better compared to pre-WWII Imperial Japan and its contentious relationship with the United States. First is the rising cult of militarism, despite China's lack of credible external threats and its total lack of combat experience stretching back decades. Second is the extreme nationalism and sense of racial superiority that arises when an ancient civilization modernizes that quickly. Third is Beijing's fear of having its strategic lines of communication permanently choked off by opposing naval powers led by the United States—a fantastic scenario that would quickly cripple the global economy. Lastly is the regime's growing resentment over a lack of recognition of its "rightful" place as globalization's new steering force—an accurate perception that nonetheless should not sap the confidence of a culture known for strategic patience.

All these historical similarities suggest inevitable conflict between China and the United States, but here is the key difference: in the Interwar period, Japan was the sole rising power in East Asia, whereas today "risen" China is surrounded by a quintet of great powers with advanced military forces (Japan, South Korea, Singapore, Australia, and India)—all of whom are major purchasers of US military hardware. Asia has never witnessed this number of great powers coexisting in peace—a legacy of the US military's decades-long role in providing the security "glue" that kept Asia from unduly fracturing amidst so many rising economic pillars. That achievement allows Washington to readily offset China's growing regional military strength through arms sales and military-to-military cooperation.

As I argued across my stint at the Knowfar Institute for Strategic and Defence Studies, Beijing has a generational opportunity to lock in its strategic standing within globalization—until India eclipses it. China can exploit that window for the world's, and its own, long-term benefit or merely hoard it for its immediate ideological needs. Invading Taiwan speaks to the latter path and raises the question of the Communist regime's continued existence. Once engaged in that war, Beijing's rulers will be fighting for their political lives—like Putin over Ukraine.

For a longer-term expression of Beijing's ongoing effort to revise global rules, we turn to Yan Xuetong—dean of Tsinghua University's Institute of International Relations—and his 2019 book, *Leadership and the Rise of Great Powers*. In it, Yan proposes a rising China can overtake far wealthier (per capita) America as the world's dominant power. His highly Confucian argument: superior national leadership projecting superior moral authority abroad. By efficiently ruling at home through progressive reforms, Beijing's leaders have, in his estimation, closed the power gap with America.

But what closed that gap even more, in Yan's analysis, has been the inferior quality of America's political leadership, specifically their inability to effect necessary domestic reforms. Hard to argue there.

Thus, China's growing advantage in political leadership capability gives it greater "strategic credibility" as a global leader. While American political leadership yo-yos between withdrawal (Barack Obama, Joe Biden), aggression (George W. Bush), and erratic untrustworthiness (Donald Trump), Beijing's current ruler, Xi Jinping, appears a paragon of stable progress. Per this logic, Xi's deep embrace of dictatorship is excusable as a necessary means to those greater ends of stability and credibility.

In Yan's analysis, China's growing leadership advantage, along with its consistently improving standing vis-à-vis the United States, allows for a new type of international leadership to emerge, one based on "humane authority" instead of brute force (e.g., US military power). In time, this new international authority can generate new international norms and a new international structure. China does not have to defeat America militarily; it must consistently outperform it on global authority and leadership by being more dependable, trustworthy, and moral.

Steeped in ancient Chinese political thought, Yan's theory makes the best of an admittedly poor hand: he acknowledges China's lack of (a) election-driven democracy; and (b) separation of executive, legislative, and judicial powers. He argues that since such absences are contradicted by his nation's rise, then clearly it must be credited elsewhere—namely, to its superior political leadership. By following ancient Chinese principles and practices ("rites" as he calls them), Beijing's leaders have strengthened their nation-state, which in turn commands great global respect. Consider it a rites-make-might-makes-right approach. Meanwhile, America's political system produces leaders of low moral character—again, a tough criticism to deflect nowadays.

If, as an American, you reject Yan's claim of China's superiority in "governmental morality," I totally agree that we win in a head-to-head comparison—not even close. But dismissing Yan's argument outright would be a mistake. Operating under the benevolence of US-style globalization, China lifted hundreds of millions of its citizens out of poverty they had long endured. There are moral consequences of such a profound economic accomplishment.

You may also bristle at Yan's casual assumption of America's inability to once again reform itself across another Progressive Era we so desperately need.

But what should really disturb you is Yan's assumption that, over time, China offers any nation in this world something far better than America ever could: personal security through steady economic progress and social order—however brutally, invasively, and arbitrarily enforced. For a recently elevated global middle class, these are not trivial offerings. So, ask yourself: How does America beat that package? Or is it simply the case that it is now China's turn to rule the world?

20

National Affiliation Does Not Grow Out of the Barrel of a Gun:
Irredentism as Superpower Brand Failure

Globalization is all about mutually and voluntarily reducing trade barriers, with states freely joining trade blocs or economic unions. Forcible integration is a twentieth-century relic.

Irredentism is an ideology focused on past grievances, specifically the loss of genuine—or merely self-declared—"homelands." It is a powerfully motivating belief system favored by authoritarian governments for its us-versus-them symbology and easy association with existential threats (*If we don't fight, they will destroy us completely!*). European fascism and irredentism went hand in hand across the early twentieth century, as both Italy's Benito Mussolini and Germany's Adolf Hitler made that quest the centerpiece of their political ascents.

Modern globalization suffers similar irredentist impulses in Russia and China. Vladimir Putin famously described the Soviet Union's dissolution as "the greatest geopolitical catastrophe of the century," while Xi Jinping never tires of referencing China's "century of humiliation" at the hands of imperial powers. These historical grievances drive geopolitical decision making in both Moscow and Beijing to a disturbingly irrational degree. Within these emotion-driven dynamics, we locate the most plausible pathways to strategic nuclear war, if for no other reason than that leaders couch these struggles in existential terms.

Russia's revanchist push to reconstitute its empire seeks to counter the EU and NATO's ongoing accumulation of "stars." Pay attention to the steady rhythm of Moscow's hostage taking (using the Russian names for each region):

★ Pridnestrovian Moldavian Republic (Transnistria), 1992 (from Moldova)
★ Union State of Russia and Belarus, 2000
★ Republic of South Ossetia, 2008 (Georgia)
★ Republic of Abkhazia, 2008 (Georgia)

- ★ Republic of Crimea, 2014 (Ukraine)
- ★ Kharkov People's Republic*, 2014 (Ukraine)
- ★ Donetsk People's Republic, 2014 (Ukraine)
- ★ Odessa People's Republic*, 2014 (Ukraine)
- ★ Lugansk People's Republic, 2014 (Ukraine)
- ★ Federal State of New Russia* (Donetsk and Lugansk), 2014 (Ukraine)
- ★ Kherson Oblast, 2022
- ★ Zaporozhye Oblast, 2022

(* signifies later dissolution)

Since the USSR's collapse, Moscow has methodically carved out enclaved micro-states along its borders, the 2022 Ukraine invasion extending the pattern.

Putin's messaging here is clear: "greater historical Russia" clawing back imperial territories threatened by an expanding Europe and, in each instance, sabotaging the targeted state's aspiration for membership in NATO by freezing a territorial conflict—only to later reignite it at an advantageous moment. After failing at regime change in Kyiv in 2022, Putin's default strategy was to link up annexed portions of Ukraine's east (Lugansk, Donetsk, Zaporozhye, Kherson) with Crimea (already annexed), Odessa, and Transnistria (already recognized), and, by doing so, landlocking a Ukrainian rump-state. Only the major seaport of Odessa remains free of his grasp—for now.

Because Putin's attempts to create EU and NATO clones have spectacularly failed, he was forced to propagandize this competition for affiliation as an existential conflict: *NATO seeking to dismantle and destroy Russia!*

In the end, the lessons of Ukraine have less to do with military strategy and more to do with brand failure, signified by how the failed invasion triggered an exodus of young Russians who now prefer life anywhere outside Russia. The world could have cared less if, like Belarus, Ukraine had voluntarily "unionized" with Russia. (Similarly, Taiwan's peaceful and voluntary union with China would little alter the East-West strategic balance—save to indicate the growing attraction of Beijing's brand.)

There are, of course, good historical reasons for fearing a wider conflagration whenever Eastern Europe serves as the target of military conquest by Germans or Russians, the most obvious being that both world wars started in that manner. Still, there are stronger reasons to temper fears over this latest conflict.

First, Putin's invasion of Ukraine only proves that nuclear superpowers still reserve the right to do what they want in their self-declared spheres of influence—without triggering WWIII even as they reflexively threaten it.

Second, Russia's invasion of Ukraine was entirely the result of Putin's monomaniacal fixation on reconstituting the historic Russian Empire. Remove him from the equation and there is no driving pan-Slavism in today's Russia.

In response to Putin's aggression, Germany's recent national-security reawakening (known as the *Zeitenwende*, or "turning point"), while surprising, was both historically overdue and a partial reaction to America's strategic retreat from the Middle East and growing dissatisfaction regarding its NATO commitment. The Russia-Ukraine war has triggered, according to *Washington Post* columnist David Ignatius, "an extraordinary cultural shift for Europe," with NATO's center of gravity moving east into Poland and the Baltic states and north toward Sweden and Finland.

Fourth and most importantly, the West's poor habit of blaming itself first is completely misplaced here—specifically the notion that NATO's enlargement strategy forced Putin's hand on Ukraine.

Neither Europe nor the United States did anything wrong by extending NATO membership to former Soviet satellites (Albania, Bulgaria, Croatia, Czech Republic, Hungary, Montenegro, North Macedonia, Poland, Romania, Slovakia, and Slovenia) and former Soviet republics (Estonia, Latvia, Lithuania). These nations were highly incentivized to seek the strategic protection of America's "nuclear umbrella," knowing full well that Russian revanchism would someday resurface. Did the West exploit Russia's weakness upon the Soviet Union's collapse? Absolutely, for if we had not, we would today face the same struggle—just farther westward.

The blame-America-first types marveling at Putin's Machiavellian "genius" were a national embarrassment. NATO made the right call. The most compelling proof? Longtime NATO partner states Sweden and Finland, after decades of remaining committed to a quasi-neutral stance vis-à-vis Moscow, immediately applying for full alliance membership following Russia's invasion of Ukraine.

The real lesson here for Europe and America is this: Western Europe "conquered" Eastern Europe and the Baltics with the lure of economic and political affiliation. That is what drove these buffer states into NATO's open arms—despite the attendant dangers. At this point, all fourteen of these nations have either joined the EU or been granted candidate status, with twelve having previously or simultaneously joined NATO. Point being when Eastern Europe and the Baltics were given the opportunity to choose their future—as free agents—these nations unanimously selected the EU and NATO over Moscow's meager offerings.

That is what winning looks like in this century: *They choose you.* If you must conquer a state to "win," you lose the superpower brand war. But if that state seeks out affiliation, you are winning—no matter the frictions triggered. Remember: allies empower you, while subject nations burden you.

The key, of course, is being open for business and willing to deal. The EU is open to new affiliates and it cuts deals; America is barely open for new citizens and has recently broken a lot of deals. The EU is both building and winning its future; America is attempting to re-create its past and retreat there. The EU is growing and expanding its geopolitical brand; America is trashing and narrowing its global appeal. Europe has its problems and obstacles but also ambition and vision. America has neither and we stoop to call that "winning."

There is no mystery why Putin thought he could get away with invading Ukraine, or why China prepares for Taiwan. Both view America as closed.

Globalization has altered the definition of winning. The EU has cracked the twenty-first-century code of geopolitical affiliation. The Kremlin resurrects its nineteenth-century version, while Beijing aggressively markets its economic variant. We await India's eventual South-centric offering. Sadly, America stubbornly disavows its own long-standing (1787–1959) code of attracting, welcoming, and admitting new member states, despite the stunning economic success of our Union.

America was built for this era of globalization's consolidation. Our political brand of rule by the middle—for the middle—is exactly what the world needs right now. The model and the hour have met.

21

Stuck in the Middle with You:
When the Middle Class Is
Happy, Everybody's Happy

When America's middle class thrives, we are a tolerant, caring, dutiful, and generous nation. To successfully manage climate change, we must apply this lesson to the global middle class.

America's Civil War is often described as our nation's "second revolution," not just for ending slavery but for subsequently ushering a middle class into political prominence. According to economist Benjamin Friedman in his 2005 book, *The Moral Consequences of Economic Growth*, American democracy has thereafter functioned best when that middle class has experienced sustained economic growth. Conversely, our politics succumb to Americans' worst instincts when that middle class suffers income stagnation. Surveying Europe's history, the author demonstrates that America is hardly alone in this pattern.

Friedman argues that Americans fundamentally shortchange our democracy when we "think of economic growth in terms of material considerations versus moral ones." Within the American model of economic integration, material advance "more often than not fosters greater opportunity, tolerance of diversity, social mobility, commitment to fairness, and dedication to democracy."

When your middle class is happy, your nation is happy. Your people and their politics are more kind, less self-centered, more open to outsiders, and more generous with the less fortunate and the wider world. Those are the profound moral consequences of economic growth: ours is a better, truer, and higher-functioning democracy when we collectively focus on satisfying the needs and ambitions of our middle class.

Consider American history since World War II: roughly three decades (1945–1973) of economic expansion triggering all manner of political ambition to fix our society while actively defending the Free World; then two decades (1973–1993) of political backlash on both scores (e.g., smaller government, less regulation, social conservatism, military rebuild); then another economic boom

(1993–2008) leading to an explosion of immigration, liberal idealism, and overseas military activities; only to see the Great Recession of 2008 plunge us into our current bout of political polarization, anti-immigrant fervor, culture wars, and a profound rejection of overseas military burdens. Notice how little of this pendulum swinging actually has to do with the global security environment!

Today, the dominant concern of America's middle class is the nightmare of backward mobility, exemplified by negative net worth (i.e., owing more than you own with little hope of paying off your debts). That fear is personified throughout the Millennial and Gen Z cohorts who now struggle with the twin afflictions of student and consumer debt (owing too much) and the gig economy (little money, no benefits). As politically open-minded and culturally diverse as those generations are, we cannot assume they will step up to sustained progressive leadership so long as America's middle class is beset with all manner of fears for its future, for therein lies the enduring appeal of strongman rule.

Those fears clearly shape Americans' ambivalent relationship with globalization itself, which has clearly done so much good across the wider world while helping deplete the ranks of the middle class back home. Here it is important to understand differences in definition: most development experts define the global middle class as anyone spending more than $4,000 per year (measured in 2011 purchasing power parity)—a standard that encompasses 95 percent of Americans. By that definition, the global middle class recently reached the unprecedented milestone of majority status. Meanwhile, the US middle class, referencing America's higher threshold of $10,000+ per capita spending, has seen its national share shrink to just over 50 percent. Aspiration and identity matter here, as roughly 70 percent of Americans still view themselves as belonging to the middle class.

But many Americans also now view globalization as the primary threat to their economic status—namely, jobs being "shipped out." The truth is more complex. Studies indicate that two-thirds of US wage declines since the 1980s were in industries experiencing rapid automation. This is not a bug but a feature of capitalism: one stays ahead of the competition by reducing production costs. Globalization imposes external competitive pressures, but so does the American economy—all on its own. Any firm that does not heed such competitive pressures—no matter the source—quickly goes out of business.

America now endures one of those technological accelerations where too few winners are created amidst too many losers. Our historic answer for skyrocketing income inequality has been progressive reform that regrades the economy into a more level playing field between employers and employees (consider, for example, the recent resurgence of unions). We need another Roosevelt to emerge, but given the nasty state of American politics, such progressive populism is hard to execute. Joe Biden's attempt to cast himself as the second coming of FDR has been fought at every turn by a know-nothing, do-nothing Republican Party laser-focused on pointless culture wars.

But there is a larger danger in play right now: when Europe's middle class first arose at the turn of the twentieth century, it was confronted by communism (rule from the Left on behalf of the poor) and fascism (rule from the Right on behalf of the rich). Vladimir Lenin's Bolsheviks sought to prevent the rise of the bourgeoisie, fearing in their emergence the extinguishing of all hope for socialist revolution, while Adolf Hitler's Nazi Party promised to protect shopkeepers from the radical, property-appropriating Left. Europe's deadly combination of communism and fascism birthed both World War II and the Cold War.

With the rise of a predominantly non-Western middle class, humanity now replays that scenario on a truly global stage. At home, notice how little the labels have changed: Democrats call Republicans "fascists" while the GOP brands Democrats "socialists" and "communists." With Vladimir Putin having vowed Ukraine's "de-Nazification," history veers from the sublime to the ridiculous.

Globalization approaches a collision between an irresistible force (climate change) and an unmovable objective (lifestyle demands of a South-centric middle class). This forces a revamp of North-South politics, a dynamic sure to be exploited by political actors of all stripes. Americans cannot merely condemn authoritarian models; we must show how democracy fosters better solutions.

Fig. 10 | The dramatic growth of the global middle class in recent decades is largely driven by India and China.

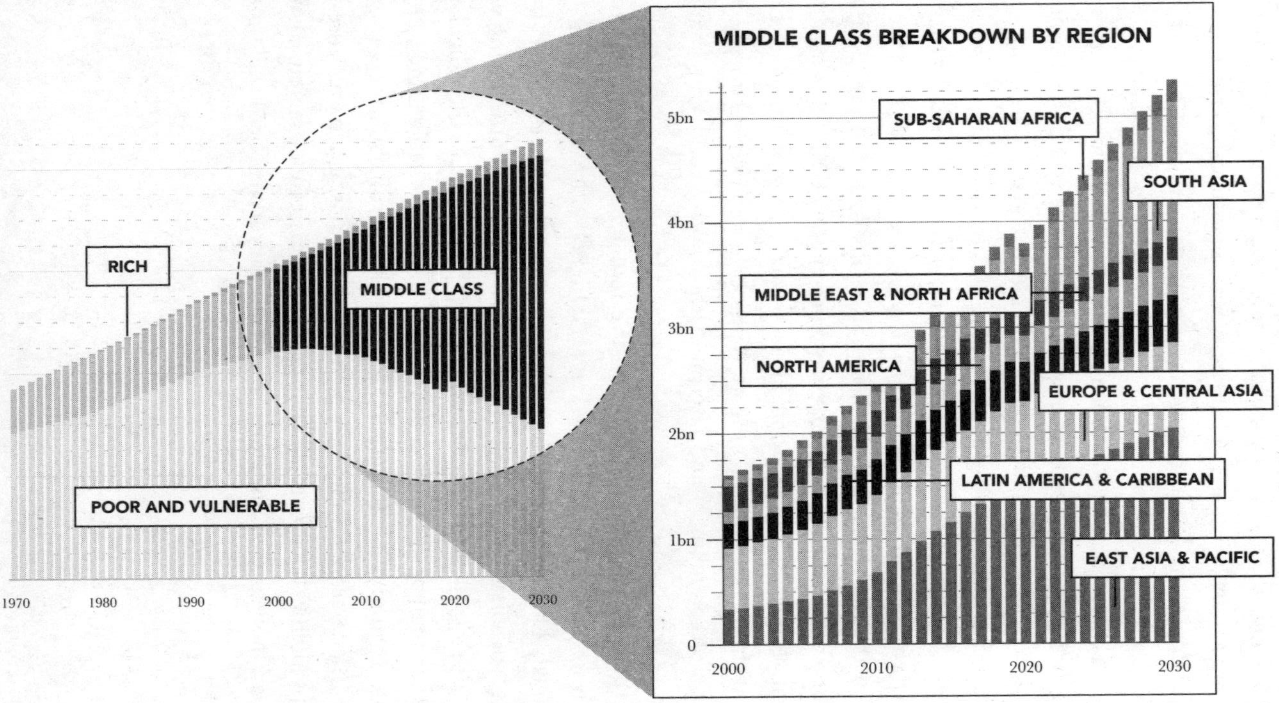

8bn
6bn
4bn
2bn
0
1970
1980
1990
2000
2010
2020
2030
RICH
MIDDLE CLASS
POOR AND VULNERABLE
MIDDLE CLASS BREAKDOWN BY REGION
5bn
4bn
3bn
2bn
1bn
0
2000
2010
2020
2030
SUB-SAHARAN AFRICA
SOUTH ASIA
MIDDLE EAST & NORTH AFRICA
NORTH AMERICA
EUROPE & CENTRAL ASIA
LATIN AMERICA & CARIBBEAN
EAST ASIA & PACIFIC

22 *Go, China. Go!*
Beijing's Methodical
Approach to Geopolitics

The warning "don't bring a knife to a gunfight" instructs us to arrive properly prepared for conflict, yet the choice of weapon depends on perceptions of the game being played.

Before a superpower engages its peers in conflict, two decisions must be reached: (1) determining the game at hand, and (2) matching the opponent's assets. The latter calculation is simple, the former harder than it seems. Competitors view conflict differently, resulting in vastly different playing styles.

America approaches international conflicts with a mindset best likened to poker. We judge our hand (cards held), estimate our opponent's, then either call (match their bet), raise (surpass it), or fold (withdraw). By estimating risk (forfeiture of bet) versus reward (winning the pot), we engage our opponent across sequential showdowns, sometimes bluffing our way (feigning a good hand). As a nation of traders, Americans gravitate to the implied bargaining dynamic at poker's core—namely, *how bad do you want this pot?*

Russians view international conflict as chess, a game that appeals to their mathematical prowess. In chess, a player moves after calculating (a) the threat at hand, (b) their own weaknesses, (c) their opponent's weaknesses, and finally (d) their best opportunity to exploit any perceived advantage presently enjoyed. The goal, logically projected over a sequence of future moves, is to trap the opponent within an untenable situation (checkmate). Like Russia's political culture, chess is hierarchical, meaning pawns are sacrificed to protect the ruling elite.

Ukraine exemplifies these fundamental differences in American and Russian approaches. On one side, Washington persistently raising the bet with each hand (sending in more potent weaponry), daring a depleted Moscow to call. On the other, the Kremlin, willing to spend pawns ad infinitum, methodically targeting Ukraine's pieces (key cities), seeking to dismember its statehood until king Kyiv is effectively checkmated. Different games seeking different outcomes.

While such East-West cold wars are daily declared in the media, China quietly pursues a different contest across a wider playing field. Go is a two-person board game invented by the Chinese four thousand years ago. Played on a 19-by-19 square grid (compared to chess's 8-by-8 layout), individual moves involve placing a single stone to claim a slice of territory (the intersection of two lines). The goal is to capture more territory than your opponent while claiming their stones whenever yours surround them, thus denying their "liberty"—a most apt term of art. The game ends when the board is fully captured and there is nothing left to scour.

Go involves no bluffing because nothing is hidden. Instead of being hierarchical (e.g., certain game pieces wielding special powers), it is imperial and zero-sum. Go is a logical grand strategy for a nation advantaged in resources (people, money) because it rewards persistence while eliminating randomness. It is perfect when playing against an unwitting, inattentive, and erratic opponent given to obsessing over the here and now.

Today, America insists on bringing a knife to the gunfight that is the superpower brand war—a game China is winning stone by stone. Oblivious to Beijing's strategy, Washington frames the contest along familiar lines—namely, the poker-like military showdown over Taiwan. While Washington dutifully marshals its defense budget to prepare for the next generation of high-tech warfare (knife), Beijing calmly executes its Belt and Road Initiative to lock in its stealthy access to local police and security systems worldwide (gunfight). Both imagine a path to supremacy playing different games: America hunkers down while sharpening the pointy end of its military spear, while Beijing methodically maximizes its worldwide political, economic, and security presence, seeding work-arounds for feared disruptions to come.

With globalization becoming increasingly digitalized, ask yourself which strategy seems more appropriate.

23

One Belt to Rule Them All, One Road to Find Them, One Initiative to Bring Them All and Infrastructure Bind Them

China's Belt and Road Initiative (BRI) seeks to capture major portions of the world economy within an alternate globalization that secures Chinese access to resources and markets.

Beijing's ambition for the BRI echoes Washington's following World War II. Recognizing the Communist Bloc's rapid expansion, the United States coalesced those European rimlands still free of Moscow's grip into a competing partial-world economy known as the Free World. That strategy's infrastructure scheme (most prominently, the Marshall Plan) seeded the first sprouts of US-style globalization, which sought to insulate those allied nations from future Soviet pressure by making them economically strong in a "peacefully rising" manner.

Decades later, rising China, recognizing America's long-standing pre-eminence as globalization's architect and rule-setter, seeks to stitch together a competing partial-world economy that will insulate the regime from future US pressure (e.g., military responses, economic sanctions) by integrating crucial regions within China's expanding global value chains.

China does this by concentrating its integrating efforts where (a) US presence is historically weak (Central Asia, Sub-Saharan Africa); (b) US influence recedes thanks to its diminishing military interests (Middle East); (c) the United States is considered an antagonist (Russia); and (d) the United States arrogantly takes its historical influence for granted (Latin America, Europe). While Washington's strategic attention regularly wanders among various familiar threats (*Terrorism! Nuclear proliferation! Resurgent Russia! Risen China!*) and the poker-like standoffs they regularly trigger, Beijing patiently tends its global Go board, laying down its stones—intersection by intersection, stringing them together over time.

In other words, hyperactive America plays the players; patient China plays the board.

Beijing altruistically pitches the BRI as a mutually beneficial scheme to address a widely recognized "infrastructure gap" plaguing many developing economies. While a real problem, China's strategic drivers are first and foremost internal. Over its decades of FDI-fueled development, China's coastal provinces achieved a level of infrastructure saturation in stark contrast to its vast, impoverished interior. The Chinese Communist Party now views developing and integrating those western provinces, with crisscrossing infrastructure networks, as necessary insurance against future domestic unrest—development as security.

The BRI is also China's belt-and-suspenders approach to securing access to Persian Gulf energy flows by augmenting vulnerable seaborne traffic with land-based pipelines. The BRI aims to do the same with the natural resources of the former Soviet republics—Russia chief among them.

By extension, the BRI expands China's infrastructure networks into East Africa and Europe—in particular, the latter's vast consumer market.

All these investments provide Beijing with a productive opportunity to deploy its currency reserves and unmatched demand along bilateral lines. Instead of negotiating multilaterally with groups of nations, China prefers to bargain on a one-to-one basis with far smaller economies, giving it the clear upper hand on every negotiation. In financial terms, China's push to become the lender of first resort makes perfect sense: as the latest economic superpower integrated into globalization's networks, China is best positioned to further extend those networks as it climbs the production ladder from manufacturing to services, repositioning itself as an intellectual property giant like America and Japan before it—Xi's ultimate goal.

To achieve that elevation, China must increasingly outsource the lower-end manufacturing that initially powered its rise. To a Chinese Communist Party obsessed with preserving its rule, that means both constructing and ruling over a global network of upstream (natural resources), midstream (cheap labor, factories), and downstream (retail enterprises) value-chain partners. Nothing less will do in securing China's rise to unparalleled leadership of a next-generation globalization of its own shaping. Toward that end, Beijing welcomes the West's self-pitying judgment that "globalization is dead," because it leaves the playing field that much more open for China's penetration and networking.

China's strategic logic here is sound, fitting where the nation now stands in the evolution of globalization and where the global economy's networks need to expand next—namely, westward (South Asia, the Middle East) and southward (Africa) from today's center of gravity (East Asia). On many levels, the future health of the global economy depends on China's success in implementing the BRI to the mutual benefit of all involved—to include Beijing becoming a leading and trusted source of globalization's new rules. That strategic credibility is built when the investing power allows those integrating economies to benefit on a preferential basis—like affording them privileged export access to its more mature consumer market. This is how America encouraged postwar Japan's "peaceful rise," and how Washington and Tokyo subsequently accomplished the same with China.

But therein lies the rub, as Beijing does not exhibit that sort of commercial restraint—much less strategic responsibility—when it comes to spreading its style of globalization. Instead, China structures its BRI investments to its maximum benefit, too often bribing local officials, who, in turn, are encouraged to accept China's social-control security offerings to help tamp down any domestic opposition to, or unrest emanating from, the ultimately exploitative relationship. Researchers estimate that China's BRI scheme has suffered local domestic pushback on one-third of its projects, typically stemming from corruption scandals, labor issues, and environmental damage.

The biggest advanced-economy gripe against China's BRI "investments" focuses on the fact that the vast majority are really loans (versus grants or official development assistance) that, when an economic downturn arrives, effectively "trap" the recipient under a mountain of sovereign debt that Beijing exploits by (a) locking in repayment as long-term, below-market resource flows to China; or (b) assuming operational control of the collateral via decades-long leases (consider, for example, Sri Lanka's Hambantota Port). While such arguments presume that BRI participants are not savvy enough to negotiate on their own behalf, such opportunistic collateralization effectively shifts project risk from Beijing to its partners. Already, several dozen BRI partners owe China sovereign debt greater than one-tenth of their annual GDP. To critics, that is Beijing's debt-trap diplomacy at work—highlighted by indebted Sri Lanka's political and economic collapse in 2022.

A secondary fear concerning China's BRI scheme is that it strikes many outside observers as woefully uncoordinated—a messy reality masked by Beijing's lack of transparency in structuring its bilateral developmental relationships with far smaller economies. A quartet of Chinese state banks and more than a dozen government ministries are major players, with individual provinces pursuing their own competing agendas. As a result, most of the transactions and resulting debt are shaded from public scrutiny, making it difficult to calculate risk against gain. There is, for example, no single, authoritative accounting of BRI deals globally executed to date—this in a scheme projected to cost in the trillions of US dollars.

Add it all up and China's BRI is a mixed bag for the world. Beijing is globally deploying its resources in a manner that respects globalization's underlying economic logic of investing it forward. It is just doing so in a manner negatively reflecting its internal political fears and its strategic suspicions regarding America's presumed desire to sabotage its "rise"—hence China's often predatory trade practices that deny equal access to others. Understand that Beijing views its me-first approach as entirely justified, given its long and tortured history with Western imperial powers. Can we expect Beijing to temper that approach over time? Given China's frighteningly fast demographic transition, that is unduly optimistic. Beijing knows its biological clock is ticking.

China's BRI experiment is well underway and will not be contained—much less stopped—by globalization's old guard, who, in the form of the G7 intergovernmental forum, have floated alternative schemes designed to raise and direct vast sums of private capital in a competitive manner.

While America should prod China on greater transparency and debt forgiveness, it should not seek to sabotage the BRI. The global economic costs of the BRI's failure will greatly outweigh any ephemeral strategic benefits America might accrue. The more China takes on in terms of regional responsibilities, the more it will be forced to learn, adapt, and compromise—a process we are already witnessing. We should encourage just enough local blowback to produce that positive evolution without crashing the entire scheme. China may well succeed in carving out various closed loops within globalization, but that will be less of a challenge to America than China's collapse as a superpower, at least until India has sufficiently risen by midcentury to supersede its neighbor as globalization's next stabilizing pillar.

I realize that is not a one-word grand strategy as straightforward as *containment*. But globalization has evolved past the point of such simplicity. Attempting to shape the rise of fellow superpowers is a difficult but essential business. Just ask Winston Churchill.

No matter China's success or failures, the United States is incentivized to limit those effects by offering something more strategically credible to those world regions it seeks to insulate from Beijing's integration scheme. Since China's debt-financed diplomacy resembles that of turn-of-the-twentieth-century European imperial powers, whose predatory behavior prompted Theodore Roosevelt to propose his economic corollary to the Monroe Doctrine, it is historically consistent to argue that America should make it a strategic priority to spare the Americas from either fate—but only by offering something more valuable in terms of security, prosperity, and affiliation.

China is presently on pace to become the single largest holder of sovereign debt in Latin America. If we cannot adequately outcompete China in our own hemisphere—an environment that gives us every strategic reason to do so—then there is little point in our attempting it on the other side of the world.

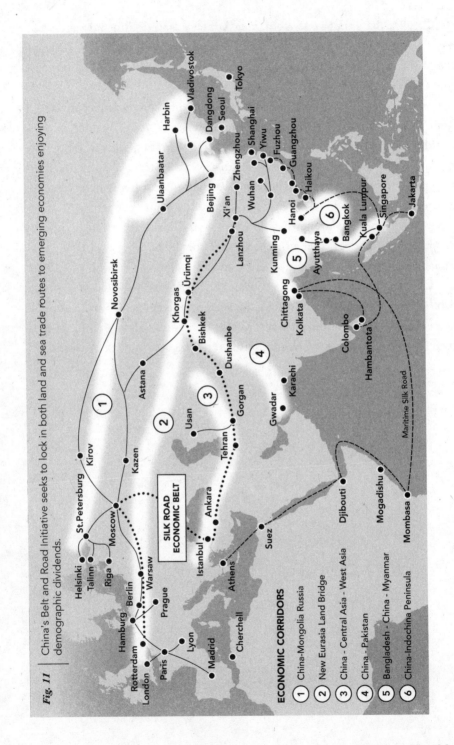

Fig. 11 China's Belt and Road Initiative seeks to lock in both land and sea trade routes to emerging economies enjoying demographic dividends.

SILK ROAD ECONOMIC BELT

ECONOMIC CORRIDORS

1. China–Mongolia Russia
2. New Eurasia Land Bridge
3. China – Central Asia – West Asia
4. China – Pakistan
5. Bangladesh – China – Myanmar
6. China–Indochina Peninsula

Maritime Silk Road

24 *Crouching Tiger, Hidden Dragon:* Is Asia Big Enough for Both Rising India and Risen China?

America views its rivalry with China as <u>the</u> superpower competition of the twenty-first century, but that dynamic takes a back seat to Beijing's always tense ties with "heir apparent" India.

America has played global hegemon long enough for its citizenry to view international developments through the narrow prism of challengers—as in, we analyze every great-power action in terms of its capacity to "challenge the US-led world order." In truth, America must come to grips with its diminished control over globalization in the same way that Whites back home must adjust to their diminished control over developments there: founding something does not grant you eternal control over the resulting enterprise.

America's fixation over who constitutes our next Cold War opponent is misplaced. The twenty-first century's coldest war will directly involve not the United States but China and India—the two rising economic behemoths of our age. In that rivalry, neither side requests our presence even as our strategic interests require it.

For now, America outpaces India and China's combined defense spending by two and a half times—a gap certain to shrink as the two Asian powers' strategic horizons expand while ours narrow. Nowhere is this more apparent than in the Middle East, where George W. Bush's nation-building effort in Iraq soured Americans on "forever wars." That growing reluctance to intervene there yielded Barack Obama's "leading from behind" approach to the Arab Spring, when, for example, Washington pressed NATO to assume the burden of putting boots on the ground in Libya. With the ascension of Donald Trump, our businessman president essentially licensed out American security strategy to our regional proxies. Given America's emerging energy self-sufficiency over this time frame, these developments were no surprise. At the same time, China's skyrocketing imports of Persian Gulf oil naturally triggered an increase of its state presence across the Middle East. In superpower terms, that constitutes a change in strategic ownership.

The United States draws one-eighth of its shrinking crude oil imports from the Persian Gulf, while ever-thirsty China pulls half and India two-thirds. Washington may still have its Central Command, but Beijing and New Delhi increasingly command the attention of Riyadh, which sends ten times more oil to Asia than to the Americas. All that crude travels the Indian Ocean, and most passes through the Malacca Straits. China has good reason to build the world's largest naval fleet.

For much of the twentieth century, British geographer Halford Mackinder's "heartland theory" animated a significant segment of East-West strategic thinking. At the start of that century, Mackinder argued that Eastern Europe constituted the great strategic pivot of the entire Eurasian landmass, meaning whichever great power controlled that region could extend its control over that continent's vast "rimlands" stretching from West Europe to East Asia. This theory explains both Nazi Germany's WWII push to secure that region and Joseph Stalin's later insistence that the Soviet Union achieve the same in any postwar settlement. Today, we can credit China's Belt and Road Initiative (BRI) with similar—but more peaceful—ambitions.

In many ways, China and India view the Indian Ocean as the maritime obverse of Mackinder's heartland theory—updated for globalization. Given their growing consumer power, both states believe that naval hegemony over Eurasia's maritime rimlands confers some measure of control over that vast landmass's economic networks. This is why Beijing lays down a constellation of naval bases spanning the southern rim of the Eurasian landmass—the so-called "string of pearls" strategy. In reply, India seeks to encircle China with its similarly naval-centric "necklace of diamonds" strategy.

Applying the same strategic logic, America recently renamed its Pacific Command as the Indo-Pacific Command. But here is the challenge: we play an "away game" (i.e., the far side of the world for us) to India and China's "home game" (adjacent seas), and that is decisive when it comes to maintaining naval presence (i.e., ships patrolling seas) decade after decade. America needs to convince itself of an extraordinary force-sizing requirement that India and China instinctively feel compelled to meet. The US Navy is keen to develop unmanned naval vessels for precisely this reason; otherwise America will eventually find itself priced out of this strategic competition.

India's relationship with China is complicated by their long-disputed mountainous Himalayan border, where the two fought an intense but truncated war in 1962. India and China have never formally agreed on the matter, which is why they have engaged in countless skirmishes over the decades concerning the Line of Actual Control—a diplomatic oxymoron for a border suffering frequent incursions from both sides.

Elevating the matter in importance: China's side of the border comprises the Tibet Autonomous Region annexed by Beijing in 1959. Mao Zedong famously intimated that China would eventually reclaim the "five fingers of Tibet"—namely, the independent border states Nepal and Bhutan, along with one Indian territory (Ladakh) and two Indian states (Sikkim and Arunachal Pradesh).

If that was not enough, Tibet's mountains are the starting point for seven rivers that flow into India—all subject to dam-construction and flow-diversion schemes pursued by an increasingly water-insecure China.

Beijing, keen to present itself as law-abiding, nonetheless sits atop several thousand years of historic expansionism along its borders. In this never-ending endeavor, China has mastered what the West has dubbed "salami slicing" tactics (in Chinese, *nibbling like a silkworm*), wherein soft- and hard-power schemes combine to incrementally advance their lines of control in an unstoppable sovereign "velocity" not unlike climate change's creeping advance.

Add in Beijing's BRI, and India's paranoia over Chinese encirclement seems strategically warranted. Two of China's planned "economic corridors"—one to India's west (involving fierce rival Pakistan) and the other to its east (linking Bangladesh, Myanmar, and India to Southern China)—effectively box in the subcontinent in conjunction with Beijing's Maritime Silk Road Initiative. With all that going on, India's clear reluctance to participate in China's vast infrastructure schemes reminds one of Mexico's lack of enthusiasm for financing Donald Trump's border wall: it feels like an invitation to build one's own prison cell.

That is the history, but this is the inevitability both sides now face: India's economic rise, fueled by favorable demographics once similarly exploited by China, will require massive foreign direct investment (FDI) flows from abroad to achieve its full potential—just like China did. As the world system's primary saver these past three decades, Beijing sits on more than $3 trillion in currency reserves—almost six times India's holdings and fourteen times America's total.

For now, China's FDI in India in no way matches its trade volume, because New Delhi is highly fearful of Chinese ownership (much like the United States is today and was in decades past regarding Japan). While such concerns are natural, they put India's economic rise at risk. Right now, one million Indians enter that country's workforce every month, meaning New Delhi faces the same bide-your-time prelude to its rise that (a) Deng's China faced with America, and (b) Alexander Hamilton's America once faced with Great Britain. Tricky stuff indeed.

I have long advocated for America to accommodate China's "peaceful rise," no matter the subsequent challenges. The alternative would have been both immoral and self-destructive to our larger strategic goals. China's embrace of export-driven growth constituted globalization's inflection point, propelling the planet past the have/have-not divisions so long assumed to be humanity's never-ending fate. The resulting economic competition is a small price to pay for US-style globalization's supremacy. That is America wisely playing the board.

If the United States is to play a beneficial role in managing the China-India competition, it will be in steering both sides toward a mutually beneficial relationship wherein last-in China now sponsors next-up India. We may assume that Beijing will resist this economic logic because, after all, America long invested in China, only to later feel "betrayed" by its lack of Americanization. Beijing has its own ideological expectations alright, but, as we will see, China does not leave such things to chance in its globalization strategy.

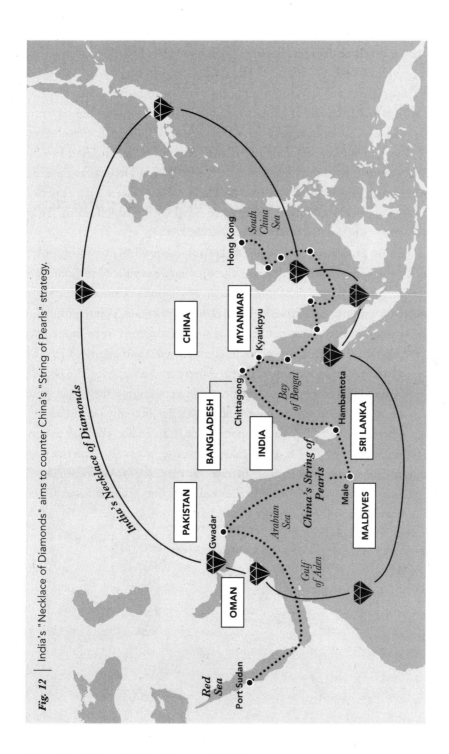

Fig. 12 | India's "Necklace of Diamonds" aims to counter China's "String of Pearls" strategy.

25 *Leave the Gun, Take the Biometrics:* How China and America Project Power Differently

America focuses on neutralizing bad actors to shape an environment—a top-down approach. China's bottom-up variant shapes an environment to prevent bad actors from emerging.

Ours is an era of insurgencies. Given globalization's brutally integrating forces, this is only natural. As a rule, insurgents seek independence, blaming their minority's lot on a distant, uncaring, and corrupt regime ruled by an oppressing tribe. Elevate that dynamic to the nation-state and you locate today's democratic recession—the insurgency-like rise of ethno-nationalism and xenophobic populism. Here, newly hardened regimes blame their lot on a distant, uncaring, and corrupt system they dub globalism. In their desperate telling, global elites "mongrelize" their tribe by forcing integration—the Great Replacement Theory adopted by ethno-religious fundamentalists across the North.

In a world teeming with insurgencies, great powers reach for counterin-surgency strategies. Some, like Russia (in Chechnya, Syria, Ukraine) or Saudi Arabia (Yemen), use brute force—they make a desert and call it peace. In contrast, the United States prefers to swoop in, take out the bad guys, and leave (the Powell Doctrine). Then there is China, which is all about creating facts on the ground—one infrastructure project at a time. America prefers its crisis-oriented, quick-fix interventions because they fit our default unilateralism and short attention span. The Chinese prefer a crisis-avoidance, long-term invest-ment approach because it fits their ideology of noninterference. Washington has a hard time recognizing Beijing's strategy because it is so counterintuitive to our emergency-responder mindset.

After 9/11, America became obsessed with homeland security. As for threats beyond, we turned to our tried-and-true method of power projection, sending overwhelming military force to destroy them at their source. Our top-down approach is to eliminate bad actors and, on that basis, secure the environment. Do we succeed? Not really. As soon as we leave, somebody new steps in, picking up that gun—and the fight. The roster of "we got him!" supervillains is long (e.g., Noriega, Hussein, Qaddafi, Bin Laden, Baghdadi, Zawahiri); the list of countries we fixed is not.

China approaches the challenge in a bottom-up fashion. The Chinese point to their history of subjugation by outside forces as reason both to fortify their perimeter and to consider that fortification entirely insufficient. Sensing themselves vulnerable to globalization's dangers, Beijing seeks to create and enforce safe zones at home and across the world. These heavily sensored safe zones are digitally enforced (e.g., CCTV cameras, location tracking, contact tracing, facial/mood recognition, biometrics, AI). Beijing tracks its citizens like Amazon monitors warehouse workers—invasively surveilling every single human action to systematically judge its potential threat to the state (or, in Amazon's case, to productivity). It is the reduction of individuals by algorithms into controllable cogs within a high-performing system—a process of dehumanization first flagged by Karl Marx in his searing critiques of capitalism but far more frequently found in dictatorships than in democracies.

Americans are familiar with this sort of surveillance, but only in certain public spaces (e.g., federal buildings) or under certain conditions (attending exceptionally large public gatherings). To us, it is the special price of admission, but to the Chinese, it is an increasingly Orwellian staple of life. A good example is how Beijing aggressively locks down its restive Muslim Uighur population in its Xinjiang Province, where its safe-zone approach looks an awful lot like cultural genocide. This is worth remembering as China seeks to impose its integration model globally: the world witnesses its own worst-case scenario in Xinjiang today.

China's counterinsurgency model is thus akin to the classic British imperial approach known as the ink spot strategy—here, securing an environment one safe zone at a time, then linking them up over time. We can call it the "string of pearls" or the Belt and Road Initiative, but it is all the same Go strategy of filling in blank spots until you control the board far more than your opponent.

For China, every bit of infrastructure it builds and controls exemplifies a Go stone successfully laid. The same holds for surveillance systems sold to metropolitan governments. Each investment extends the safe-zone network.

Before we came into our own as a global player, America extended its power across North America in a manner echoing China's current approach. Back then our version of safe zones were small forts that eventually morphed into pioneer settlements and later cities linked by railroads and telegraph networks. We saw ourselves integrating empty frontiers, while the Native Americans living there saw us as a force of cultural—and oftentimes literal—genocide. No matter how you choose to describe it, White American settlers *replaced* Native Americans across their historic lands. Point being world history is replete with *replacement* dynamics triggered by waves of human migration and frontier integration.

With modern globalization, that frontier integration dynamic is best described as national integration into global value chains with the attendant dangers of cultural imperialism. Like any past wave of frontier integration, this variant is highly disruptive to traditional societies. When that much change hits at such a high velocity, social tumult is guaranteed; hence the accompanying requirement for some measure of reinforcing security integration. America has its historic Cold War–style offering of membership in military alliances, but that no longer suffices for an emergent global middle class more interested in personal security than national defense. That is why China's current integration offering (BRI plus social control technologies) is readily accepted across developing regions.

Would most targeted nations prefer EU/NATO-style integration? Absolutely. Would many jump at the chance to engage in some drawn-out accession process that leads to their joining an expanding United States as member states? Of this I have little doubt. But until these integration models are marketed on a geographic scale that puts them in direct competition with China, Beijing's quick-and-dirty offering wins by default pretty much everywhere else.

A good portion of that success stems from Beijing strongly supporting its big tech companies as they penetrate and capture wide swaths of the planet. Meanwhile, Washington busies itself with corralling, taming, and even breaking our own tech giants, many of which are already so intertwined with China's big tech firms as to compromise their ability to compete with them globally. America should view these firms more like our Security Industrial Complex for the coming struggle. Their collective global brand appeal is one of our great national assets.

Fig. 13 | China is aggressively building a global security surveillance network, country by country.

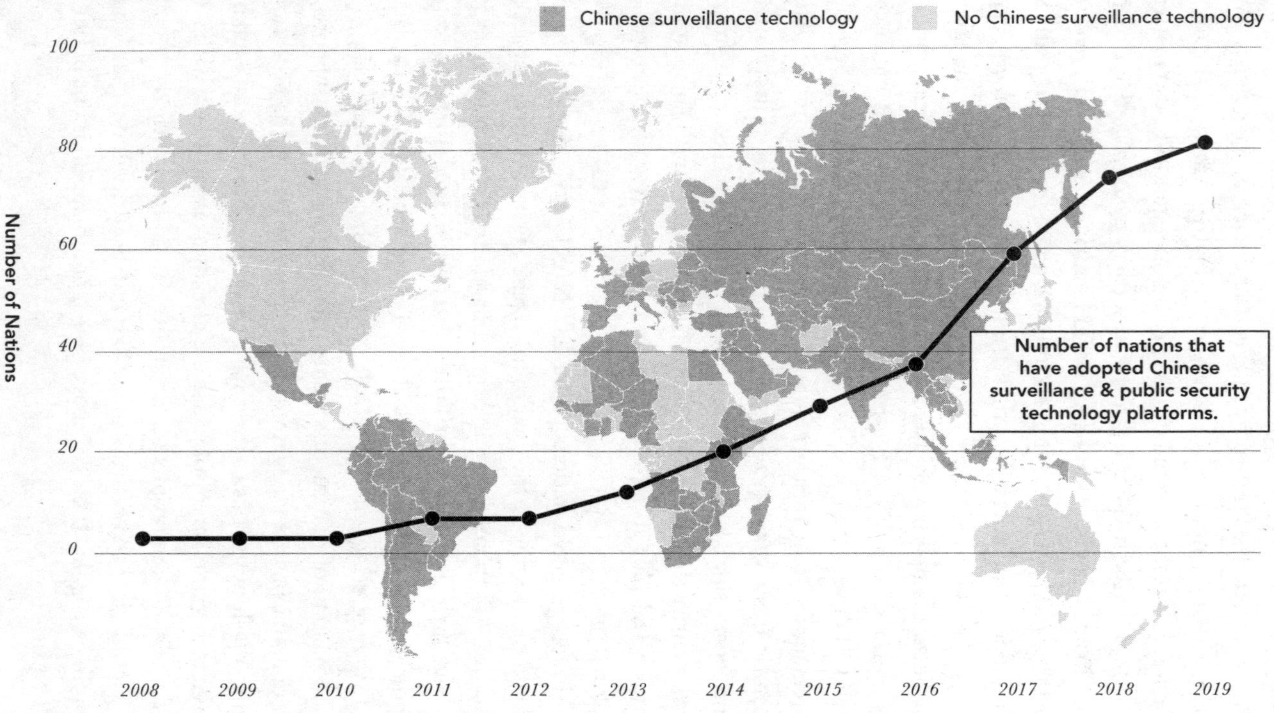

Chinese surveillance technology

No Chinese surveillance technology

Number of nations that have adopted Chinese surveillance & public security technology platforms.

Number of Nations

2008 2009 2010 2011 2012 2013 2014 2015 2016 2017 2018 2019

0 20 40 60 80 100

26 *Pacification by Gamification: Ruling the World One Cowed Citizen at a Time*

> The best-policed society is one where everyone acts as their own cop, reminding themselves at every point in their day what they are doing wrong and what they could do better.

Born in 1962, I grew up listening to, and reading, stories with a beginning, middle, and end. Passively accepting such storytelling conditioned me for linear thought: a past acknowledged, a present engaged, a future anticipated. What later drew me to strategic planning was that domain's embrace of alternative futures that liberated the present (*We have choices!*) by critically reviewing the past (*They had choices!*). That was my introduction to the multiverse—not as a theoretical abstraction but as the sum of our decisions. History constantly bends around us "butterflies" as our actions set in motion all manner of possible futures. Neither chaos nor imprisonment, we still collectively command tomorrow.

Thanks to computer games and their increasingly immersive environments, my kids have grown up exploring and manipulating stories in which the past is but a jumping-off point, the present is entirely reconfigurable, and the future remains fractiously open-ended. What my Boomer generation views derisively as historical illiteracy and relativism-gone-mad in Millennials and Gen Zs is their superpower—the ability to navigate a complex, ever-shifting storyscape, clicking their way to outcomes no one narrative can contain and moving through virtual reality (VR) environments rendered entirely pliable by their decisions. Little wonder they have grown up thinking they can change the world if their generations put their collective minds to the task.

Still, every superhero suffers some "kryptonite"—a vulnerability that inverts strength into weakness. For these generations, it is their eagerness to embrace gaming and varying degrees of VR environments throughout their daily lives, rendering them susceptible to the biggest ideological threat our world faces in coming years: political pacification of citizenry through the gamification of state instruments of social control.

Gamification involves applying game components (e.g., points, badges, levels) and dynamics (rankings, credentialing, access) to a real-world activity, organization, service, or system to make it seem more like a game. For Boomers, the classic example is airline miles and the status-granting privileges they unlock (*I get to board first!*). Gaming-native Millennials, Gen Zs, and Gen Alphas have embraced this mindset throughout their environment, from the trivial (relative status in an online community) to the highly consequential (credit score).

All this gamification of daily life dovetails with the rise of Big Data collected from our expanding universe of smart devices: our past comprehensively archived, our present invasively tracked, our future algorithmically predetermined and spoon-fed as the pop-up sum of all our choices to date (*Are you sure you're not ready to buy that . . . ?*). The more we connect, subscribe, and network, the more we surrender personal information and subject ourselves to externally determined rulesets. That is the price of living in an interconnected world, whether you are an individual, enterprise, or even a nation-state.

Advanced authoritarian governments like China increasingly grasp the potential for gamifying their citizens' daily lives as a virtual means of totalitarian control. Chinese technology companies are required by law to share with the government everything they collect on citizens, enabling security agencies to calculate a "social credit score" that captures any activity or association deemed more or less acceptable by the Communist Party. Have a friend who openly criticizes the government? You lose points. Noticed searching "harmful" ideas online or geo-located at a street protest? You lose points. Conversely, like the right pro-government post? You gain points. Same for ending associations with "antisocial" people.

By design, point totals trigger real-world consequences. You try to buy that train ticket to Province X but are told your rating does not allow such travel. Your attempts to access a more exclusive housing complex are rebuffed without explanation. Meanwhile, you look around and realize that friends who toe the party line increasingly live in an entirely better universe than yours, going to places off-limits to you and engaging in activities beyond your grasp.

Pretty soon you find that you are self-correcting to raise your point total. Frowning in public is captured on face-recognition cameras, so you smile vaguely whenever outside your apartment. You avoid friends with lower scores.

You realize that your every movement, act, and even emotion is being held against you, determining the size of your virtual cage. The government no longer needs to actively control you—just remind you of your score. After some time, you are your own police, your own jail-keeper, your own minder. You have been gamified into complete submission within the Matrix.

China peddles that Orwellian vision around the world to frightened governments eager to control their restive middle class and tech-savvy youth. It is also why Beijing vacuums up Big Data on everyone on this planet to predictively identify those who are, or may become, a threat to Communist Party rule—*Minority Report* on a global scale.

Now imagine an America in which any online comment you offered in support or criticism of the January 6th Insurrection determines whether Fannie Mae approves your mortgage. Or when your online search for abortion services suddenly shuts down your Tesla as you attempt to drive out of state.

Gaming, VR, and the cyber realm offer users an escape from the limitations and strictures that govern the real world. As environments optimized for self-discovery, free association, and thought experimentation, they are naturally threatening to autocracies that are reflexively determined to extend their instruments of social control throughout these media, in the process strengthening their already firm hold over their citizens in the real world. China observers have taken to describing Beijing's social credit scoring system as Mao Zedong's Cultural Revolution digitalized, which makes Beijing's aggressive pursuit of society-pacifying gamification systems an even greater threat to a world well conditioned and incentivized for their pervasive application.

The danger here is Beijing's successful commoditization of social intangibles like freedom and security, transforming them into generic products (like gasoline, flat-screen TVs, or budget air travel) undistinguishable by their source (democracies vs. autocracies). To a nervous global middle class seeking certainties in a seemingly uncertain world, China promotes the image that its freedom-and-security offering is not all that different from America's—just cheaper, more reliable, and easier for emerging-market governments to implement and operate.

That is how democracy dies in the twenty-first century, not with a bang but with a bargain.

Fig. 14

STOP TIER 2 WARNING

You have read more than 50%
of an unsanctioned book.

42 Negative themes encountered.

16 Instances of lingering on pages
containing negative themes.

4 Suspicious interactions with other
low-score readers of this text.

YOUR CURRENT SOCIAL SCORE

Down by 20 points
in 48 hours.

Transportation privileges have been
revoked until score improves.

OPTIONS TO CORRECT YOUR SCORE:

1 Stop reading immediately.
5% additional score drop.

2 Surrender book to your nearest
Free Speech Center.
25% score boost.

3 Ignore this warning.
50% score decline.
ATM access suspended for 2 weeks.

27 *Sensor Chip Meets Censorship:* China's 5G Telecom Offering Is a Trojan Horse

> With the Internet of Things (IoT), the pervasive use of sensors throughout environments triggers an inflection point for the surveillance of, and thus government control over, societies.

We spend a lot of time today debating the issue of censorship: whose views are legitimate for public expression and which views, doing far more harm than good, warrant suppression by authorities. This timeless argument expands exponentially with the pervasive sensoring of our lives (embedding of sensors within everyday objects) made possible by the combined rise of the Internet of Things (the connectivity of all those smart devices) and fifth-generation (5G) broadband cellular networks (delivering digital services ten times faster than 4G). Put simply, the more sensors there are, the greater the potential for censoring speech and behavior.

This is why the US government is so concerned about China's domination of 5G networks being rapidly constructed around the world today, particularly those involving its national flagship companies Huawei, world-leading provider of 5G "backbone" telecommunications infrastructure, and Hikvision, world-leading provider of video surveillance equipment. Eventually, the IoT will develop into the Artificial Intelligence of Things (AIoT) in which cognitive computing mimics the human brain, allowing AI networks to operate with minimal human intervention and develop on their own.

If that strikes you like the jumping-off point for conscious computers to overthrow their human masters per the *Terminator* movies, then let me just note that Beijing calls its nationwide video surveillance system "Skynet." It turns out you really can make this stuff up, and China aims to get there first by being the leading worldwide hardware provider for 5G, the IoT, and the AIoT.

While America maintains its lead in software, China's aggressive global marketing of its hardware is paying off. By massively subsidizing firms like Huawei and Hikvision as they piggyback their global sales on China's Belt and Road Initiative (BRI), Beijing has succeeded in building in "backdoors" throughout the world's expanding surveillance networks, leading US government officials to accurately label Huawei a 5G "Trojan horse."

Fighting back, the Trump administration sanctioned Huawei and other Chinese tech giants, forbidding any firms using US technology from producing components for their hardware products. The US ban immediately crashed the firm's smartphone sales outside of China's vast domestic market. Huawei has since pushed into global markets less dependent on US technologies: energy conservation; electric cars; and AI to run factories, mines, hospitals, ports, power plants, and other industrial enterprises.

With Joe Biden's dramatic expansion of those curbs, to include broad restrictions on selling semiconductors and chip-making equipment to China, we approach the limits of what we can do with non-financial sanctions. In the global economy, the dollar's supremacy as a reserve currency gives our financial sanctions genuine heft in a hierarchical system where we sit on top. But the same cannot be said of America's standing in the technology realm, where we are far from dominating either supply or demand in value chains that are far more distributed and thus amenable to adjustments and work-arounds. For example, the US government is just beginning to promote a standards-based alternative (Open Radio Access Network [ORAN]) to supplant Huawei's proprietary hardware in lower-end 5G cellular network markets. The problem is, America is trying to enforce a global ruleset on telecoms even though no global cellular equipment firms are US based and our market is already saturated—not impossible but a hard nut to crack without a level of multilateralism rarely achieved by Washington nowadays.

Look at it from the perspective of an emerging Southern market: you know climate change will render your economy less attractive to Northern investment over time, so you are already on the clock. When it comes to global crises (Great Recession, climate disasters, COVID-19), you have watched China either match or do no worse than America's performance. Now, while the United States continues to self-immolate over bizarrely narrow culture wars, Beijing offers you the magical combination of top-flight network connectivity and the social control means to manage the politically disruptive dynamics that inevitably accompany any great leap forward. In contrast, Washington offers its usual finger-wagging sanctions and bromides about democracy and free markets. There is no mystery here: you take the Chinese deal—backdoors and all.

That choice is defensible even before we add in Chinese bribery that enriches local leaders. The same holds for China's internal use of such surveillance systems on its minority Uighurs. Most illiberal regimes face such destabilizing internal dynamics, rendering China's offering more attractive. Most emerging markets likewise suffer weak legal systems, which make China's social control technologies an appealing shortcut. Finally, developing economies invariably need help managing rapid urbanization, something Chinese state enterprises offer in abundance, having just done the same on a massive scale throughout China. Add it all up and China's umbrella BRI scheme is a compelling offering cleverly co-marketed with Huawei's Safe City/Smart City solutions sold to dozens of major metropolitan areas (e.g., Islamabad, Nairobi, Belgrade, Marseille, São Paulo, Santiago) around the world—Beijing's Trojan horse readily accepted.

American fears of a bifurcated technology world are legitimate. Beijing offers its cyber-sovereignty model amidst globalization's ongoing consolidation of the goods trade, enabling it to lock in network supremacy across great swaths of the developing world. In so penetrating these states' media ecosystems, Beijing seeks, in the words of longtime observer Joshua Kurlantzick, "to influence who gets selected as political leaders, what topics are discussed in those states' domestic politics, how their universities approach issues related to China, and how their local media operates and covers many topics relating to Beijing."

America ruled the several-steps-forward period of globalization's rapid expansion (1990s–2000s) because its then-unparalleled consumption forced the global economy to revolve around its demand and tastes. But with China's demographic dividend now being cashed out, globalization enters a one-step-backward regionalization phase triggered by East Asia's transformation from the global economy's "factory floor" to its preeminent demand hub.

Today, China occupies that same sweet spot that America enjoyed last midcentury when our combination of a vast domestic market and unmatched manufacturing capacity allowed us to promote national flagship companies as de facto global brands. By effectively capturing worldwide construction of 5G networks while successfully marketing both its BRI and associated city-security solutions, Beijing is poised to steer globalization's next expansive phase. If America does not want to live in China's world, we must—once again—carve out and propagate a competing integration model; otherwise we lose by default.

Fig. 15 | Huawei's 5G offering serves as a Trojan horse for China's security surveillance technologies.

Confirmed Huawei
Network / Vendor

M.O.U. or Testing
with Huawei

Confirmed
Huawei Ban

Globalization's Consolidation Is Hemispheric Integration: America's Goal of Stable Multipolarity Preordained This Era

THROUGHLINE FIVE

America built globalization to encourage and accommodate the peaceful rise of other powers. Now we compete to see which superpowers' integration schemes work best.

From the Cold War's end until the Great Recession, globalization spread like wildfire. Global GDP tripled, the value of traded goods increased fourfold, and foreign direct investment (FDI) jumped tenfold. However, starting with that 2008 crash, goods-based globalization flatlined across the board, leading analysts to argue we are in a period of de-globalization—or at least globalization's stagnation.

Compared to the decoupling effects of last century's two world wars, the stagnation label seems more apt. Measures of trade and integration have stalled but not reversed. Great powers are reassessing their interdependencies as they grapple with the trade-offs between vulnerabilities revealed and capabilities enabled. This is only natural after an extended period of rapid trade integration.

Several elements complicate that ongoing reassessment. First, there is political opportunism during an era of populist anger. This leads to showy and self-destructive displays of diplomatic unilateralism, exemplified by Donald Trump's spiteful withdrawal from several international agreements (e.g., Paris Climate Agreement, Iran nuclear deal, Trans-Pacific Partnership), an arms treaty (Intermediate-Range Nuclear Forces Treaty), and UN organizations (UN Educational, Scientific, and Cultural Organization [UNESCO], UN Human Rights Council [UNHRC]). This effort at political and security decoupling is contradicted by America's still formidable economic and technological interdependencies, but it feels good and wins elections.

Second, any slowdown of globalization (what the *Economist* dubs "slowbalization") is a de facto re-regionalization—namely, when multinational corporations opportunistically shorten their global value chains to avoid proven or suspected political risks while exploiting closer-in sources of inputs or labor. When those strategically uncertain moments present themselves, certain great powers smash and grab what they can—while the getting is good. In invading Ukraine, Putin felt he understood what the current superpower "market" could bear. He was wrong, but his aggression naturally spooked multinational corporations on their supply chains.

Third, our superpower competitors occupy different strands in this timeline: America retreating; the EU regrouping in the face of Russian aggression; Moscow inexorably falling under Beijing's economic thrall; China methodically laying down markers worldwide, while eyeing Taiwan; and India beginning its internal dialogue on becoming a full-spectrum superpower. As none are on the same wavelength right now, too many experts feel compelled to declare a *world in chaos*!

Fourth, COVID-19 pushed every global enterprise to reconsider its supply chain—great powers included. China is way out ahead with its Belt and Road Initiative, while America engages in an historically high rate of re-shoring manufacturing jobs. Thanks to Putin's invasion of Ukraine, the EU finally moves to ditch its energy dependency on Moscow.

Fifth, there is climate change's ticking clock. India faces by far the greatest environmental threat, as that nation's southern half extends into Middle Earth's danger zone. In many ways, India plays the role of "canary" in the climate "coal mine": alerting the world to looming tipping points. China, too, will see its southern lands decimated. Our Arctic powers, while advantaged with new arable land, likewise face extreme migration pressures. All these strategic dynamics incentivize great powers to pursue vigorous regional consolidation efforts, if only to get one's own neighborhood in order for the crises to come.

Finally, there is growing awareness that globalization is not so much stagnating but morphing into something new—namely, a digitalization makeover that promises to put the service sector through the same competitive wringer previously suffered across manufacturing. You might think this digitalization would further erase the world's sense of time and distance—as globalization's manufacturing version once did—but this is unlikely given how superpowers view cyberspace as both a field of military conflict and a medium for domestic political control. Authoritarian regimes are no longer willing to suffer connectivity whose content they cannot control—user privacy succumbing to cyber sovereignty.

That natural competitiveness among our five superpowers is the primary reason why globalization will "vertically" integrate across latitudes versus harden "horizontally" into a North-South divide. China did not rise to fit itself within a US-defined international order, nor will India. Stipulating Russia's continued antagonism for the foreseeable future, not even Europe is all that eager to follow America's lead anymore. As the United States loses itself in internal strife, why should Europe do anything but look out for itself?

While there are places in the North still worth competing over, like the Arctic and Central Asia, they do not come close to offering the same wide-open competitive space that the South does. Political allegiances across the North are largely set, while in the South they are far more fluid and thus purchasable.

The South is where the global middle class will experience the most growth in coming decades, along with the most environmental stress. These vulnerable nations are desperate for answers concerning their future viability as states. Travel Middle Earth today and you will hear leaders discussing the same thing: food security as the great fear. That is climate change talking— hungry for deals.

Where will Middle Earth find those deals as climate change worsens? We can pretend that all trade is neutral and all counterparties equal. But when push comes to shove on climate-driven mass migrations, Northern powers will be far more incentivized to deal with their own portion of the South than with those threatening their competitors. That will be true whether we are speaking of reactive food assistance, preventive developmental aid, or foreign direct investment. Pain prioritizes.

The North has a long history of ignoring the South's plight and pleas for a more equitable global order, typically citing bigger problems to address amidst their various great power rivalries. But eventually the North will collectively face such an overwhelming security threat from Middle Earth's instabilities—and the refugee flows and terrorist movements they trigger—that each of our superpowers will be forced to act out of desperation to preserve statehood and standing.

The longer it takes for that global dynamic to command the North's attention, the more intense will be the resulting scramble and competition. The race to vertically integrate various North-South zones of the global economy will determine which superpowers are still competitive in the second half of this century—and which no longer warrant the title.

28 *Nations in the Cloud:* Globalization's Digitalization Meets Cyber Sovereignty

China's championing of cyber sovereignty tells us that Beijing aspires to shape—even to rule—globalization's digital realm by building its structure and establishing its norms.

Most of us visualize globalization as this nonstop flow of container ships crisscrossing oceans. We define it as an interregional material trade unfolding in real time across real space, involving goods such as agricultural commodities, steel, cars—tangible items all. All of that is still true; it just no longer captures what expands globalization today.

Globalization now includes the Weeknd song downloaded 3.4 billion times around the planet via Spotify—the world's largest music-streaming service. It is also a Nigerian schoolchild receiving online tutoring from Canada, a 3D printer in Brazil pulling designs from Europe, and China's video-based social media platform TikTok serving as a psyops war zone for competing global narratives on Russia-v-Ukraine. All these online transactions involve service delivery and money changing hands—even when they are nominally "free" to users (e.g., mapping, navigation, email, videoconferencing).

The globalization of the 1990s and 2000s was a goods-intensive phenomenon, which, since the Great Recession, has flatlined. Today's globalization, rising phoenixlike from the ashes of that worldwide financial crash, features service-intensive trade with exponentially expanding data flows. Global data flows were negligible at the turn of the century. Per the McKinsey Global Institute, they now account for more value added to global GDP than do traded goods—the effective digitalization of globalization. Remember that the next time some pundit declares globalization dead and buried.

In the decade surrounding the 2008 crash, cross-border data flows and cross-border bandwidth-in-use jumped forty-five-fold. If the previous era's globalization leveraged cheap transportation, then this one capitalizes on cheap communications. Every global transaction today contains digital content, even as we do not yet possess good methods for measuring data flows—much less policing them.

The economic drivers behind globalization's transformation from goods-centric to service-centric make clear that we are in a period of globalization's intraregional consolidation. The driver here is China, where skyrocketing consumption captures more of what its domestic economy produces, leaving less for export. This is becoming true of many emerging markets, where domestic and regional supply chains rapidly expand to meet middle-class demand that is increasingly addressed with just-in-time delivery mandating the nearshoring of certain segments. As (Anything)-as-a-Service business models proliferate, the line between goods and services blurs, while the latter's role in global value chains expands, likewise favoring shorter, more intraregional networks that improve speed-to-market timelines.

China's economic maturation has put it on par with advanced economies regarding trade dependency—the essence of any nation's relationship with, or subjugation to, globalization. The EU, for example, conducts two-thirds of its trade within its union, leaving only one-third exposed to external forces. America's inter- and intrastate trade accounts for three-quarters of its GDP, leaving a mere quarter exposed to global trade. In the early 2000s, China depended on foreign trade for two-thirds of its GDP. Today that share sits at one-third, meaning Beijing can now plan for a globalization that increasingly adjusts its value chains to revolve around China's demand signal.

Point being all these consolidating trends are a logical, system-wide response to the emergence of a global middle class located overwhelmingly in emerging markets, which, until recently, lacked the infrastructure—both physical and virtual—for these levels of consumption. No economic law states value chains must always be world-spanning to constitute "real" globalization. If anything, business logic argues for supply chains to be no longer than necessary to efficiently serve any market. That is the "de-globalization" we witness today: the emergence of more efficiently regionalized value chains to serve new demand centers—China chief among them.

None of these developments are US-centric, which is why, from our perspective, globalization seems more fragmented, when, in truth, it is more vibrant than ever. We simply do not yet appreciate the size and scope of today's digital iteration. This is odd considering the United States is the undisputed global leader in digital content production and export platforms. Chalk that up as another example of technology and economics outpacing our political and security understanding. On that, see the *Saturday Night Live* skits showing elderly US politicians lacking basic understanding of today's digital landscape—not a good sign as global value chains grow knowledge-intensive and national governments become more territorial in the cyber realm.

The doctrine of cyber sovereignty argues for state control over a nation's portion of the World Wide Web. For example, Russia and China have instituted localization requirements whereby data gathered on their citizens must reside on servers within their borders—largely to ensure government access. Many states also censor and restrict content flows (consider, for example, the Great Firewall of China)—nothing new there. But national privacy rules likewise proliferate for a host of legitimate fears, even as most consumers, especially younger ones, gladly surrender personal data to sustain their access to convenient mobile services.

With all these data flows (and corresponding "dams") being difficult to track, globalization's digitalization will remain in its Wild West phase for some time, particularly as artificial intelligence joins the fray. As with any ruleset gap, we should expect some political-military crisis to arrive—like the long-dreamed-of cyber-Pearl-Harbor, crystallizing the world's urgency to conclude Geneva Conventions–like treaties concerning data handling, personal privacy, and national cybersecurity. For democracies, there is nothing like a hard punch to the face (consider, for example, 9/11) to motivate rules creation.

In the meantime, China plows ahead in frontier-integration mode when it comes to globalization's digital realm. Today, Beijing exhibits the same ambition America once acted upon when establishing both the structure and norms of globalization's initial, post–World War II order—the free trade of goods across a Free World. When it comes to establishing digital globalization's structure and rules, China wants to capitalize on the unsettled nature of both to justify its creation of what is essentially an unfree web for an Unfree World.

China's logic in championing cyber sovereignty mirrors its case for national sovereignty: in seeking total political control of its citizenry, Beijing spends vast resources on firewalling the nation from globalization's liberalizing influences—no matter the delivery mode. China's offering here, while decidedly authoritarian from a US perspective, still appeals to more of the world than we care to admit.

As with the BRI and social-control technologies, China's version of the internet promises to transform the targeted country into a "walled garden" safe from the dangers and uncertainties of a chaotic world. If yours is a traditional society hoping to modernize—but not too fast, such state control is a welcome tool. If you are an authoritarian ruler, enforcing cyber sovereignty is essential given today's under-governed internet, particularly social media.

Pragmatically speaking, we should expect and accept some level of cyber sovereignty as a natural response to globalization's stunningly rapid digitalization, especially when it is justified as economic nationalism or just cultural preservation. Ditto for dark web content that no self-respecting society should have to endure. But when all that Big Data is pulled into citizen-control mechanisms like China's social-credit scoring system, Beijing's promotion of cyber sovereignty has less to do with protecting Chinese culture than preserving Communist Party rule.

As with all Chinese offerings, America cannot counter with simple admonitions to resist. The competition here is not between China and perfection but between some security and no security—between belonging and going it alone. If America wants the world to say no to Chinese social-control technologies, then we need to offer something better and equally tangible: belonging that delivers similar security with less loss of liberty.

29 *The World in Three Vertical Slices:* Why America Should Choose the Door Marked "West"

Resurgent isolationism checks America's instinct to manage the world. Climate change plus multipolarity compel us to split the difference by focusing on our hemisphere.

I n its own strategically intuitive way, the Pentagon has mentally prepared itself for the world of tomorrow. Consider a global map of US Combatant Commands and you quickly notice that the dominant lines run north-south, using oceans (Pacific, Atlantic, Indian) to divide the world into three vertical slices: the Western Hemisphere (Northern Command on top, Southern Command below), Asia (Indo-Pacific Command), and the busy Center slice comprising European Command on top, Central Command in the middle, and Africa Command below.

The US Navy has long ruled the open oceans as the world's preeminent "blue water" fleet, meaning we possess the only navy that can swiftly mass forces anywhere in the world and conduct large-scale operations for long periods. In today's strategic landscape, the notion of superpower navies contending for "sea control" is limited to individual regions, such as China-v-America in the Western Pacific or China-v-India in the Indian Ocean.

As a result, when we view the American military's regional "areas of responsibility" (AORs), we find in each instance that the most troubled seams are found within those vertical slices—not between them. For example, America's immigration crisis is currently fueled by the climate-ravaged Northern Triangle states found along our Northern/Southern Commands' seam. In the Center, we locate (a) Russia versus EU/NATO (European Command); (b) Central Command working the Middle East terrorism/Iran beat to limit spillover into the European and African AORs; and (c) Europe's Mediterranean climate-fueled migrant crisis pitting it against both North Africa (Africa Command) and the Persian Gulf (Central Command). Finally, in Asia (Indo-Pacific Command), we find China taking on all comers—but particularly India—within what could be called Indo-China Command because of that dyad's signature rivalry.

While it diminishes over time, the United States retains its role as external balancer in both the Center and Asia slices. But as we saw with Russia-v-Ukraine, our safest path forward in such conflicts is serving as an "arsenal for democracy"—Franklin Roosevelt's pre-WWII policy that balanced America's strong isolationism against Washington's strategic instinct. Preemptively performing the same role with Taiwan vis-à-vis China, rendering the island nation an un-swallowable "porcupine," seems another wise move by the Biden administration. We live now in a world of sufficient multipolarity where we can always find a worthy side to pick in any conflict without getting directly involved. In effect, this approach resurrects the 1980s Reagan Doctrine of bankrolling insurgent forces resisting a hostile superpower's imperial strategies: it is relatively cheap and often effective.

America's eventual acceptance of this verticalized strategic landscape is preordained by climate change. With their persistent focus on Russia and China, Boomers and Gen Xers may find that preposterous, but Millennials, Gen Zs, and Gen Alphas will live—and lead—in a midcentury world defined by US-style globalization's greatest structural success (multipolarity without system-level war) and its worst collateral cost (Middle Earth's environmental devastation).

There will be plenty of operational distractions along this journey, and we will hear numerous calls for various "walls" to be erected, "curtains" lowered, and "cold wars" declared. So long as Cold War Baby Boomers cling to power, America will remain trapped in the story lines of that generation's youth—particularly its nostalgic fantasy of restoring past greatness.

America is better served by moving on to more suitable definitions of twenty-first-century greatness. Let us reach that conclusion by process of elimination.

Will America be the primary agent of regional integration in Asia?

While we played the security "glue" role in previous decades, China's rise clearly supersedes that dynamic, so no. There is no stopping China's emergence as Asia's economic hub, and any talk of doing so to spare our regional allies that fate is fantasy. Yes, our nuclear umbrella will still extend there, and we can certainly rally the region's democratic pillars (India, Australia, New Zealand,

South Korea, Japan) through coordinated policies, arms sales, and military cooperation. But each of these powers will invariably need to strategically accommodate Beijing's economic domination, and those individual choices will define Asia's future far more than any US strategy. This is not a dire situation: our allies constitute a powerful economic bloc backed by strong militaries. They are entirely incentivized to press their strategic interests with our support.

Will the United States be the primary agent of integration in wider Europe?

If Russia's Ukraine misadventure proved anything, it is that Europe can—and must—stand on its own as a global superpower, so another no. This is not a loss of US influence so much as Europe finally coming into its own. Again, our nuclear umbrella remains intact, as does our leadership within NATO. We have long wanted this positive outcome, and, thanks to Putin's poor choices, we should welcome it without triggering self-doubt—much less self-recrimination.

Will America again aspire to comprehensively fix and integrate the Middle East?

That is a hard pass for long enough to allow numerous would-be regional integrators (e.g., EU, Russia, Turkey, Iran, Saudi Arabia, UAE, Israel, Pakistan, India, China) to pursue efforts that effectively preclude any significant US security burden as we witnessed during our Global War on Terror. The George W. Bush administration's "big bang" theory regarding Iraq worked—just not as advertised. The administration's goal was to blow up the Persian Gulf's ossified security landscape by toppling Saddam Hussein—mission truly accomplished. But because Washington insisted on limiting all these regional powers' influence over postwar outcomes in both Iraq and Afghanistan, we only yielded to such cross-regional networking—too many years later—out of sheer exhaustion. The Middle East, now more controlled—in overlapping fashion—by that cluster of far more engaged and always competitive regional hegemons, is better off without America's military-heavy unilateralism. Our work there is largely done.

Will the United States ever become Africa's lead integrating force?

Given Europe's colonial ties, the investment ambitions of the Persian Gulf monarchies, India's long-standing immigrant presence, and China's BRI, that horse left the barn long ago. Yes, our Africa Command will continue to hunt down bad actors, but ours remains a strategy of limited regret (i.e., do not risk much, do not regret much).

Which leaves the Western Hemisphere as the only regions (Arctic, North America, Central America, Caribbean, South America) where the United States enjoys a clear and compelling advantage as North-South vertical integrator.

No, this vision does not disavow our natural ambitions to shape and steer developments across the other two slices. It does, however, argue for fixing our nation, as well as things in our neighborhood, before launching any extended crusades elsewhere. This is a pragmatic and plausible path forward in this era.

So let us admit to ourselves that China is already the hegemon of Asia, and that the current Game-of-Thrones dynamics unfolding across the Center slice are too numerous and complex for us to definitively manage from afar.

Let us also admit to ourselves that America is in danger of losing its long-standing hegemony over Latin America. First, there are America's self-inflicted wounds (e.g., anti-immigrant xenophobia, broken immigration system, pointlessly punitive War on Drugs) that continue to sour intra-hemispheric relations and postpone logical economic integration schemes (e.g., Free Trade Area of the Americas) that should have succeeded long ago.

Second, there are the growing incursions of competing superpowers: the EU based on historical/cultural ties and better trade pact offerings; China with its BRI, demand for commodities, cheap exports, and 5G offerings; and Russia's aid relations with regional outcasts Cuba, Venezuela, and Nicaragua. Amazingly, America willfully underperforms as an integrating force in the one region where we enjoy real advantages—for now.

Let us admit all these realities so that America can move to genuine solutions, in turn animating a new grand strategy that improves our political and economic offerings while enlisting the ambitions and heartfelt efforts of our upcoming leadership generations. Right now, we swim against history's tides, wondering why we make no progress, why we disappoint allies, and why we lose our will. Meanwhile, a greater United States awaits our determined action.

30

In Globalization, Demand—Not Supply—Is Power: So, the Biggest Markets Command the Most Power

> Throughout most of history, we have naturally viewed *having something* (supply) as connoting more power than *wanting something* (demand). Globalization inverts that power relationship.

T
hink back to the OPEC oil embargo and the 1973–74 "energy crisis" it triggered in the United States. Back then, global energy markets were inflexible, with supply choices limited by, and locked in through, long-term government ties. When OPEC nations sought to punish the United States for its military support of Israel, they triggered a decades-long American obsession with our "dependency on foreign oil." That genuine strategic vulnerability pushed Washington into deep engagement with the Middle East's conflicts and rivalries—right through our Global War on Terror.

But the global economy mounted its own response to OPEC's power play, as nations and companies capitalized on that perceived risk by investing in new forms of exploration, alternative energy sources, and oil-conserving technologies. Neither a straight nor short journey, we nonetheless today enjoy a far more diversified energy market as a result. Now the most powerful player in global energy markets is not exporting Saudi Arabia but importing China. Meanwhile, the United States is energy independent and therefore much less motivated to police the Persian Gulf.

Globalization flipped that supply/demand power relationship thanks in part to the rise of the global middle class, who have unlimited demand for mobility, communications, education, entertainment, electricity, food, healthcare, pets, vacations, bandwidth, air-conditioning, and so on. As globalization exploded across the 1990s, that worldwide demand signal became the most powerful communication on the planet, reshaping all manner of markets. The business world likewise awakened to the purchasing potential of the "bottom of the pyramid," economist C. K. Prahalad's revolutionary reframing of the world's working poor—located just beneath that global middle class in terms of daily income—as a surprisingly vast pool of discretionary spending.

Recall the old business bit, "If only I could sell one [product] to everyone in China!" Well, the radical expansion of Chinese mass consumption has clearly opened Pandora's box. On the dark side: Chinese consumers desiring body parts from endangered species (e.g., elephant tusks, tiger penises); Chinese farmers being encouraged by the state to domesticate wild animals for meat production, expanding transmission of their viruses into the human population (zoonosis); and Chinese females being trafficked as unwilling brides in response to the nation's gender imbalance. More benign: China's love of pecans and walnuts blowing up US nut exports.

Most impactful and positive: Beijing's concern over worsening domestic air pollution pushing the government to mandate that electric vehicles (EVs) constitute 40 percent of domestic sales by 2030. Think about how long Americans have waited on Detroit to pursue that initiative and then recognize why suddenly the Big Three car companies are all-in on all-electric vehicles, along with an EU that now says it will allow only EV sales after 2035. It is no mystery: China's new car market is 50 percent larger than ours and double that of the EU. Beijing now wants EVs, which means consumers all over the world are going to get them, too. That is the supremacy of demand over supply in globalization—wanting trumping having.

What China produces in the future is less important and influential than what China consumes. The country's authoritarian leadership knows that they are caught in a political trap of their own making. The Communist Party, comfortable in its authority, nonetheless fears for the legitimacy of its rule. That legitimacy is increasingly based on the continued increase of China's standard of living (expanding consumption); to continue that advance, Beijing must build and secure global networks to ensure its access to resources, markets, and investment opportunities. In sum, because China's demand function is so vast, Beijing has little choice but to fully embrace globalization and even aspire to become its preeminent security guarantor—domestic-consumer power *demanding* more international power. Xi Jinping is quite open about this linkage, proposing, in the 2022 Communist Party Congress report, his new "comprehensive national security concept" and linking it to Beijing's "global security initiative." That is how a world power speaks today.

But also remember this: Beijing's leadership fears its own citizens more than us. Chinese history is full of "bad emperors" succumbing to palace coups, internal rebellions, and civil wars. Global security ensures national security, which in turn secures Party rule—a one-way street.

Regarding the Middle East, China's mindset today recalls that of Cold War America, raising Beijing's risk of involvement in that region's future conflicts. In many ways, Beijing still thinks like a middle-sized power vulnerable to supply shutoffs instead of the demand superpower without peer that it is. Frankly, the scariest global economic scenarios going forward all center around a potential disruption of Chinese consumption—however achieved. On all these points, China's recent brokering of a Saudi-Iranian detente is a positive sign.

Understanding China's needs (e.g., economic stability, meeting rising consumption) and domestic deficits (farmland, water, energy, clean air, willing mothers) should temper our fears of spreading Chinese hegemony, if only because Beijing is operating under the same, now-outdated logic that long drove our global policing. This is how a superpower imposes imperial overreach on itself: the desire to secure everything results in nothing being truly secure.

The problem comes down to historical timing.

The optimist says Beijing will eventually recognize its profound demand-centric global power, encouraging it to remain soft power–centric in its external relations (benevolently hegemonic) and more open to legitimacy-enhancing reforms at home. The pessimist says China invariably resorts to aggression abroad out of the fear of domestic unrest if serious supply disruptions were to unfold. Much depends on how China's leaders view their nation's standing in the world—the Asian concept of "face" (always to be saved, never to be lost).

How should the United States handle China's volatile ego? Again, the oft-cited historical analogy is early-twentieth-century Britain mentoring brash America as the latter supplanted the former as global hegemon. But that relationship unfolded during an era when production still trumped consumption, if for no other reason than that industrial capacity determined which great powers won wars (consider, for example, US military production in World War II).

Direct great-power wars do not unfold in US-style globalization, thanks to economic interdependency *plus* nuclear weapons, and that is the core reason demand power now reigns supreme. America must accept that our primary competition with China lies not in military technology but in regional integration schemes and the security they offer states in an era of heightened global turbulence.

If the United States wants to restore our global leadership, then we need to scale up to play up to China's true challenge—the power of its consumer demand.

31

Strength in Numbers: America Does Not Stack Up Well Against the Competition

China and India's combined purchasing power is now 80 percent greater than America's. By midcentury, the duo's global share will grow to three times larger, dropping the US from second place to third.

For over six decades after World War II ended, the United States owned the largest share of the global economy, as measured in purchasing power parity (PPP)—an amazing streak. In 2016, however, China surpassed America in national gross domestic product (GDP), despite having a far smaller per capita income (one-quarter the US rate). Before 2050, India will accomplish the same feat with a similarly lower per capita GDP.

Come midcentury, the US share of annual growth in global consumer spending will be but a small fraction of our Chinese and Indian counterparts. Consider: In 2000, Chinese consumers accounted for 7 percent of growth in global spending while Americans drove one-third. In 2040, America is projected to produce a mere 12 percent of growth versus China's whopping 44 percent—a reversal of fortune and global influence.

As such, America could end up with stunningly little influence over world consumer trends amidst the tectonic collision of an ascendant global middle class and climate change's crescendoing impact—two momentous dynamics driven by global consumption. Each development is arguably the biggest structural change the world system has yet endured, and so, in combination, they constitute the most impactful geopolitical turning point in human history.

The United States will not have the numbers to steer globalization's next, highly contentious phase. By midcentury, China and India will add roughly 1.5 billion new middle-class consumers between them—while both societies grow far wealthier on a per capita basis. Meanwhile, America will get wealthier but increase its consumer pool only marginally. After World War II, when we set about to alter the global system's structure and norms, America controlled half the world's GDP. A century later, China and India can combine to wield a similar level of influence—relative to our diminished standing.

Today, Washington speaks boldly about beating China versus merely containing it. To beat China, we first need to enter its weight class, and that is a numbers game—one we are set to lose. There is a reason the so-called Chinese Dream does not aspire to any form of universality: it is a big enough dream all by itself. The same holds true for the Self-Reliant India movement. Their consumption is their greatest power; they do not need to grow their ranks.

How might America punch at the same economic heft as both #1 China and #2 India in 2050? The Americas are home to just over one billion souls (723 million non-US). Add those states' $10 trillion in projected 2050 GDP to our own ($32 trillion), and we would sit midway ($42 trillion) between China's $54 trillion and India's $33 trillion.

Based on the EU's lengthy—but so far unsuccessful—effort to secure a free trade agreement with South America's Mercosur trade bloc, Europe spots terrific value in tapping into its old colonial roster there. Based on the moribund Free Trade Area of the Americas launched by Bill Clinton in 1994, our United States remain—with one clear exception—unaware of how such numbers could factor into future competition with China and India.

The EU does not admit former Soviet vassals for reasons of economic efficiency. The Union admits these less-developed states to prevent them from becoming future security problems—short-term tactical generosity yielding long-term strategic advantage and expanded market strength. The EU understands that its future influence in global affairs depends mightily on numbers. Moreover, if the EU had not locked in Eastern Europe and the Baltics, Russia eventually would have.

America needs to view Latin America along the same defensive lines, because eventually those nations will choose to collectively align themselves with what they perceive to be the best (for them) superpower brand out there. Right now, the EU and China are working that angle with vigor, while America contents itself with merely updating the North American Free Trade Agreement (NAFTA)—an effort that did little to rekindle the hemispheric trade ambitions once exhibited by the Clinton administration during globalization's go-go '90s.

The World Bank recently noted that Latin America and the Caribbean were lapsing back into an extended phase of weak economic growth caused, in large part, by a lack of investment in transportation infrastructure. The bank's prescription? "Increased integration in international trade and global value chains." Guess who's coming to that dinner—China's Belt and Road Initiative. If both China and the EU see the value in North-South trade integration with Latin America and the Caribbean, why can't the United States? Are we not the superpower with the most to lose or gain in these regions' economic trajectories?

The one American state that fully recognizes Latin America's potential contribution to our nation's future economic might would be Florida, with its thirty-four ports of entry (fourteen deep-water ports and twenty airports). Already home to the "capital of Latin America" (otherwise known as Miami), Florida is the top state trading partner of every Latin American and Caribbean country save Mexico, whose top state trading partner is Texas. That is because Florida possesses all the necessary soft business–development infrastructure (e.g., social networks, cultural knowledge, language skills, venture capital) to go along with all those South-North supply-chain networks. The state also features a population entirely representative of the Western Hemisphere, while somehow remaining entirely and quite oddly American—the sort of national asset that could well determine our initial success in attracting Latin American and Caribbean economies to next-level hemispheric value-chain integration.

As eccentric as it may seem to the rest of America, Florida is our nation's best gateway to the economic future our country most needs.

32

You Will Be Assimilated, Resistance Is Futile: America Is Finally Forced to Join Its Own Neighborhood

> Thanks to globalization's regional consolidation, America's racial makeup will come to mirror that of the Western Hemisphere as a whole, forever ending our outlier status.

Whites of European origin constitute 15 to 20 percent of today's world population, a share certain to decline. America, as presently defined, will never approach that profile. However, these United States will soon enough resemble the Western Hemisphere, where the current population holds at approximately 45 percent White.

Two observations arise from this: First, America is in no danger of losing its identity within globalization's ongoing regional consolidation. We will merely mirror the racial profile of our Americas as it already exists. This is hardly reverse colonization, as we are all survivors or products of European colonialization. The United States is not an outpost of European civilization but the cornerstone of an Americas civilization.

Second, extending the American Union north and south would not appreciably change our nation's inevitable racial profile. As such, we should consider that scenario based on its merits rather than the existential fears it elicits.

Through our consumption to date, the North has set much of Middle Earth on a trajectory toward un-inhabitability—meaning a significant portion of them will come north, seeking a sustainable life. We can pretend this is a "clash of civilizations" or globalist-engineered "genocide," but infantile fantasies of various zombie apocalypses waste time, money, effort, and—most of all—our imagination regarding winning solutions. Those Northern powers prepared to manage these inevitabilities will rule globalization's verticalizing stage. The choice is between bridges and walls.

Among our superpower quintet, America and Europe are built to handle climate migration. Both are home to the world's largest stocks of immigrants (50 million in America, 37 million in the EU). That equates to 15 percent of the US population and just under a tenth of the EU's. The United States is also lightly populated at 35 people per square kilometer, compared to the world at 59/km² and the EU at 112/km². Russia is a wash, having hosted as many immigrants as it has sent abroad (11 million each way). Given its extremely low population density (8/km²), Russia is a huge target for future climate refugees. Densely populated China (149/km²) and India (428/km²) possess no appreciable immigrant cohort, instead sending millions abroad. Expect China to integrate its way northward through Russia, followed by India through Central Asia.

In the early twentieth century dominated by longitudinal migrations, America assimilated tens of millions of South and East European immigrants then widely, if incorrectly, considered to be of inferior genetic stock—particularly the oft-rejected Ashkenazi Jews. We later came to recognize our culpability in the horrors that ensued from our unthinking embrace of "scientific" applications of social Darwinism, plenty of which still circulate in our body politic.

As a synthetic nation with a multiverse of cultures, America has historically processed immigrants by first demonizing them as "invaders," then condemning them as "parasites," then criticizing their slow assimilation, then mocking their entry on the lowest rungs of the economic ladder, then begrudging their ascent, then accepting them into sports and entertainment, then admitting they are "not so bad once you get to know them," then allowing them into the corridors of power, and finally admiring their "immigrant journey." Outside of Anglo-Saxons, every immigrant group has traveled this pathway once reaching America, their consolation being that any inbound population is immediately granted a status superior to Blacks—the enduring target of Armageddon-triggering, ultra-right-wing visions of race war.

Despite such successful assimilation, America then spent decades attempting to lock in our racial profile through a quota system—the Immigration Act of 1924. Effectively barring immigration from non-White countries for decades, the act reflected that era's profoundly entrenched institutional racism. Our quota system lasted until the peaking of the Civil Rights Era, when the 1965 Immigration and Nationality Act abolished the National Origins Formula, finally allowing America to recast its racial profile in the image of the world it purposefully created with its brand of globalization. In 1960, Europeans made up four-fifths of US immigrants, but by 2010 that figure had reversed, as non-Whites expanded to four-fifths of that flow.

The arguments offered by today's anti-immigration lobby are the same propagated during the previous great migrant wave a century ago: *they* drive down wages and do not assimilate. Neither is true today.

In the previous wave, European immigrant laborers competed directly with native-born workers then aspiring to join the middle class. In contrast, today's heterogeneous immigrant mix complements America's middle class by being split between high- and low-tech workers. Thus, economic "replacement" is an illusion because today's immigrants cluster in professions where jobs would otherwise go unfilled for being too high-skilled or too low-paying and thus undesired by the native-born.

As for assimilation, comprehensive studies indicate that while today's immigrants are, on average, less assimilated when they first arrive, compared to Europeans landing a century ago, they nonetheless assimilate faster over the years that follow—particularly in cultural terms. Where today's immigrants lag in terms of assimilation are in the economic and civic realms, logically reflecting (1) this era's polarized politics on the subject, and (2) the reality that one-quarter of our immigrant population is presently undocumented.

In any event, the longer immigrants live in the United States, the more they resemble the native-born on health, education, marriage, fertility, home ownership, crime, incarceration, and—most importantly—political preferences, thus refuting the assumption that immigrants equate to a win only for Democrats. As a rule, immigrants come to America seeking not to change it but to preserve it; they come here not to stick out but to fit in.

Regardless of what unfolds on immigration, America is already locked into becoming a majority non-White nation. Persons of color accounted for the entirety of America's population growth across the 2010s, as the White population experienced an absolute decrease for the first time in our nation's history. The two biggest sources of that growth were Latinos and persons of mixed race. In many regions around the country, Latino immigrants filled in where otherwise the local population would have dropped—in large part because of low White fertility.

Here is where it really gets interesting: recall that America classifies Latinos as an ethnic group and not a race, even though we often break them out in statistics as though they were a race (i.e., comparing them to non-Hispanic Whites, Blacks, or Asians). As an ethnic group of multiple races, Latinos intermarry with non-Latinos at an unusually high rate the longer they live in the

United States. Whites intermarry roughly 10 percent of the time, while Blacks do so at a rate of 20 percent and Asians approach 30 percent. In comparison, while only 15 percent of first-generation Latinos intermarry with non-Latinos, that share jumps to 40 percent in subsequent generations—a rate surpassed only by native-born Asians at 46 percent.

Point being if today Latinos are one-sixth of Americans, by midcentury, given all that intermarriage, those who self-identify as partially or fully Latino will constitute one out of three American voters. This is worth keeping in mind as we contemplate our future ties with the rest of the hemisphere.

Our choice of bridges versus walls is a powerful signal to our Southern neighbors, the former indicating our openness to salvaging as much of Middle Earth as possible to sustain viable statehood there. Better to link infrastructure development to a pathway for eventual membership in expanding North-South political unions than to simply hand over trillions of dollars in a UN-sponsored global "loss and damage fund" certain to aggravate the North's angry populism while succumbing to all manner of waste, fraud, and abuse at the hands of local governments ill equipped to manage such spending. By signaling such long-term political intentions, the North creates a far more secure investing environment to the benefit of all. In other words, an effective response here focuses on incentivizing and mobilizing the private sector more than the public sector.

This is where the confluence of climate change and an ascendant global middle class creates a unique historical opportunity: climate change generates geopolitical "orphans" (non-viable states, migrants) at exactly the point when that South-centric middle class seeks maximum belonging (protection of newly acquired status and wealth). That tectonic collision of fear and hope defines this century, demanding that superpowers move beyond their strategic fixation on national defense and embrace a far more expansive definition—and delivery—of security in all its forms.

Throughout all such strategizing, Americans need to keep in mind just how lucky we remain in geopolitical terms. The Eastern Hemisphere faces primarily Russia as it turns northward, while the Western Hemisphere lucks out with Canada. The same holds with the South: North America is gifted a rather culturally coherent Latin America, while Eurasia's superpowers have to manage the decidedly more complex array that is Africa, the Middle East, Central Asia, South Asia, and Southeast Asia. Ours is by far the easier row to hoe.

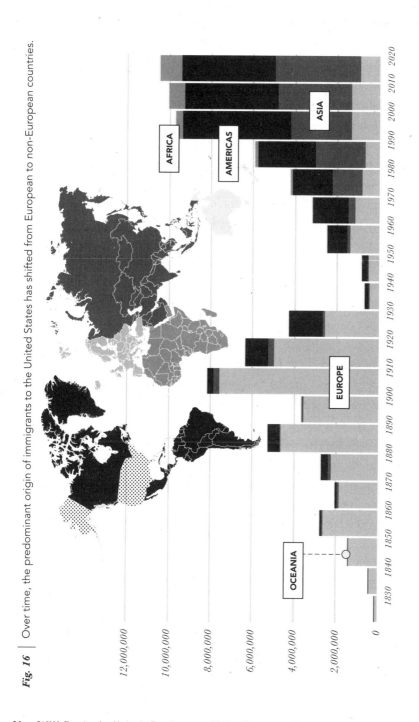

Fig. 16 | Over time, the predominant origin of immigrants to the United States has shifted from European to non-European countries.

33 *The Geopolitics of Belonging:* The EU's Model of Political Integration Works

Using the accession "carrot," the EU incentivizes political and economic reforms, avoids the usual mistakes and wastefulness of foreign aid, and reduces strife across its eastern rimlands.

When polled, Americans consistently overestimate the amount of economic aid our government sends developing economies, typically conflating it with our vigorous flows of military aid. Egotistically, we express disappointment—even betrayal—that such interactions have not been enough to Americanize those societies, much less their politics. China is the classic example here (*Nixon goes to China and all these years later they're still communist!*), but the same recriminations were offered about Russia after it invaded Ukraine (*All those Starbucks and McDonalds didn't change them one bit!*). You either become America's political and cultural clone and slot yourself under Washington's global leadership, or *we were all duped by idealists and their wishful thinking!* There are no partial or even temporary wins, as anything short of replication is abject failure in our eyes. Given America's snail-like pace on correcting its chronic racial, gender, economic, and political inequities, our arrogance on this score is breathtaking. Surveying the world from our glass house, we have an endless supply of bricks to toss.

In offering such withering judgments, we assume cultural superiority: to develop is to Americanize—to surrender one's culture completely and forever. For a good stretch of globalization's spread these past decades, that argument went unchallenged. Indeed, the blistering counterclaim of America's cultural imperialism was offered the world over. Now, with China's aggressive global branding, America confronts a new competitive landscape in which the geopolitics of belonging is back in play—to wit, Xi Jinping peddling China's development model as a "new choice" for humanity. Last time it was business (class conflict); this time it is personal—winning hearts and minds. The global middle class, no matter where it calls home, is all about belonging.

Globalization's spread and maturation involve the economic and political integration of "frontier" (i.e., less-connected) nation-states. For countries long on the outside and looking in, opening up one's society and economy to globalization's transformational effects is a daunting prospect. Trade and investment are not enough to secure that profound transition, nor is Washington's pat on the back a big enough prize for achieving it. What is needed is a clear and present pathway to political and security integration. Europe, in the form of the EU and NATO, understands this reality; America, not so much.

To join the EU is to avowedly "Europeanize" your society, economy, and state. That is the accession process: inculcating European norms and values by—most prominently—adopting, implementing, and enforcing all current EU rules (the "acquis" or European body of law). That is a huge ask, but it is tied to a huge give—full state membership in a union of shared sovereignty.

The EU's accession policy of methodically prepping candidate states for full membership is the most successful display of soft power ever wielded by a multinational union. It helps transform dictatorships into democracies (e.g., Greece, Spain, Portugal) while fast-tracking the economic development of poorer states (former Soviet satellites). Most importantly, it offers globalization's fragile frontier states the political safe harbor of pooled or networked sovereignty at the time they need it most. The EU offers a home to states seeking one, and it willingly provides relevant financial, administrative, and technical assistance throughout that integration process—brilliant!

Simply put, this is where globalization goes next.

While China aggressively supplies hard-infrastructure connectivity and a social-control model through its Belt and Road Initiative, America offers little beyond its nuclear umbrella and preferential access to its vast market. What we expect in return is your state's marketization, democratization, and Americanization. If you do not achieve all, you may one day find yourself demonized as an existential threat to our way of life. In *Star Trek* terms, we sell ourselves as the United Federation of Planets but too often act like the Borg.

Right now, the United States is not seriously competing in the superpower brand-affiliation contest despite owning history's most attractive brand, which we presently go out of our way to trash every chance we get. Thus, America is reduced to the role of offshore balancer, defensively countering Russia's and

China's every move. America no longer leads; we merely react, like the reactionaries we have let ourselves become.

Remember when America owned the future instead of fearing it?

Consider the EU's description of why and how it admits new members, as delineated in its *EU Accession Process: Step by Step*:

> A credible enlargement policy is a geostrategic investment in peace, stability, security, and prosperity in Europe. It is based on fair and rigorous conditionality and the principle of own merits. It requires candidate countries to implement complete reforms in many areas such as the rule of law, the economy, the fight against corruption and organized crime. Reconciliation, good neighborly relations, and regional cooperation are of utmost importance.

That is how you take ownership of your future.

Now think of how that vision matches what Washington currently espouses regarding Latin America's best possible future and yet does so little to facilitate. Instead, we sabotage any such progress with a gaggle of ill-considered national policies—the War on Drugs being the most painfully counterproductive. In our usual patronizing manner, we ask for magnificent effort while offering virtually nothing as payoff.

There is a Pentagon saying that strategy without budget is hallucination. Europe has a strategy for today's superpower brand wars, while China has a budget. Meanwhile, America is lost in a hallucination of grievances. Despite two centuries of frontier integration and state-building-leading-to-accession, the world's oldest and most successful federal union remains clueless as the latest iteration of the superpower game passes us by. The United States builds a wall; the EU builds a superpower. Tired of winning, America? Or just whining?

To the EU's credit, and despite its current limitation on geographic eligibility, it offers non-European states international arrangements that allow some integration with the Union, to include adopting the euro currency and tariff-free access to EU markets. A dozen or so North African and Middle East states already enjoy these privileges, as do the so-called Eastern Partnership states—all former Soviet republics (Ukraine, Georgia, Azerbaijan, Moldova).

Within the EU, it takes an average of five years for a state to migrate from candidacy through negotiations to accession. Negotiations comprise thirty-five chapters across six clusters (Fundamentals, Internal Market, Competitiveness and Inclusive Growth, Green Agenda, Resources & Agriculture, and External Relations). Having enlarged from six signatories in 1957 to twenty-seven members today (post-Brexit), the EU now has ten nations in process: two applicants (Georgia, Bosnia & Herzegovina), one potential candidate (Kosovo), two confirmed candidates (Moldova, Ukraine), and five in negotiations (Albania, North Macedonia, Montenegro, Serbia, Turkey). Imagine the EU with thirty-seven members.

Now imagine a visionary EU someday housing more member states than stuck-in-the-mud America.

The point here is less destination than journey. Europe has not conquered anybody, yet it has successfully marketed its superpower brand in those neighboring regions most important to its long-term security, stability, and prosperity. In return, acceding members have boosted their international influence, increased their security, grown their economies, and modernized their governments—all while maintaining sufficient individual sovereignty (let us call them states' rights).

That is not to say that EU membership does not come with costs and issues (e.g., Hungary's soft fascism), just that those problems are a vast improvement over the globalization challenges new members faced prior to accession. That is all we are talking about here: not a perfect solution or painless pathway but an offer that beats the competition—even more the option of going it alone.

Not convinced?

Check out the UK economy post-Brexit, for it is far less globalized and trails the EU's GDP per capita growth.

Better yet, ask Ukrainians if they would prefer suffering Brussels's bureaucracy over Moscow's missiles.

Fig. 17 | The EU's accession process is supremely detailed, structured, and deliberate: "Europeanizing" a candidate state before admission.

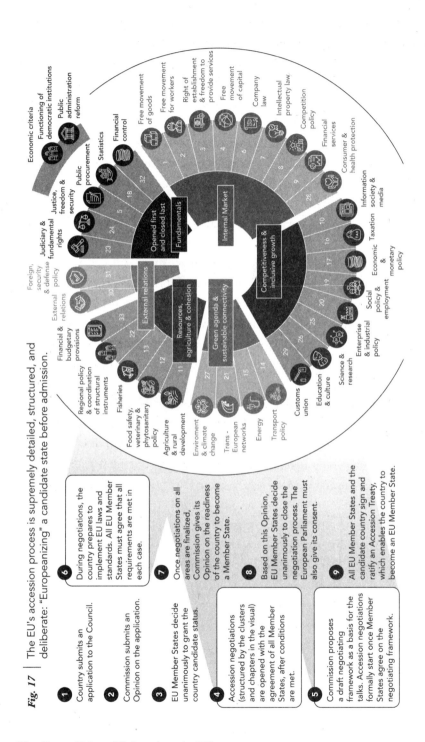

1. Country submits an application to the Council.

2. Commission submits an Opinion on the application.

3. EU Member States decide unanimously to grant the country candidate status.

4. Accession negotiations (structured by the clusters and chapters in the visual) are opened with the agreement of all Member States, after conditions are met.

5. Commission proposes a draft negotiating framework as a basis for the talks. Accession negotiations formally start once Member States agree on the negotiating framework.

6. During negotiations, the country prepares to implement EU laws and standards. All EU Member States must agree that all requirements are met in each case.

7. Once negotiations on all areas are finalized, Commission gives its Opinion on the readiness of the country to become a Member State.

8. Based on this Opinion, EU Member States decide unanimously to close the negotiation process. The European Parliament must also give its consent.

9. All EU Member States and the candidate country sign and ratify an Accession Treaty, which enables the country to become an EU Member State.

The West Is the Best: Our Hemisphere Is Advantageously Situated for What Comes Next

THROUGHLINE SIX

The Western Hemisphere is well resourced for adapting to climate change. The Americas are ripe for regional integration. The United States needs to recognize this strategic imperative.

I magine the story of globalization's ongoing regional consolidation as a romantic comedy with America as the male lead. Burned-out-but-age-appropriate Europe plays our cynical ex, while glittering-but-distant Asia is stereotypically cast as our exotic desire. As for Latin America? She plays the all-too-familiar girl next door, standing right in front of us but maddeningly unable to escape her taken-for-granted friend zone status . . . until the third act.

Latin America has never enjoyed much strategic attention from the United States—not since we built the Panama Canal. Yes, we clean house there now and then (e.g., changing regimes, responding to disasters) and we work our catastrophic-for-all War on Drugs, along with immigration. But compared to other regions, Latin America strikes us as more burden than boon, more responsibility than opportunity.

This must end if the United States wants to restore its global leadership.

Climate change rotates America's strategic perspective from East-West to North-South, "verticalizing" our worldview. Globalization, of late suffering a series of system perturbations, compels our recalculation of supply-chain risks. Those are threat-fear reactions. Our Southern neighbors deserve a better identity, in both our deeper recognition of their value and their improved standing.

Our hemisphere's shared, truly Western civilization marks us as supremely more capable than either the Asia or Center zones when it comes to vertical integration. If for no other reason, Americans should view our hemispheric partners in a far better light. We are entirely blessed to have these neighbors.

No matter where you hail from across the so-called New World, we are all products of globalization's imperial era—either as those being replaced or those doing the replacing. In our familial past, some of us know what it is like to have our homelands destroyed by global forces beyond resisting. Others know the horror of forced relocation through enslavement that lasted centuries. The rest of us know what it is like to take everything you can carry and escape an environment that pervasively denies our pursuit of happiness.

Point being we all endured such cataclysms, earning a certain shared resilience for the daunting future we now collectively face. We have paid our dues.

Blessed with 30 percent of the world's land, the Americas spaciously distribute one billion souls in a manner that India and China can only dream about. As the world's "tallest" landmass, extending to both poles, we enjoy the benefits of unmatched biodiversity. Reflective of that environmental richness, we enjoy a surfeit of water resources that are the envy of the world. These are some of the reasons why our continents dominate the global food trade, feeding the five-times-more populous Eastern Hemisphere. As for mineral reserves, we lack for nothing and share our surpluses with the world.

All these shared characteristics mean the Americas collectively tread a far easier path than either the Center or Asia verticals when it comes to the North-South dynamics triggered by climate change and demographic disparities. We *Americanos* have fewer divisions, deeper similarities, and less daunting geographic obstacles. Our West is the best resourced and thus prepared for the hemispheric integration that lies ahead. We simply need to recognize our shared identity and strengths, leveraging both to form a more suitable union for the unprecedented challenges we have already begun to encounter.

On this path toward a future worth creating, we bring an established and time-tested model of political and economic integration known as the United States of America. Beyond a few administrative reorderings of our island territories, we have not employed this state-accession model in over six decades— the longest and only such drought in our nation's history. Given the recent and persistent integrating activities of our superpower rivals, we need to reopen *these* United States for the business of uniting states.

As we shall see (**Thread 41**), America already offers an array of citizenship levels to its 330-million-plus subjects, along with a tiered membership status to our collective state, tribal, and territorial entities. In our past, when we spotted mergers and acquisitions worth concluding, we did so with great speed and the utmost flexibility—oftentimes putting cash on the table. We are born dealmakers.

As the world's most synthetic civilization, constructed across the world's most artificial nation, we must recognize our strengths when it comes to integrating and expanding our American Union. It should come as little surprise that we will be the first postindustrial great power to experience a stunning decline in our majority racial group; we are, after all, the most mongrel of populations. While some spot a profound social weakness in that lack of genetic uniformity, the entire history of our species says otherwise. Our civilization is strong precisely because it is so heterogenous—so willfully and avowedly diverse. There is no threat that we cannot absorb, digest, and put to good use.

But what truly sets us up for success this century is the fact that we in the Western Hemisphere actually like each other, and so blend rather easily. Our histories of state-on-state conflicts pale next to our far deadlier civil strife, meaning we tend to dislike our own more than one another. Europe cannot say that, nor can Africa, the Middle East, or any subregion of Asia. There, in each instance, we can readily spot far more historical, cultural, religious, tribal, and ideological divisions to be overcome in any North-South integration.

American workers have a right to feel abused by globalization's recent past, to include the flatlining of the goods trade that, in combination with Washington's misguided trade protectionism, has stagnated the flow of foreign direct investment (FDI) into our economy and depressed our trade openness relative to other advanced economies—a combination that weakens our global competitiveness while making imports more expensive. During tougher economic times, advanced economies tend to open themselves up even more to globalization to stimulate growth, and this go-around has been no different—except for outlier America.

Despite those unwise policies, Americans should feel optimistic about globalization's digitalization amidst a superpower brand competition over an ascendant global middle class. We are the world leader in digital content generation, befitting our status as the superpower with the most widely popular brand—even with all our recent self-harm. Of the top 100 most valuable corporate brands in the world, just over half (51) are American, still double that of second-place China (24).

A second American Century is within our reach, but it requires our determined effort—just like the first. Climate change and globalization's consolidation focuses our effort on our own hemisphere. Done right, our modeled behavior in integrating North and South will constitute powerful, *prove-it* global leadership. This is our contest to lose.

34 Energy Independence Ain't All It's Fracked Up to Be, but It's Why the United States Stopped Obsessing Over the Middle East

America's dependency on "foreign oil" disappeared over the last two decades, reshaping US foreign policy and tanking the strategic rationale for our military activism in the Persian Gulf.

Ours is a rare country when it comes to mineral rights—the exploitation of underground natural resources. In most of the world, the state owns subsurface resources no matter who owns the surface property. Americans, in legal possession of any such blessed land, can lease mineral rights to extractive companies in return for royalties paid. This ruleset, inherited from English common law, fueled the so-called fracking boom of the last two decades. By so incentivizing private landowners, America's energy companies were able to aggressively scour the country to exploit new reserves using new technologies.

The "fracking" (hydraulic fracturing) of previously inaccessible oil and gas deposits involves drilling into "tight" deep-rock formations and fracturing them through the high-pressure injection of liquids (water mixed with sand and chemicals). This process frees oil and gas deposits that flow up to the surface, along with the wastewater, and are subsequently captured and transported via pipelines. While fracking comes with more environmental costs than traditional oil and gas drilling, it has revolutionized the US energy sector, elevating it to first place in the world in both crude oil and natural gas production for the first time in decades. In the early 2000s, fracking accounted for less than 10 percent of US oil and gas production; it now accounts for more than half of each.

If we add in the rest of the Americas' oil output, then the Western Hemisphere collectively outproduces Russia and Saudi Arabia combined. In natural gas, the Americas collectively outproduce #2-ranked Russia by 80 percent and #3 Iran by five times. None of this means that our hemisphere can rule over either product's global market—far from it. Saudi Arabia still owns the lion's share of excess oil production capacity and known reserves, while Russia possesses by far the most conventional natural gas reserves. That ability to manipulate energy markets matters during crises, like when Russia, after invading Ukraine, restricted its natural gas exports to Europe and the Saudi-led OPEC subsequently cut oil production in solidarity.

Thanks to fracking, the United States is now immune to such direct economic warfare. In the early 2000s, America imported more than half of the crude oil we consumed. Today we produce as much as we consume. America also now produces more than 90 percent of our natural gas consumption. That recently made us the world's largest liquid natural gas (LNG) exporter—a share certain to expand as Europe looks to radically reduce its pipeline dependency on Moscow. Thanks to hydraulic fracturing, the United States is now a net energy exporter for the first time since the 1950s.

In the next decade, North America will likewise switch from net primary energy importer to net exporter, marking us as the sole region to accomplish that feat this century and bringing us in line with our net-exporting neighbors to our south. This changes the way America looks at other superpowers: we now no longer share Europe's continuing reliance on energy imports—much less China and India's ballooning dependency. Russia's energy sales, which account for more than half its export earnings, flow overwhelmingly to the EU and China, linking their fates. America stands alone as a diverse-but-energy-independent economic superpower.

In combination, the Americas enjoy an even more enviable energy situation: we produce one-third (33 percent) of the world's natural gas and crude oil but consume a smaller share in each (30 percent in gas, 29 percent in oil). Those margins are projected to comfortably expand through 2050. Compare that to Asia's situation: led by China and India, this region presently consumes five times what it lifts in oil, and one-third more than what it produces in natural gas. By midcentury, Asia will need 50 percent more natural gas than it can locally produce and nine times more oil. Historically speaking, such extreme dependencies result in imperial overreach.

Four-fifths of America's crude oil imports come from Canada, Mexico, and Latin America, whereas China imports half its oil from the Persian Gulf, which, in turn, directs 85 percent of its oil exports to Asia. Put those facts together and it makes sense why Washington feels less responsible for, and less willing to ensure, stability in the Middle East, while China and India grow far more incentivized. In terms of US strategic interests, this is addition by subtraction.

The Western Hemisphere's situation on natural gas is especially important, as gas will soon surpass oil and coal as the planet's primary energy source. Global natural gas reserves are split between dry natural gas (7,300 trillion cubic feet [tcf]) and shale gas (7,600 tcf). In dry gas, the Americas collectively possess half that of Russia, the world reserve leader with 1,700 trillion cubic feet. But in shale gas—whose global reserves match that of dry natural gas—the Americas' reserves (3,200 tcf) are eleven times larger than Russia's (285 tcf) and almost triple that of world reserve leader China (1,115 tcf). In the United States alone, natural gas has already surpassed oil as a percentage of total energy production, and the two are tied in consumption. With our nation's electricity generation increasingly dominated by natural gas, along with our automobile fleet moving in the direction of electric vehicles, America's "age of oil" ends after seven decades of supremacy. This eliminates a primary driver of US overseas military interventions since the Vietnam War—a truly liberating development that should not be squandered by Washington's reflexive default to a Cold War mindset vis-à-vis either Beijing or Moscow.

America's movement down the pollution-emitting carbon chain from coal and oil to cleaner natural gas is laudable, but it comes with caveats. First, energy self-sufficiency does not insulate America from turmoil abroad. What happens in the Middle East still impacts Asia's economic health, which indirectly impacts ours. For now, the same holds true for Russia's supply relationship with Europe. Second, hydraulic fracturing comes with a bevy of significant environmental costs.

The fracking boom can only last so long in an industry known for its cyclical busts. Its primary value to America is the flexibility and time it provides us to execute the strategic pivots forced by climate change, to include our economy's—and the world's—continued movement from more intense greenhouse-gas-emitting energy sources to cleaner ones. That alone should steel our confidence regarding the challenges lying ahead.

Fig. 18 | Not just the US, but the entire Western Hemisphere is presently energy self-sufficient.

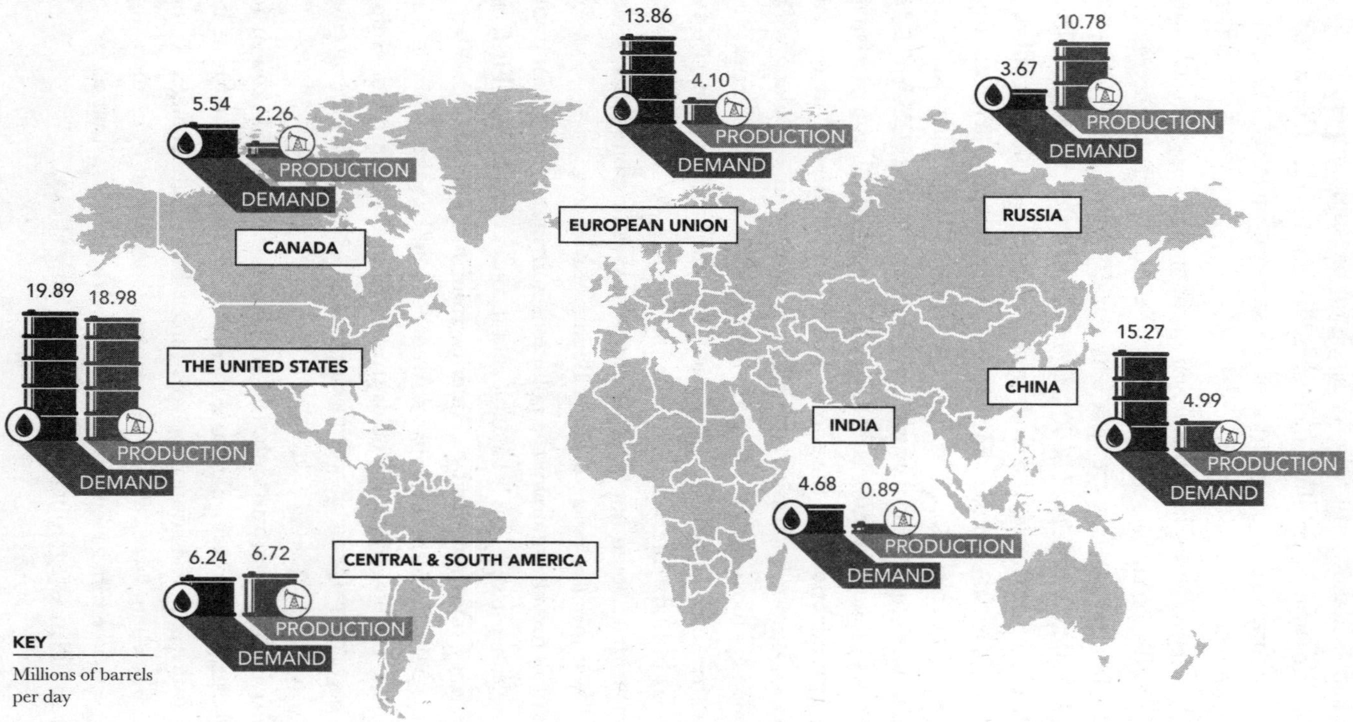

RUSSIA
PRODUCTION 10.78
DEMAND 3.67

CHINA
PRODUCTION 4.99
DEMAND 15.27

INDIA
PRODUCTION 0.89
DEMAND 4.68

EUROPEAN UNION
PRODUCTION 4.10
DEMAND 13.86

CANADA
PRODUCTION 5.54
DEMAND 2.26

THE UNITED STATES
PRODUCTION 19.89
DEMAND 18.98

CENTRAL & SOUTH AMERICA
PRODUCTION 6.72
DEMAND 6.24

KEY
Millions of barrels
per day

35 *Water, Water Everywhere but Not Enough to Drink:* Why Tall Now Beats Wide

> Climate change radically redistributes natural resources, here stealing from water-poor lower latitudes and giving to water-rich higher latitudes. It is now good to be a tall continent.

It is common in policy circles for water to be described as the "oil of the twenty-first century." Frankly, that undersells the strategic importance of the world's freshwater resources—particularly in their varying impact on regions. Masses of humanity were never put on the move by fossil fuel scarcity—much less perished on that basis. Nor have crude reserves ever achieved any migration velocity.

On Earth, the water that humanity sustainably consumes is but a tiny fraction of the world's total supply, 97 percent of which resides in the oceans as salt water. Outside of desalinization (which is getting less expensive but remains energy intensive), that leaves 3 percent as fresh water, two-thirds of which is frozen on Greenland and Antarctica. Humanity makes do with that remaining single percent.

Per our planet's water cycle, some portion of that unfrozen fresh water is a renewable resource—as in, continuously exploitable. However, so-called "fossil water," ancient underground bodies of water undisturbed for millennia, is more like oil and gas. When humans tap those supplies, they are effectively depleted—at least along a human timescale. The same can hold true for ground-water held in aquifers closer to the surface when local demand far outstrips their capacity to recharge—oftentimes measured in decades.

Global water use has more than tripled since 1950 but has slowed this century to a 1 percent annual increase, thanks to growing efforts to stop treating fresh water as a cost-free economic input and start pricing it appropriately. As the water-stressed state of California continues to demonstrate with its innovative policy responses (e.g., usage restrictions, wastewater reclamation), humans are entirely capable of consuming this precious resource with far more efficiency—when suitably incentivized.

Such innovation is crucial, because when it comes to exploitable fresh water, humanity survives on increasingly tight margins. Of that tiny renewable freshwater share, three-quarters goes into agriculture while a tenth goes into industry, leaving about 15 percent for direct human consumption. What comes through our pipes and faucets is thus a mere one-sixth of 1 percent of the world's water—our most precious natural resource now being globally redirected and redistributed by climate change.

Examples of such "climate velocity": The world's subtropic regions, home to the biggest deserts, expand five kilometers poleward each year while squeezing the equatorial rain forest/jungle band. In its continuous growth, the huge Sahara Desert is a tenth larger today than a century ago. In North America, the wheat belt marches twenty-five kilometers northward every year as the Canadian permafrost annually retreats two to three kilometers, meaning we will harvest that crop outside of Fairbanks, Alaska, midcentury. That alone tells us why Canada and Russia matter plenty in the future.

Not all these shifts are latitudinal. America's so-called 100th Meridian (100° west longitude) historically marked the transition from our dry West (where drought-resistant wheat reigns) to our wet East (where thirsty corn is king). Since 1980, it has slid eastward well over 200 km. The same happened with Tornado Alley, once known as Oklahoma but now centered in Alabama— an 800-kilometer shift over three decades (27 km/year). Remember: With climate change, the *what* is not as unprecedented as the *where*.

Humans naturally concentrate themselves according to where exploitable water is more abundant—to wit, history's great civilizations began along major river systems, where today two-thirds of us remain clustered. But when you compare regional shares of world population with those of freshwater supplies, it quickly becomes apparent that, on a global scale, our ascendant middle class faces a decidedly water-stressed future.

While Europe (10 percent of humanity living on 16 percent of fresh water) does fine and Oceania (1 percent living on 2 percent) covers its needs, both Africa (17 percent on 9 percent) and Asia (59 percent getting by on 28 percent) already face water insecurity that climate change will considerably exacerbate. Meanwhile, the Western Hemisphere is sitting pretty: 13 percent of humanity enjoying 45 percent of the world's replenishable freshwater supply. That is a huge advantage going forward.

Our surfeit of water does not mean the Americas escape being tested and stressed by water shortages. We already witness that stressing dynamic in the American West, Central America's Northern Triangle, and South America's Andean Mountain states. It does mean, however, that those challenges are surmountable through intra-American means. Compared to Europe, Africa, and Asia, our solution set is far more easily imagined and executed.

Consider, for example, the challenge of far more severe and lengthier droughts highly concentrated along that Middle Earth band stretching 30 degrees north and south of the equator. Climate change speeds up the water cycle through faster evaporation and transpiration (evaporation via plants). That leaves less moisture for the soil, which makes it harder for plants to grow. Less plant coverage means greater ground absorption of solar radiation, raising surface temperatures, which helps generate more high-pressure weather systems (fewer clouds), which depresses rainfall and boosts solar absorption further, which leads us back to drier soil . . . in a cycle that grows more vicious with each passing year.

Droughts are the sneakiest of disasters: with no clear beginning or end and no single cause to correct, they simply unfold and spread and deepen on their own. Droughts kill crops and livestock and can eliminate riverine transport (consider, for example, the Mississippi River in 2013 and 2022). Their extreme heat destroys infrastructure, particularly roads, and fuels wildfires. Droughts overstress power grids and rob them of their hydroelectric sources. They also hamstring industrial development and activity. Droughts simply make life unbearable, putting people on the move—something Americans have not witnessed at scale since the 1930s Dust Bowl.

Based on scientific projections of the next few decades, the most severe droughts will call into question the political viability of numerous states throughout our planet's lower latitudes. Recalling that most of the world's population is concentrated along the 27° parallel north, it should be no surprise that the UN already classifies half of humanity as living in agricultural zones subject to significant water shortages.

Rising saltwater sea levels paradoxically increases water insecurity by ruining coastal freshwater aquifers. This intrusion used to happen only with storm surges but now regularly unfolds as "sunny day floods" reflecting high tide.

With sea levels set to rise along US coasts by one foot come 2050, Americans are looking at a doubling of flood events within the current thirty-year home mortgage window. That will surely trigger huge public infrastructure costs.

All such changes to how fresh water moves around our planet means the long-standing geopolitics of oil are being replaced with local, national, international, and global hydropolitics. While negotiations concerning water use have long been practiced as a near art form in America's Southwest (consider, for example, arbitration over states' rights regarding the completely consumed Colorado River), the world witnesses growing political struggles concerning upstream dams and downstream agriculture across a host of historic—and mostly Asian—river basins. These situations will prove particularly difficult for national governments to collaboratively manage, inevitably leading to charges of "hydro-hegemony."

In the Western Hemisphere, our water advantage plays out with far less interstate tension. While hydropower (dam-generated electricity) constitutes a mere 16 percent of electricity generation worldwide, Canada (60 percent) and Latin America (45 percent) lead the way on tapping this renewable energy resource. The United States is the fourth-largest producer of hydropower—following world-leading China, Canada, and Brazil, but it accounts for only 6 percent of our electricity.

The trick, of course, will be maintaining that high rate of exploitation amidst climate change's intensification of precipitation in higher latitudes and droughts in lower latitudes. In South America, states along the Pacific coastline will see their hydropower increased, while nations leeward of the Andes Mountains will suffer a decrease. Meanwhile, ever-wetter Canada, which already supplies a significant amount of hydro-powered electricity to America's northern states, plans to vigorously cash in on the Biden administration's push to reduce the role of fossil fuels in US power generation.

Experts fear that Latin America is on the verge of yet another "lost decade." If the United States wants to keep Latin America's portion of Middle Earth as politically viable as possible, despite climate change, then we must encourage such cross-border cooperation and infrastructure investment to ensure our hemisphere equitably exploits our global advantage in water. We in North America either extend such capacity southward or resign ourselves to receiving climate refugees in far greater numbers.

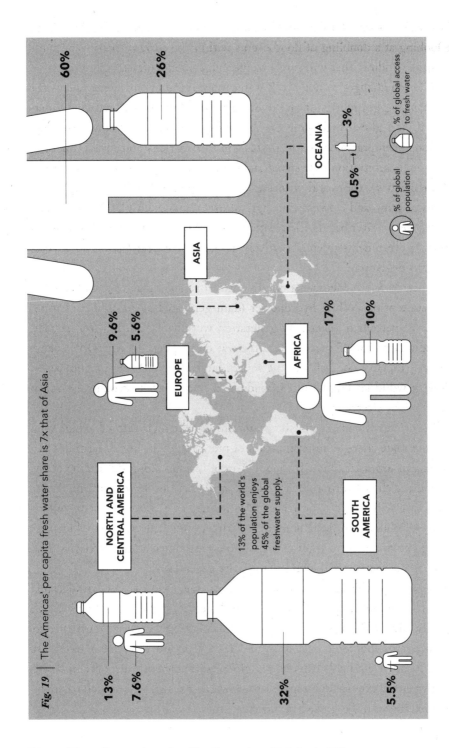

Fig. 19 | The Americas' per capita fresh water share is 7x that of Asia.

ASIA
60%
26%

NORTH AND CENTRAL AMERICA
13%
7.6%

EUROPE
9.6%
5.6%

SOUTH AMERICA
32%
5.5%

AFRICA
17%
10%

OCEANIA
0.5%
3%

13% of the world's population enjoys 45% of the global freshwater supply.

% of global population

% of global access to fresh water

36

The West Feeds the Rest: Climate Change Elevates Food Security to National Security

An expanding global middle class eats better while consuming more food. But the regions acutely experiencing that growth are also where climate change most ravages agriculture.

I n the mid-twentieth century, humanity's per capita supply of calories stood at approximately 2,000 per day, to include all food spoiled or left uneaten at the retail, restaurant, or household levels. Since then, humans have increased that combination of direct and indirect consumption by half. Most of that growth was concentrated in lower-middle income (36 percent increase) and upper-middle income (60 percent) states, while both rich and poor countries advanced far less (20 percent).

Today, the world's per capita supply of food approaches 3,000 calories per day (including food waste). Given its surfeit of fresh water relative to population, the Americas unsurprisingly enjoy the highest average rate at 3,300 calories per day. With the global middle class projected to expand by two to three billion people by midcentury, we should expect other regions to further converge in that upper range, promising us a future of increasing food equality.

In global food production, that demand translates to 50 percent growth by 2050. At that point, experts expect a leveling off of consumption. Global population growth will plateau at ten or so billion and, even with rising incomes across emerging economies, our global middle class will reach the same calorie-saturation point that we have witnessed with high-income societies (i.e., obesity).

That is the good news on food.

The worrisome news naturally concerns climate change, which promises that today's uneven food security landscape will grow dangerously more imbalanced. Thanks to climate velocity, the bulk of humanity will find itself increasingly reliant on distant agricultural production centers that are ever more clustered toward the poles. Those places in the world that cannot feed themselves today—that Middle Earth band stretching 30 degrees north and south from the equator—will need to import a lot more food in the future as their populations surge and it becomes increasingly less feasible to grow crops there. The youthful, climate-vulnerable Middle East, for example, already imports half its consumed calories.

The world's primary grain exporters are projected to enjoy modest yield increases from global warming, but that means the wider world is relying on a small pool of states (America, Canada, Argentina, Brazil, Russia, Ukraine, Kazakhstan, Australia, New Zealand) to export far more food. That will not be easy in a world experiencing unprecedented droughts, truly extreme weather, pests and diseases spreading at climate velocity, and rising seas reclaiming long-productive coastal farmlands. Global agricultural trade doubled over the past quarter century; we must work for the same over the next—despite all such complicating variables.

Keep in mind also that the world's food system is already highly interconnected, so when America engages in "trade wars" or Russia decimates Ukraine, these perturbations quickly damage export relationships decades in the making. Problems in any of the major exporting countries can, at the very least, spook their trade partners and, at the very worst, suddenly send those partners' food prices skyrocketing to the point of political instability. Recall the Arab Spring was preceded by bread riots across North Africa—the *Les Misérables* effect repeated throughout history.

Three basic grains (corn, rice, and wheat) combine to provide half the world's caloric intake. In first place, corn accounts for one-fifth of global consumption. The top three corn exporters are found in the Americas: #1 United States, #2 Argentina, and #3 Brazil. In all, the Western Hemisphere supplies 60 percent of the world's corn trade. China, the world's second-biggest corn producer (after America), is nonetheless the world's biggest importer of corn (alongside Japan).

Point being there is what you produce, there is what you consume, and there is what is left over to feed others across this world. The Western Hemisphere has plenty left over; Asia, home to more than half the world's population, does not. Given China's long history of famines triggering unrest, imagine just how much that strategic reality preys on the minds of Beijing's leadership.

Tied for second, rice and wheat each provide one-sixth of the world's calories. Asia dominates the production and exportation of rice (75 percent)—a grain highly vulnerable to climate change. Europe, thanks to #1 exporter Russia, provides 60 percent of the wheat trade. The Americas occupy second place in both instances (rice at 15 percent, wheat at 33 percent).

Other commodity markets where the Americas' exports dominate are soybeans (95 percent) and sorghum (85 percent). In both cases, China is the biggest importer—by far.

Reviewing our quintet of competing superpowers, we spot a clear dividing line between those who dominate global food exports (America, Russia) and those who loom large in imports (China, EU). In between sits India, both a huge producer and consumer that, for now, feeds itself and may feed others if it effectively combats climate change with technology—a very big *if*.

I have long singled out the American farmer as the single most important stabilizing force on the planet. Thanks to climate change, Canada will eventually rival the United States on that score. Already the world's second-largest exporter of wheat (after Russia), Canada will see its western provinces' wheat belt dramatically expand in coming decades. Russia will be less fortunate, as its newly accessible northern lands will not offer the same rich soil of its Black Sea regions, where more severe droughts may well cancel out any gains from an expanded belt.

China, as the world's biggest producer, consumer, and importer of food, seeks to methodically shore up its security in that domain. One route is to position itself as the technological leader in transforming meat production from a water/grain/farmland sinkhole into a laboratory-as-factory process. Beijing, which clearly views food security and national security as one and the same, formally called for rapid development of "future foods" (e.g., cultivated meat, plant-based eggs) in its most recent Five-Year Plan. As the biggest global market in both foods, such policies can easily become globalization game changers.

Beijing's second track is to expand its farm footprint through overseas purchases of arable land. In doing so, China follows in the footsteps of other rich-but-food-insecure powers such as Japan, South Korea, Saudi Arabia, and the United Arab Emirates. A decade ago, China signed a deal with Ukraine to lease, for half a century, one-tenth of its arable land. That investment surely shaped Beijing's muted response to Moscow's brutal invasion of Ukraine: a short-term loss of imports balanced against preferring Moscow's firm control of that breadbasket.

Call it neocolonialism or food imperialism or a de facto water purchase. Or just think of it as a new form of state affiliation in the age of climate change. Foreigners now control 3 percent of US farmland—a tripling since 2010.

Agricultural flows are the global water trade embodied—H_2O transformed into human food. The Americas possess the most water per capita—seven times that of Asia. In the world's agricultural trade, the Americas exhibit a high level of overseas flows and a low percentage of intra-hemispheric flows. Add up all the grain left over after each continent feeds itself and what is left covers the rest of the world's growing demand. That reserve capacity is overwhelmingly (four-fifths) located in the Americas—meaning our West feeds the Rest.

That growing East-on-West dependency drives China's investment across the world, pushing it to lock down arable land across both Russia and the global South. To achieve its strict definition of food security, Beijing must go everywhere in a Go strategy of laying down as many markers as possible.

In a globalization where demand typically trumps supply, food insecurity constitutes its own universe of fear because of the vagaries of weather and—now—climate. Energy reserves are not shifted by climate. The same holds true for manufacturing and technology. Food is unique, and our West is uniquely advantaged as a result—assuming we keep it that way.

With China so clearly incentivized to go global on food security, shouldn't America at least respond within our own hemisphere? It is easy to imagine Chinese agricultural firms exporting food from a climate-damaged Latin American country experiencing famine while spewing refugees northward. Ditto on their engaging in farming practices that decimate precious environments, such as the Amazon rain forest. These push-come-to-shove moments will arrive—logically in concert with Chinese security interventions, making it sensible for America to consider a twenty-first-century Monroe Doctrine corollary on food security.

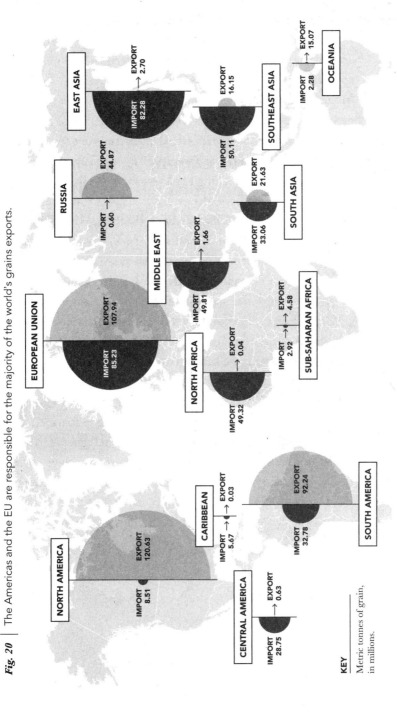

Fig. 20 | The Americas and the EU are responsible for the majority of the world's grains exports.

KEY

Metric tonnes of grain, in millions.

The West Feeds the Rest ★ 245

37

Global Value Chains Regionalize Amidst Superpower Brand Wars: America Disregards This at Its Peril

While Asia and the EU build out capacity as regional manufacturing hubs, populist America ignores Latin America's potential when the answer is more regional free trade agreements.

T hanks to Donald Trump's constant propagandizing, most conservative Americans came to view the enormously successful North American Free Trade Agreement (NAFTA) as the "worst trade deal ever made." It was anything but, quadrupling foreign direct investment (FDI) among the three economies and efficiently regionalizing manufacturing chains—most notably in the automobile industry. The follow-on United States–Mexico–Canada Agreement (USMCA) that Trump negotiated as president is described by Shannon K. O'Neil, a Council on Foreign Relations vice president of Latin American studies, as "NAFTA for populists"—introducing as many complications as improvements. Thus, America remains, in O'Neil's judgment, the "reluctant regionalist" during globalization's current phase of consolidation along regional lines.

How can this be?

When Asia emerged as globalization's "factory floor" across the 1980s, 1990s, and 2000s, intercontinental supply chains (often called global value chains) arose to take advantage of the extreme wage differential that Asia—and particularly China—offered. That wage differential dissipated, along with China's demographic dividend, around the time of the Great Recession, thus flatlining globalization's advance in terms of goods manufactured across truly global value chains. Now, with China consuming far more of its own production, it anchors an increasingly regionalized Asia manufacturing hub—much like the EU. This is how the two regions came to generate two-thirds of the world's GDP today while America's share slid from 30 percent in 2000 to 24 percent in 2021.

Trapped in a miasma of economic nationalism, security fears tracing back to 9/11, and now health fears thanks to the deadly combination of the opioid crisis and COVID-19, America stubbornly refuses to update its trade agenda to reflect globalization's current evolution. As O'Neil argues: "To keep up with and compete against Asia's expansive reach and Europe's industrial prowess, US politicians, entrepreneurs, and workers need to recognize that we do better when we work with those who are closest to us."

Citing the clear advantages offered by nearshoring our supply chains within the Western Hemisphere (e.g., similar time zones, shorter chains, fewer languages, greater certainty, increased capacity to customize products for consumers), O'Neil notes just how far we have fallen behind Europe and Asia when it comes to trade across the Americas. Whereas Europe conducts two-thirds of its trade within its ranks, Asia has reached just over half. Meanwhile, North America, despite NAFTA/USMCA, remains stuck at 40 percent. Excluding Mexico, Latin America—the only answer to our lack of regionalized value chains—remains vastly unintegrated in the mid-teens. The citizens of the Caribbean and Latin America are aware of this problem: a recent multi-state poll found that two-thirds of them are eager to jump-start regional integration, with support strongest among the young, who see it as crucial to their more inclusive and sustainable economic future.

Because Latin America is so weakly integrated with North America, it remains largely relegated to outer circles of global value chains, useful primarily as a source of raw materials and a dumping ground for cheap finished consumer goods—a replication of colonial-era trade inequities. That is the nature of the Chinese developmental threat: locking in less-advanced economies to perpetually disadvantageous global value chains. Left to its own devices, Beijing will beggar *our* Southern neighbors, diminishing their long-term economic prospects to the eventual strategic detriment of the United States, which will be left dealing with the northward migration pressures that result—particularly to the extent climate change hollows out those regions' middle class.

For America to thrive as we compete with China and the EU for the brand loyalty of that ascendant global middle class, our commercial offerings, per O'Neil, "must now court choosy consumers from Kuala Lumpur to Prague—and compete with cutthroat foreign brands on their own turf."

America's greatest economic strength is our rulesets and the long-term certainty they impart to FDI directed to our shores. Given the harshly competitive global landscape, America is best served by weaponizing that strength on a hemispheric basis to, in O'Neil's blunt prescription, generate "more NAFTAs." Why, for example, has Washington spent so much time and effort seeking to counter China's successful push for a Regional Comprehensive Economic Partnership (RCEP) in Asia—creating the largest trade bloc in the world—when it should be proposing its own Latin American and Caribbean variant? Have no doubt: some outside power will eventually do just that.

As the global leader in services and digital content generation, our national economic prospects should be bright within globalization's current evolution, but they are dimmed by our unwillingness to embrace regionalism on par with our competitors. While China, in O'Neil's description, pursues "regionalism through business" and the EU does the same "through diplomacy," Washington, with no clear trade agenda of its own, contents itself with warmed-over protectionism, with Biden continuing the bulk of Trump's misguided policies. In O'Neil's strict economic logic, our path forward is clear: "For the United States, the best way to compete with other regional manufacturing hubs is still to build its own." It is as simple as that: not trying to prevent China's ascendancy as Asia's prime integrating force but getting our own house in order. In that sense, Biden's aggressive embrace of industrial policy, replete with generous government subsidies, can be forgiven, but only if it undergirds a larger vision of hemispheric trade integration.

The United States presently possesses the security motive, economic means, and strategic opportunity to rectify decades of neglecting and abusing our Southern neighbors, in the process clearly benefiting ourselves and restoring our global leadership. Our society's ongoing racial makeover enables it. Our nation's success in the superpower brand wars depends on it. Our hemisphere's expanding vulnerability to climate change demands it.

In generational terms, we currently lack the visionary leadership and political will to achieve this transformation. That is the biggest threat Americans face today: our inability to move past our grievances with one another and the world. By refusing to put our paddle in the water, we lose our ability to move faster than the current, which means we now go wherever history's flow takes us. This is not who we are.

38

West Hem Civ 101:
**Having Outgrown Our Parentage,
the Americas Stand Tall**

As climate change forces North-South integration across this century, the Americas are uniquely advantaged by a blended hemispheric culture born of an earlier globalizing era.

Across the fifteenth through eighteenth centuries, Europe's colonizing conquest of the New World drove a genocide among our Indigenous populations, wiping out 90 percent of their ranks in an historical blink of an eye (the first 150 years). What ensued was a vast influx of European settlers, enslaved Africans, and Asian immigrants—the Eastern Hemisphere's major racial groupings. All three widely interbred with one another and the hemisphere's remaining Indigenous peoples, leading to today's mixed and multiracial landscape—a complicated legacy full of institutionalized racism that is more readily recognized across Latin America than White-centric Anglo America (Canada plus the United States). Call us mutts if you must, but our pervasively mixed heritage makes what comes next far easier to navigate.

Our New World is the product of the Old World's forced attempt at globalization. Being the first in the world to be so comprehensively colonized, we were the first to thoroughly de-colonize our ranks in a series of unprecedented anti-imperial uprisings stretching from 1776 through the nineteenth century.

We are the children of those revolutions. As such, our hemisphere is full of countries where those of European descent live peacefully in the minority. Compared to the fractured Eastern Hemisphere with its long history of warring races, we of the far more peaceful Americas are living proof that racial integration forced by global dynamics can nonetheless birth a blended civilization of unique characteristics—*E pluribus unum*.

White America naturally traces its primary culture heritage to Europe, but so does the rest of the Western Hemisphere. The "transatlantic relationship" was just as strong across Latin America as Anglo America. A telling example: nothing defines America more than our West and its associated cowboy culture, yet that was gifted to America by Mexico, which in turn traces the role of the vaquero (horse-mounted livestock herder) back to medieval Spanish haciendas. Today, that remarkably similar frontier culture still stretches from Canada to Argentina—sadly to include its vigorous gun subculture.

As a result of such cultural blending, our West possesses the most varied music and art forms in the world. We Anglo-Americans believe ourselves unusually tolerant of outside additions to our culture, but we have nothing on Hispanic American culture. Both of us can legitimately hoist the "melting pot" banner.

Facilitating our future integration, a mere four European languages (Spanish, English, Portuguese, and French) dominate our landscape, while we are unusually concentrated along one religious axis—Christianity (four-fifths of the total Americas population), and within that, Catholicism (three-fifths). Still, our societies are known for religious pluralism, and tensions among our faiths are minimal.

That relative faith uniformity cannot be underestimated as a hemispheric advantage for what lies ahead. Consider America's growing conservative resistance to both immigration and the racial justice movement. That aggressive impulse now coalesces around a Christian nationalist movement and, within that, an increasingly hardline Catholic subset that finds its most powerful expression in a Catholic-majority US Supreme Court (seven of nine justices). There, six conservative Catholic justices (five practicing, one former) methodically blur the distinctions between church and state to preserve a Christian cultural identity by promulgating a sort of Catholic *sharia* (religious law) that many non-Christian and secular Americans deem both unconstitutional and anti-democratic.

This growing effort to carve out a safe political space for Christians is a predictable reaction to the looming reality that America will cease being majority Christian at some point in the 2060s—a mere generation after Whites slip into majority-minority status in the 2040s. An example of how this spills over into inter-American relations: the Supreme Court's 2022 dismantling of *Roe-v-Wade* now triggers a new Latin American drug trade in abortion pills largely sourced in Mexico and mailed throughout the United States, attaching this white-hot culture war to the Drug War and its associated anti-immigrant fervor.

Genuine Christian nationalists, as opposed to those cynically cloaking their racism with religion, should welcome future North-South integration in the Western Hemisphere, as it would strengthen their ranks. Specific to Catholicism: while the Eastern Hemisphere possesses almost six times the West's population, half the world's Catholics are found in our hemisphere, with #1 Brazil and #2 Mexico besting #3 America for the top global spots. With two-thirds of the Western Hemisphere's population concentrated in those three states—all of which have recently experienced Trumpist populism (no coincidence)—they alone could form the religious core of an Americas Union that addresses preeminent hemispheric issues in a manner that assuages conservative fears of lost religious identity.

Such arguments acknowledge the tricky path ahead: if the Western Hemisphere is going to come together over climate change and how it will devastate and remap our shared environment, a key motivation will be any population's instinct to preserve core identities even as they are forced to merge with new ones. To maximize our speed of adaptation, the Americas as a whole will need to openly address such divisive fears.

Beyond that baseline effort, America's success in the superpower brand wars will be determined by our demonstrated willingness to welcome, and make space for, culturally distinct members. One cannot become Chinese or Indian, but anyone can become an American—anywhere in our hemisphere—because each of our states lacks an exclusive racial identity. There is no singular Canadian, Costa Rican, or Chilean "race" to preserve. Our hemisphere's entirely synthetic national identities, rightfully criticized as masking pervasive forms of institutional racism, nonetheless constitute our greatest strength—the ability to evolve faster than our competitors. Racism and multiculturalism are natural bedfellows, meaning you cannot have one without the other. That is just human nature resisting change.

The combination of Anglo America and Latin America is by far the easiest human merger forced by climate change. We earned this; we are built for this.

39 *Nobody Does It Better:* These United States as Globalization in Miniature

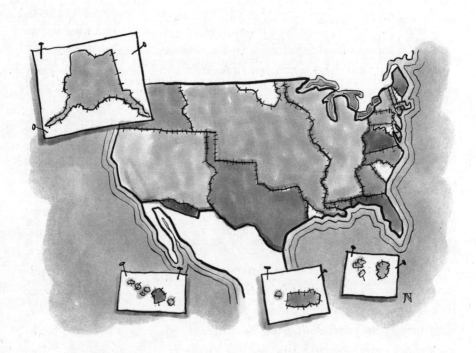

In growing from thirteen colonies to fifty states, America mastered a skill critical to our future success: the ability to assimilate new members and incorporate them as full partners.

America is both the creator of modern globalization and its most experienced practitioner. Our blueprint is one of states uniting, economies integrating, and networks spreading under the protective umbrella of collective security and common laws. The European Union fancies itself the first supranational union in history, but that title really belongs to us. By knitting together thirteen distinct colonies—each with its own army, navy, flag, laws, paper money, and origin story—into a constitutional republic, we imposed a supranational federated structure over states that, to this day, still fiercely defend their rights within our American Union. Whether you welcome or despise the notion, the first seeds of world governance were planted by us.

Building our Empire of Laws was no mean feat, and it contained numerous legal inducements for westward expansion. The 1783 treaty that ended our revolutionary war with the British crown codified the claims of several of our newly independent states to the trans-Appalachian West, putting them in direct competition with one another, in addition to Britain, France, and Spain, for control of the continent. There, our westward settlers effectively pioneered modern globalization's most devastating dynamics—namely, the engulfing and near-eradication of Indigenous societies by American-style market economics.

More than anything else—even more than religious freedom—immigrants came to America in search of land they could own. American expansion was, first and foremost, an expression of economic will—a human motivation we need to keep in mind during the North-South integration to come. Nothing defines citizenship like land ownership. America is, after all, the "*land* of opportunity."

Recall also the fierce, decades-long struggle between free and slave states to claim and then settle their shared-and-constantly-extending frontier for their diametrically opposed economic systems. That Cold War–like conflict, where both sides viewed the other as seeking to destroy their way of life, found only partial resolution in a bloody civil war whose monuments divide us still.

Point being the American Union was hardwired for expansionism from the very beginning. George Washington's farewell admonition to avoid "foreign entanglements" had less to do with intervening in European wars than focusing our national energies on continental conquest. No surprise there, as he and other Founding Fathers built their personal fortunes on frontier land speculation. Washington himself began his history-bending career as a land surveyor.

The American System, first enunciated by Alexander Hamilton and later coined by statesman Henry Clay, served as ideological DNA for our continental integration schemes of the nineteenth century and their subsequent extension to the global stage following World War II. Hamilton's vision centered on the state's direct financing of "internal improvements"—namely, public infrastructure. His goal was a decades-long integration of our young nation's disparate regions into a *single market*—now the EU's term of art for the free movement of products, services, finance, and people throughout the European Economic Area.

While Hamilton's original vision of the American System was continental in scope, his true target was imperial Britain. By constructing our inland empire, Hamilton, and later Clay—whose Whig Party specialized in promoting railroads—envisioned America challenging Britain's overseas empire or, at the very least, deterring its further expansion into the Western Hemisphere.

That same logic motivated President James Monroe to articulate, in 1823, his doctrine of opposing any European political interference in the Americas as a security threat. Decades later, Theodore Roosevelt's "corollary" declared America's right to intervene if European powers tried to strong-arm indebted nations—as China does today.

Abraham Lincoln, who idolized the "great compromiser" Clay, began his political career proposing an "Illinois System" to transform the Prairie State with roads and canals. Those plans presaged his strategy of rapidly integrating the West as the ultimate reconstruction of American identity following the Civil War. As president, he front-loaded that transformational process with the

Homestead Act (free land to settlers), Pacific Railroad Act, Morrill Act (creation of land-grant colleges), and the Legal Tender Act establishing the first single-currency US notes—our "greenbacks" predecessor to the EU's euro. Popularly dubbed a "Man of the West," Lincoln's notion was to center the US political system on that frontier-integrating ideal—a geographic precursor to America's middle-class ideology that divides the citizenry into "hardworking" types and nefarious "special interests," both rich and poor, inhabiting society's margins.

Fast-forward to the World's Columbian Exposition of 1893: America's coming-out party as a world power. University of Wisconsin history professor Frederick Jackson Turner presents his "frontier thesis," which traces American identity to its history of westward expansion. With that frontier now "closed," fears spread that America would be swamped by, and lose its core identity to, an ongoing deluge of European immigrants, most of whom were then considered to be non-White.

Enter Theodore Roosevelt, self-invented Western cowboy. TR's fears of the "stationary state," in which Americans' natural ambitions were boxed in by imperial powers claiming the world's remaining frontiers, pushed him to declare an "open door" policy toward China, then being devoured by colonizing powers. It was the first time any US president had extended the Monroe Doctrine's logic of curtailing European imperialism outside the Western Hemisphere.

In doing so, TR previewed the grand strategy employed by his cousin Franklin Delano Roosevelt in the waning days of World War II: America would guarantee Europe's access to global markets, preventing those nations' imprisonment behind Moscow's Iron Curtain. Like TR's promise of a "Square Deal" to America's middle class, Harry Truman delivered an international variant of his predecessor's "New Deal" designed to sustain and expand the postwar capitalist economies' vulnerable middle class. America won the Cold War because its mini-globalization model vastly outperformed the Soviet Bloc's alternative. Having succeeded on continental and international stages, the American System informed the world system now called globalization, defining its on-ramp for emerging economies.

The American System is all about gearing up your economy to compete on a global stage—not about how you behave once you have arrived there. In that all-important journey, the American System allows for a protectionist government role in economic development that first stitches together the national economy and then connects it to the outside world on decidedly favorable terms. This catch-up strategy will strike competitors as "cheating," which it is. But for the global economy, it is far better to allow such short-term cheating because the result is a much bigger economic "pie" for all to divide.

America was considered the world's most thieving and cheating economy of the 1800s, just like Japan, the Asian Tigers, and then China in the late– and post–Cold War eras. In globalization, everyone cheats their way to the top by not becoming a fair trader until they are strong enough to play on that highly competitive level. It is then—and only then—that the American System's logic yields to that of the Washington Consensus, emphasizing the widest possible integration of a national economy to the global economy, along with legal protection of patents, brands, and intellectual property.

When I have here referenced established world powers successfully mentoring the rise of states that ultimately become their competitors, that process invariably involves turning a blind eye to their catching-up efforts. That is how America enabled Asia's peaceful rise these past several decades: short-term magnanimity extended for long-term gain. We must adhere to this pragmatic logic in any economic integration with Latin America because it is the same visionary thinking that the EU applied to post-Soviet Eastern Europe.

It is often difficult for Americans to realize just what an amazingly integrated multi-state economy that American System created in North America. The countries listed on the map on the following page comprise more than two billion souls—seven times today's US population. A supranational union capable of stitching together all that economic power into a single overarching ruleset must know a thing or two about unleashing the cumulative creative power of its member states and their citizens.

America's historical record clearly indicates that we possess the structures, norms, and instincts for state integration on a grand scale. We did it across the continental United States and beyond, and then successfully implanted that ruleset in a global economic order that, seven decades later, has recast our planet—literally. If America can do it on both a continental and global stage, then we should proceed with replicating it on a hemispheric scale with genuine confidence in both our skill set and our ultimate aims. We are more than clever enough to pull this off.

Fig. 21 This map overlays states with nations that have comparable GDPs, and multipliers to indicate the relative populations that make up each.

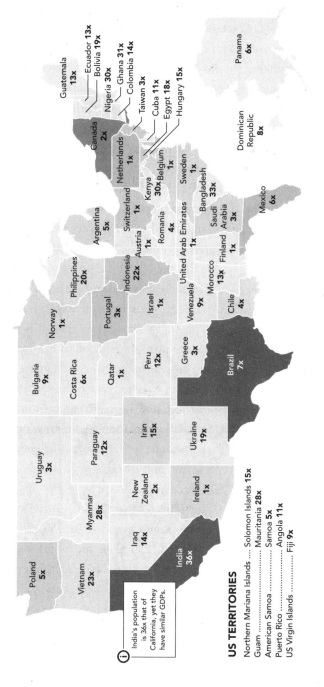

US TERRITORIES

Northern Mariana Islands	Solomon Islands **15x**
Guam	Mauritania **28x**
American Samoa	Samoa **5x**
Puerto Rico	Angola **11x**
US Virgin Islands	Fiji **9x**

India's population is 36x that of California, yet they have similar GDPs.

Canada **2x**

Guatemala **13x**
Ecuador **13x**
Bolivia **19x**
Nigeria **30x**
Ghana **31x**
Colombia **14x**
Taiwan **3x**
Cuba **11x**
Egypt **18x**
Hungary **15x**

Netherlands **1x**
Belgium **1x**
Sweden **1x**

Argentina **5x**
Switzerland **1x**
Kenya **30x**
Austria **1x**
Romania **4x**
United Arab Emirates **1x**
Bangladesh **33x**
Saudi Arabia **3x**
Finland **1x**
Mexico **6x**

Philippines **20x**
Indonesia **22x**
Morocco **13x**
Venezuela **9x**
Chile **4x**

Norway **1x**
Portugal **3x**
Israel **1x**
Greece **3x**

Bulgaria **9x**
Costa Rica **6x**
Qatar **1x**
Peru **12x**
Brazil **7x**

Uruguay **3x**
Paraguay **12x**
Iran **15x**
Ukraine **19x**

Myanmar **28x**
New Zealand **2x**
Ireland **1x**

Poland **5x**
Vietnam **23x**
Iraq **14x**
India **36x**

Dominican Republic **8x**

Panama **6x**

GROSS DOMESTIC PRODUCT (GDP) $32.94 B  $2,515.31 B
(in 2020 USD)

40 Winning the Twenty-First Century: Citizenship Is About Identity, and Identity Is About to Change

BUILD YOUR CHARACTER

As globalization digitalizes into a metaverse of virtual realities, citizens' allegiances grow more diverse, cross-cutting, and fluid, allowing them to manipulate their national identities.

During every off-season in the US professional sports leagues (basketball, football, baseball, and hockey), there is a period of free agency in which players whose contracts have expired are allowed to sign new deals with other teams. As a thought experiment, imagine something similar for countries: regardless of geographic location, consider what would happen if, during such a free-agency period, each nation had the opportunity to join some larger team—at no political penalty or security risk and with the hope of economic advancement. Let us designate those teams as the United States of America, the European Union, the Russian Federation, the People's Republic of China, and the Republic of India.

To make it more interesting, let us afford the same side-switching privileges to member states or provinces within each of our five major franchises. In other words, Norway can join the United States, Hawaii jump ship to China, Xinjiang defect to India, and Russia's Amur Oblast sign with Beijing. Consider this a democratic choice in which citizens' sum desires hold sway.

Weighing everything we know about each team's deficiencies, strengths, backstory, and prospects, which rosters end up larger at the end of this free agency, and which are smaller? My prediction is that the United States and EU skyrocket in membership, India and China hold steady, and many Russians *unsubscribe*!

In today's real world, this is a fantastic notion, but in tomorrow's virtual worlds, far less so. As globalization increasingly technologizes, digitalizes, and virtualizes our collective existence, humanity approaches the point where subscription challenges citizenship as a more accurate and fungible construct of membership, identity, belonging—even allegiance.

Among older generations, this notion can be ridiculed as "citizen of the world" drivel. But think about it—for most people, citizenship is a subscribed identity with the annual fee in the form of taxation: *I prefer this identity to others and so I pay for that privilege.* Or, if I am rich enough, I shop for another political identity that charges me less (say, tax-free Monaco or the Bahamas). US citizens engage in this sort of thinking all the time when they choose to leave a high state income tax environment (e.g., California) and move to a no state income tax environment (Texas).

Then there are those (typically wealthier) citizens who want to balance their political-identity portfolios, so to speak, by subscribing to additional political identities in the form of legally maintained multiple nationalities, citizenships, and passports. If one citizenship-provider is tanking, then the opportunity to effectively switch one's primary allegiance is always there for the taking.

Suffice it to say there is a transactional calculation here: *How much is this political identity worth to me?*

As for when you judge that a political identity costs you too much or delivers too little: if you are an average person, that is when you and yours emigrate. Soon, such choices will unfold in both real-world and virtual-world dimensions. In the former, consider that Spain now offers special long-term visas to foreign remote workers (dubbed "digital nomads") and their families if they meet certain income thresholds and are willing to relocate. But for many trapped by real-world circumstances, be they economic or political, virtual realms will offer the most feasible options for tuning out a bad life situation—as in, Ready, Player One?

Here we must account for the onrush of the metaverse: an evolving iteration of today's internet that will be home to all manner of virtual worlds within which users can interact with computer-generated environments and other users. To the extent the real world increasingly disappoints younger generations—particularly in diminishing their sense of national pride and citizenship—we should expect these digital natives to seek something better (community, belonging, identity, etc.) in the metaverse—to include the forging of new forms of political allegiance.

This is already happening all around us. A key example is foreign governments cyber-meddling in America's elections, which are becoming a superpower battleground unto themselves. Vladimir Putin has succeeded in capturing, by virtual means, the hearts and minds of a significant portion of America's Republican Party base—a stunning achievement demonstrating the power of this dynamic. Then there are extremist groups that recruit new members through internet chat rooms and propagandistic YouTube videos. QAnon, for example, is but the latest in a long line of apocalyptic American cults prepping adherents for an End Times–like spasm of "righteous" violence.

Per the old Leninist term, the internet presents an endless supply of "useful idiots" eagerly awaiting activation. Seemingly overnight, citizens can be swayed to switch political and even national allegiances—bodies cyber-snatched by unseen, un-present forces. It is a national security nightmare: Who can be trusted when allegiances are so easily converted within that nebulous realm?

Our quintet of superpowers, along with a host of lesser great powers, invest vast sums of money and brainpower to address this challenge, to include firewalling national networks. But the numbers of individuals escaping from closed to open networks will only expand, as will determined efforts by governments to poach allegiants from opposing networks. Cybersecurity experts emphasize the threats posed to hard infrastructure (e.g., shutting down a nation's electrical grid), when—in truth—those posed to our human infrastructure (i.e., social cohesion) are far greater.

Recall that kinetic warfare has migrated from the system level, down past the nation-state level, and into the subnational level, meaning the fight now unfolds overwhelmingly among individuals. The same is happening in cyberspace, where individual hearts and minds are being won or poisoned in numbers sufficient to trigger regime change dynamics in any political system—to include America's own experience with the January 6th Insurrection.

That terrifying realization motivates a lot of policy dialogues today in Washington—at least on one side of the political aisle. It triggers Beijing's intense focus on cyber-pacification of its citizenry—and of ours, too, if we are not vigilant. It also fuels China's ambition to rule 5G networks around the world, giving them a direct line into individuals' daily lives and thoughts.

If all that were not enough to put the vast bulk of the world's competing political identities in play, let us now add in climate change's remapping of our planet, the billions of refugees put on the move, and the political restructurings forced between Northern and Southern regions. Individuals, along with their allegiances, will be both mobilized and made mobile. Superpowers can treat them as either potential allegiants or enemies, but rest assured they will end up in some superpower's camp or at least put to some superpower's use.

Finally, let us also remember the numerical heft of that emergent global middle class, with its deep hunger for security and stability. Their grouped political allegiance is crucial for any state's stability, so expect national governments to align with superpowers most ready, willing, and able to deliver those intangible goods and services.

All this is to say that the world is on the cusp of an intense struggle between competing superpower models of belonging. That playing field will include both real and virtual worlds. As such, we enter a period of clashing rulesets that seems quite threatening to an America long accustomed to living in a world overwhelmingly populated with rules of its making.

This century's globalization belongs to those superpowers that propagate the best and most responsive rulesets, build and operate the most inviting and empowering networks, and win new subscribers with integration schemes that deliver what citizens most desire: predictable and unhindered access to goods and services. This is not good versus evil but efficiency versus incompetency.

In response, US leaders will instinctively call for another "moon shot," Manhattan Project, or "war on BLANK." Americans possess a deep and abiding faith in technology—especially of the military variety—to conquer all challenges, but that will not suffice here. There is no hoarding such advances in today's world. If technology yields a flat playing field, then we must win on associated human intangibles: customer service, user experience, buyer satisfaction, loyalty programs, and the like.

If you cannot beat them on silicon, beat them on carbon instead.

This struggle calls for a seminal change in our mindset. Americans are used to outsiders competing for US citizenship, not the US government competing with other nations to attract citizens—much less new member states. Nonetheless, this is the strategic challenge we face in the superpower competition already begun.

41

The Climate Redemption: Get Busy Adding Stars or Get Busy Losing Them

Globalization's original sin forces North-South integration the world over. States evolving in union with others will survive; laggards may not. America's hemispheric imperative is clear.

I have spent my entire life living under the same US flag, when, in truth, that emblem is a poor capture of our far more complex Union. The United States of America comprises 639 legal entities—and counting: 574 sovereign Native American nations, fifty member states, fourteen territories (nine uninhabited, five inhabited), and one federal district. As the American academic Juan Enriquez noted in his 2005 book, *The Untied States of America*, "There is a zoo of citizenship within the US."

How did America accumulate all these parts? Truth be told, steadily. From the year of our Constitution (1789) to the admission of our most recent member states (1959), we averaged a new star on Old Glory every three to four years. The United States purchased many future components from other nations, and fifteen of our member states, before joining our Union, encompassed lands that once claimed sovereign status. The colonial territories were added across the latter decades of the nineteenth century. Meanwhile, Native Americans were always here, suffering persistent displacement through genocidal conquest of their lands. Having seen their sovereignty endlessly violated by Washington, these First Nations have only lately received genuine value in government-to-government relationships with the United States—to include direct access to federal resources. That national redemption, along with one encompassing slavery, will never end.

No matter how we whitewash our past, America has always been a blended family of nations and their political entities—however cross-bred our population, however fused our culture, however imperfect our Union. We are simultaneously our own unique species and the single most accurate projection of globalization's endlessly fractured, frequently polarized, multicultural future.

Being deeply proud of participating in this world-steering experiment, I would not have it any other way. Life here carries more potency simply because, in the grand scheme of human history, being American is the most important identity any of us will ever know. It is a secular religion reflecting our faith in ourselves, our national community, and our shared future.

Like any religious followers, Americans are compelled to spread our faiths, many of which have long animated modern globalization's stunningly powerful spread. Our present state of domestic unhappiness reflects our growing repudiation of that global role over the disorienting change that globalization has forced upon us. We are no longer history's happy warriors. Our national self-confidence sapped, we seem more intent on tearing up our flag—and our Union—than honoring our heritage, which is all about building something bigger, adding new stars, and amazing the world with our ambition, ingenuity, and tolerance.

Per Enriquez, "Countries, like marriages, companies, and people, oft reach a break point, and split up or die." A nation's origin stories are delicate myths citizens tell themselves. They represent a country's shared beliefs and ideals. If that consensus dissolves, so, too, does that imagined state. The Soviet Union was real—right up to the moment it became unreal in its citizens' minds.

As living things, countries—like faith—either flourish or wither. History, in the form of technology and its consequences, constantly tests both. Channeling Charles Darwin, America will survive not because we are the strongest of unions but if we are "the one most responsive to change."

America's capacity for political evolution has never been more important to the world. Human technologies have spawned the most profound environmental test humanity has faced in millennia—large portions of our world becoming first economically and then politically unfeasible. We either extend new structures of belonging toward these peoples—adding their stars to our own—or they will swamp us with their desperation, dividing our Union as never before.

That ultimatum admittedly echoes the fearmongering of so many culturally conservative segments of our aging society: *They are coming to destroy us!* The difference is, I am trying to sell you a way ahead—the next logical iteration of the American Experiment—versus a fear-induced retreat to an idealized, unrecoverable past. Such nostalgia is entirely wasted on our youth—thank God. They seek more meaning, impact, and purpose in their lives than can be achieved by erecting a wall and telling Middle Earth that they are on their own. If our young people cannot locate that redemption within the American belief system, they will increasingly subscribe their loyalties elsewhere—bank on it.

Middle-aged Whites fearing "replacement" are not the problem; disillusioned youth are the problem. Again Enriquez: "Grandchildren may decide it is not worth the effort to defend the same symbols, beliefs, flags, and border of their grandparents." That is because "citizenship is buying into a national brand"—one so attractive that it commands unreasonable loyalty and even sacrifice.

In serious decline now, America's brand seems more occupied with its past than its future. Our patriotism, always forward leaning, is recast as a litany of grievances. By pathetically aping Old World nationalism, we denigrate—even deny—our unique hemispheric civilization here in the *true West*. We should have more pride in who we are, what we have accomplished, and why we still matter to this world.

Americanism as a faith strikes many of our youth as a generational con job perpetrated by their selfish, self-centered elders. Therein lies the danger, says Enriquez, because "when brands promise one thing and deliver another . . . they lose support. Old brands are removed from the supermarket shelf, old countries are removed from maps." Compare the life experiences of today's youth with those enjoyed by the Boomers and ask yourself, Will our flag command their allegiance in the decades ahead? Will we add stars or lose them?

Citizens most readily take ownership of a country they have had a hand in creating. Like a trust-fund generation, the Boomers cannibalized that which was bequeathed to them by the Greatest Generation. Gen Xers to date offer few reasons for optimism, content as too many of them seem in extending and exacerbating their predecessors' self-destructive culture wars.

No, if the American Union is going to thrive again, it will be through encouraging, empowering, and unleashing Millennials, Gen Zs, and Gen Alphas to redefine what it means to be American and what America means to become. As true globalization natives, these generations, per Abraham Lincoln, "shall nobly save, or meanly lose, the last best hope of earth."

When the UN was created in 1945, it had fifty-one signatories. Having since averaged one new entrant every seven months, it now has 193 members. As Enriquez observes, "Countries are breeding promiscuously" within globalization, often seeking to preserve their unique cultural identities within a rapidly homogenizing world. While that instinct is both admirable and understandable, there will always be more strength in the numbers amassed by multinational unions—a political art form in which America is deeply experienced and magnificently talented.

Every US generation, right through the Greatest Generation, has left America better and *bigger* than they found it. The Boomers are the first generation to lose that throughline—to our great shame. That disastrous development needs reversing, and globalization's regional consolidation, accelerated by climate change's remapping of our world, is a made-to-order opportunity.

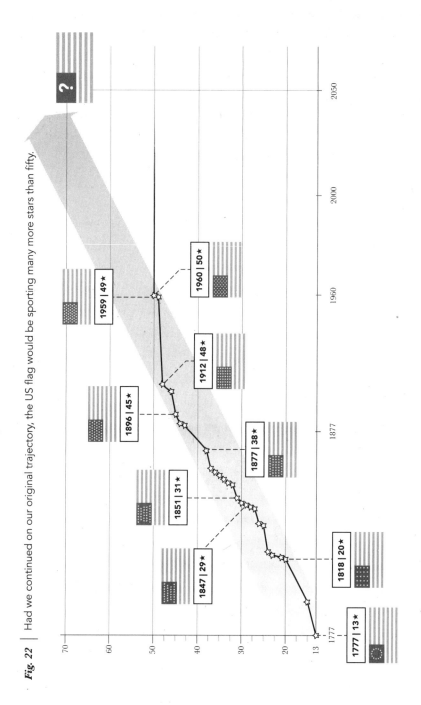

Fig. 22 | Had we continued on our original trajectory, the US flag would be sporting many more stars than fifty.

1777 | 13 ★
1818 | 20 ★
1847 | 29 ★
1851 | 31 ★
1877 | 38 ★
1896 | 45 ★
1912 | 48 ★
1959 | 49 ★
1960 | 50 ★

42 *We're Still the One:* The Durability of America's Superpower Brand Appeal

Our brand's positives far outweigh its negatives. Yet many Americans regret how those attributes shape our world. We should be more cognizant of how we model behavior.

There are many reasons for America's incredibly powerful brand appeal:

* *Political ideals*—explained in our founding documents and copied the world over
* *Sheer power*—first expressed as our nation's unprecedented domination of the global system after World War II, gracefully degrading ever since
* *Presumed global leadership*—our leaders are de facto world leaders
* *Military capabilities*—go-to disaster-reliever, global cop, and crisis responder ("Send in the Marines!"), plus the only force with genuine global reach
* *Prosperity*—huge market that has long shaped global value chains
* *English*—global reach of language, ease of use, acceptance of foreign words
* *Innovation*—persistent wellspring of technological breakthroughs that go global
* *Work ethic*—Americans live to work instead of the other way around (sigh!)
* *Education*—finest teaching and research universities in the world mean we educate the world's top talent, retaining many for life
* *Ubiquity of culture*—inescapable, loud, and constantly evolving
* *Modeled behavior*—nobody loves their own country and culture more
* *Self-confidence*—Americans walk down any street like they own it
* *Cool factor*—nobody else quite sets that global standard like we do
* *Defining youth culture*—rap and hip-hop are just the latest examples

- ★ *Representing the new*—consistent global trendsetting
- ★ *Rebel mindset*—per our origin story, a cultural throughline of iconic loners taking on the system and winning against all odds
- ★ *Freedom*—Americans live and work where they want, buy what they want, worship how they want, wed whom they want, and say what they please
- ★ *Empowerment mythology*—ethos of the self-made person
- ★ *Eat-what-you-kill mentality*—with surprisingly little social contempt for those who strike it rich and lord their wealth over the rest
- ★ *Anything can happen here*—a fear-of-missing-out (FOMO) attractor
- ★ *Empty vessel*—as anyone can make it big in America, big dreamers the world over project those ambitions onto the US landscape
- ★ *Ability to commercialize anything*—Americans can and will make a buck off anything, creating demand where previously there was none
- ★ *Responsiveness to consumers*—American business obsesses over American buyers, meaning we produce what consumers want most
- ★ *Ability to market anything*—in America, products find you!
- ★ *Lack of traditions and fixed tastes*—means we will try anything, which makes us a perfect laboratory for productization
- ★ *Sex sells*—as we are both incredibly prudish and pervasively pornographic
- ★ *IT productization*—our big tech companies lead; the world copies
- ★ *Glamour*—our influencers/celebrities shape global consumption
- ★ *Cultural velocity*—we are the royalty of virality and memes
- ★ *Icon production*—name a global icon, and odds are they're American
- ★ *Battle-tested products*—big market + fierce competition = winners
- ★ *Simplicity of culture*—we are not hard to figure out and easy to access
- ★ *Incorporating outside cultural influences*—learning how to sell to immigrants, we learn how to sell better to their homelands
- ★ *Our Xs are better than their Xs*—any nation's emigrants succeed more here
- ★ *Urban Black aesthetic*—our most consistently impactful cultural export
- ★ *Future-oriented*—our short memory means we welcome change
- ★ *Optimistic outlook*—we try anything because we expect to succeed
- ★ *Road warrior mentality*—most of us originally left everything to come here, so pulling up stakes for a new opportunity is in our blood

- ★ *Environment*—America has it all in terms of variety, and our ability to keep it reasonably clean earns us global authority in that realm
- ★ *Everything is bigger*—creating a certain shock-and-awe factor
- ★ *Masters of entertainment*—we know how to put butts in seats
- ★ *Hollywood*—70 percent of its total revenue comes from foreign markets, while 97 of the 100 all-time highest-grossing films are American
- ★ *Masters of digital content*—we know how to capture and keep eyeballs
- ★ *Musical genres*—we have invented and globalized jazz, gospel, country, bluegrass, soul, rhythm and blues, rock and roll, funk, disco, heavy metal (with the UK), electronic (with Germany), house, rap, grunge, and hip-hop
- ★ *Fashion*—prevalence of American designers and influencers
- ★ *Sports*—popularity of baseball in Latin America and East Asia, global reach of basketball and golf, expanding generational appeal of X Games
- ★ *Holidays*—spreading observance of US-style Thanksgiving, Christmas, Mother's/Father's Day, Halloween, Earth Day, Valentine's Day, etc.
- ★ *Haters*—even those who despise our culture tend to be obsessed with it

Americans veer between pride in our global influence and embarrassment over what many in our world consider to be brand detractors, such as our:

- ★ *Culture wars*—and their coarsening of public dialogue and behavior
- ★ *Gun culture*—appearing more out of control with each passing year
- ★ *Institutional racism*—pervasive despite protests, movements, and reforms
- ★ *Police misconduct*—creating levels of citizen distrust not seen in decades
- ★ *Treatment of kids*—extending culture wars to children seems unnecessarily cruel
- ★ *Treatment of lesbian, gay, bisexual, transgender, queer, and non-straight non-cisgender identities (LGBTQ+ community)*—vindictive targeting of vulnerable minorities
- ★ *Immigration system*—constantly vilified and never adequately reformed
- ★ *Obesity epidemic*—costing us plenty and constituting America's deadliest export
- ★ *Healthcare*—the only highly developed nation without universal healthcare

- ★ *Reproductive rights*—bucking the global trend of increased access to abortion
- ★ *Science denialism*—most notably on vaccines and climate change
- ★ *Political violence*—a growing fascistic quality reminiscent of Weimar Germany
- ★ *Xenophobia*—featuring an increasingly apocalyptic tone among Whites

Both lists compare well to any generated by our competitors, each of whom, if objectively calculating win-probability, would trade their brand for ours. America thus enters this contest advantaged, the only question being our will to succeed. There we must turn to leaders capable of reimagining our hemispheric relations.

The Americanist Manifesto: Summoning the Vision and Courage to Remap Our Hemisphere's Indivisible Future

THROUGHLINE SEVEN

As our demographically divided world enters the climate change crucible, now is the time for all good Americans to come to the aid of their countries, continents, and common civilization.

A spectre is haunting the Americas—the spectre of ethno-nationalism. The history of all postindustrial society is the history of identity struggles. The US-style globalization that has sprouted from the ruins of European colonialism has not done away with ethnic and racial antagonisms. It has but established a majority global middle class that, when faced with income stagnation, instinctively succumbs to ancient hatreds and fears readily mobilized by authoritarian movements and manipulated by their leaders.

Two things result from this fact:

I. Ethno-nationalism, and the xenophobic populism it spawns, is already acknowledged by all the world's advanced powers to be itself a power of great destruction to globalization's present and future. Global society as a whole is more and more splitting up into two great hostile camps directly facing each other—Integrators dedicated to preserving and growing the global commonwealth and Separators dedicated to prioritizing and preserving distinct identities that invariably privilege one group over another.

II. It is high time that Americanists—proponents of the uniquely fused civilization comprising the Americas—should openly, in the face of the whole world, publish their views, their aims, their tendencies, and confront this Spectre of Ethno-nationalism with a manifesto of their own—a grand strategy of progressive hemispheric integration.

To this end, Americanists acknowledge that climate change is driving species away from a Middle Earth that grows increasingly hostile to sustainable economics and thus eventually impractical in many instances for independent political statehood.

High-latitude powers have three choices: First, they accept these growing waves of climate refugees out of a moral responsibility, suffering their disruptive social impact while profiting from their economic contributions. Second, they wall themselves off from this disaster zone, condemning some measure of those so geographically cursed to a harsh, marginalized, and resentful existence certain to breed violent extremism. Third, they extend to these peoples and their states new forms of economic and political belonging, the material benefits of which enable a certain local resiliency that limits the poleward flow of climate refugees and contains any ungovernable spaces that may emerge.

Globalization's five superpowers will each attempt some combination of these options, with the United States, EU, and Russia able to accept climate migrants. China will continue offering new forms of economic belonging, an approach rising India eventually copies. Only Brussels and Washington can politically pursue the third option, as few states are eager to join any union dominated by Beijing, Moscow, or New Delhi.

Here the Americanist spots a competitive advantage in the superpower brand wars: the Americas are far better poised for latitudinal integration than either of the other two "vertical slices" (Center, Asia). Our winning throughlines include:

1. A long history of interstate peace and stable, undisputed borders
2. The world's #1 military power, with no peer on global reach and power projection
3. Expanding resource advantages in energy, water, and agriculture
4. All the attractions and benefits of nearshoring global value chains
5. Shared origins and histories fused into a unique hemispheric civilization that has far outgrown its source continents
6. High-latitude states featuring low population densities, high-income economies, and reasonably well-run governments
7. Core diversity factors (languages, religions, racial/ethnic identities, etc.) numbering far lower than those bedeviling Asia and the Center

8. North-South economic match that makes demographic sense labor-wise, while elevating our hemispheric market to better approximate the demand signals of midcentury behemoths China and India
9. North-South political match between continents where high measures of political and economic freedom are the norm
10. Of the three vertical zones created by climate change, the Western Hemisphere is the only one not to feature two rivalrous superpowers

For America to win this century, our views, aims, and tendencies should logically coalesce around a grand strategy of enlarging our borders, expanding our definitions of citizenship, and extending to our hemisphere a transparent pathway to sovereign statehood in a Union once again accepting new members.

This is how our nation successfully adapts our slice of the world to climate change, scales up to compete with China and India, prevents Latin America's capture by extra-hemispheric powers, gets back to the business of growing this Union, and surmounts its current disunity by creating a future worthy of our citizens' shared ambitions and passions.

Americans of the hemisphere—unite!

43 *Thesis:* American Acceptionalism

> Frozen at fifty states, America strategically retreats as other superpowers extend spheres of influence—and borders. We need to re-embrace growth, looking primarily south.

I f America does not admit a new state before I die, I will be the first Barnett—in a long line of Barnetts—to be born and die under the same flag. Barack Obama, born one year earlier, would be the first US president to suffer this fate. Track the growth of these United States across seven generations of my family:

★ Joseph Barnett (born 1754) saw thirteen colonies form a new nation, and then grow to twenty-six states total before he died in 1838.

★ His son Andrew (born 1797) witnessed eighteen states join the Union, only to see it rip apart as he passed in 1862.

★ Then came Jared (1831–1911), who, across his tumultuous eight decades, watched nine new states join, nine leave in a rebellion (only to be forcibly readmitted), and then another thirteen added.

★ Jared's boy Harry (1864–1948), who was born under Lincoln and died under Truman, had his national flag expand from thirty-five to forty-eight stars.

★ My grandfather J.E. (1896–1983) got five new stars.

★ His only son, my dad, John (1922–2004), made do with just Alaska and Hawaii.

★ As for me (1962 and counting), I am looking at bupkis (!) with all this anti-immigrant fervor and Red-versus-Blue State hostility, even as our competitors scheme to bulk themselves up.

When America's Founding Fathers dreamed of the American System of political, economic, social, and territorial integration, they were not just contemplating our horizontal slice of North America. Visionaries like Alexander

Hamilton (a Caribbean immigrant) and later Henry Clay (who coined the term "American System") imagined that expanding Union eventually accepting all—in Clay's words—"real and true Americans." It was this hemispheric ambition, clearly missing today, that got us twenty-eight different Old Glories over twenty-five decades. So why is America closed for business today?

Blame it on our Cold War containment strategy, which turned America into a status-quo-protecting power, in turn gnarling our historical roots. Thanks to 9/11 and the Cold War babies (Boomers, Gen Xers) still in charge, we have grown obsessed with defending our borders while the rest of our superpower competitors plan and act *bigger*:

★ The EU began as six states in 1957, doubled that total across the rest of the Cold War, and then celebrated its end with sixteen more (losing the UK in 2020). Ten current applicants can eventually raise the total to thirty-seven states. Do not be surprised to see the UK—or parts thereof—rejoin.

★ Upon partitioned independence in 1947, India began as a union of ancient principalities that were systematically consolidated or divvied up into twenty-eight states and eight territories, with the last state (Telangana) formed as recently as 2014. While not adding territory, India nonetheless engages in considerable state-building, not unlike how America once constructed new states and admitted new members across its western territories. India remains acutely aware of its potential for dismemberment due to (a) having summarily lost Pakistan and Bangladesh (then West and East Pakistan, respectively) to the United Kingdom's partitioning of British India, (b) continuing border tension with China, and (c) chronic internal threats from numerous insurgencies seeking state independence.

★ China, upon declaring the People's Republic in 1949, has added Xinjiang Province, Hainan Island, Tibet, Hong Kong, and Macao, in addition to expanding its borders with Russia and Tajikistan. In the China Sea, it has created and claimed new islands. Taiwan remains target #1 and the most immediate pathway to direct military conflict with the United States. Beyond reconstituting imperial China, Beijing seeks, through its Belt and Road Initiative, to execute a form of sovereignty-incursion within partner states through the widespread application of social-control technologies and networks, to which it maintains access, allowing for stealthy and discreet overseas police actions at the time of its choosing.

★ Russia, reborn in the Soviet Union's collapse, has clawed back pieces of its old empire from Moldova (1992), Belarus (1998 union), Georgia (2008), and Ukraine (2014 and 2022+). Every cycle, the West imagines Moscow might be satisfied with its latest capture and finally stop this behavior—only to be yet again disabused of such optimism. Like China's threat to Taiwan, these military interventions, while narrow in scope, nonetheless offer the most plausible scenarios for triggering World War III among nuclear superpowers.

Amidst all this, America cannot even manage to admit Puerto Rico or the District of Columbia—both of which want in. Puerto Rico would immediately become the thirtieth largest US state by population. Despite being our territory for more than a century, the island has no congressional representation, and its citizens cannot vote in our national elections. What does that say about how far America has strayed from its origins as a revolutionary, integrating force?

None of our competitors are growing their unions for reasons of economic efficiency; they do so because they find the alternative to be unacceptable—namely, ceding hegemony of their "near abroad" (Russia's term) to competing great powers. But not us. China builds and operates major ports on both ends of the Panama Canal and we do not blink an eye. Ditto for Beijing's twenty-one Belt-and-Road-Initiative partners across Latin America. Russia props up dictatorships in Nicaragua, Cuba, and Venezuela, and we refuse to even invite those states to the Summit of the Americas, as though we are above engaging Moscow on that competition even as we underwrite Ukraine's resistance.

Meanwhile, Washington continues busying itself in a bloody and counterproductive War on Drugs, Richard Nixon's most catastrophic strategic error, as our foreign policy cornerstone for Latin America. Yet we are dumbfounded to discover that the world views our government as increasingly irrelevant in our so-called backyard.

America's long history of accepting immigrants tells us everything we need to know about where our demographic future lies—namely, to our south.

Immigrants, overwhelmingly Latino, will account for all of America's population growth over this century. Without that influx, we are a rapidly aging—and thus precipitously declining—Japan in the making. With it, we continue to enjoy a nonstop, completely artificial demographic dividend that is incredibly advantageous to our economy.

Immigration is a net jobs creator while technology is a net jobs eliminator; it is as simple as that. Reconceptualizing those economic realities as the Great Replacement Theory is pure demographic escapism—magical thinking to postpone White America's inevitable acceptance of its natural diminishment within our Union's parallel diminishment within globalization. America can decide that it is done with globalization, but globalization is not done with America. No amount of wall building or political nostalgia will change that.

Accept that larger reality and we can move our nation back toward some understanding of its still-crucial role in shaping globalization's future. Run from it, and we might as well resign ourselves to junior partner status to some combination of China, India, and the EU—not *if* but *when*. This is the path trod by post-Brexit "Global Britain," now reduced to cynical dreams of becoming Europe's Singapore. Oh, how the mighty have fallen: London's "banksters" money-laundering for globalization's nefarious elites.

The alternative to this depressing and disempowering path, one still clearly within our reach, is to reposition our Union as globalization's most recognized, attractive, emulated, and accessible influencer—and thus its integrator of choice. Right now, the EU can rightfully claim to best represent globalization's model of political integration, while China aims to best reflect globalization's future economic integration. America can either sit back and enjoy that ride or decide it wants to reenter and thus reframe that competition, recapturing what Gen Zs would call its "main character energy."

If we choose to do so, we must lead with a killer app: namely, the soft-power lure of eventual membership in larger definitions of our Union. It is, dare I say, America's trump card.

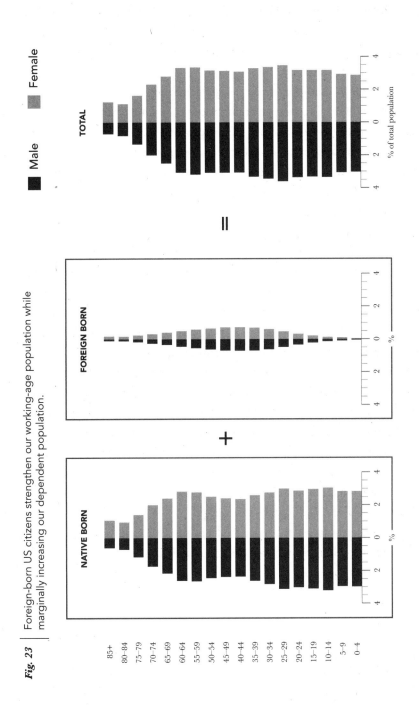

Fig. 23 Foreign-born US citizens strengthen our working-age population while marginally increasing our dependent population.

44 *Antithesis:*
American Apartheid

As America devolves into White minority rule, the fastest route back to majority rule is to accelerate—by expanding our Union—the demographics driving that authoritarian reaction.

merica's political polarization is a cautionary tale for globalization, for it arises by choice—the cherished ability of Americans to live where they want within our country. US journalist Bill Bishop famously described this self-segregation as the "Big Sort"—an internal migration where we Americans "seek our own kind in like-minded churches, like-minded neighborhoods, and like-minded sources of news and entertainment."

The result is a concentration of political like-mindedness, as Blue cities, counties, and states grow bluer, while Red small towns, counties, and states grow redder. As Bishop noted, "People don't need to check voting records to know the political flavor of a community. They can smell it."

Expand that self-selection dynamic to a global scale and realize why national governments worry so over mass migrations and how they can concentrate like-minded citizens within nations, rebalancing national identities and often polarizing them. While this is misleadingly framed by anti-immigration forces along racial lines, what they really fear is *the end of our way of life*.

That charge has been leveled numerous times across US history, starting with our revolution against British imperial rule. In the nineteenth century, the key "way of life" distinction was slavery, which sorted the Union into free and slave states—a powder-keg dynamic now dangerously replicated over reproductive rights. Across the twentieth century, mass urbanization and migration came to be viewed by many Americans as first threatening rural life, then small-town life, and finally the White "way of life" underpinning "real America." Far from "replacing" anyone, the Big Sort rearranges everyone geographically—a very American dynamic in a civilization built on, and shaped by, migration.

While America truly is a "melting pot" union, that mixing does not reach down as far in society as we imagine. Not at all atomizing identity, the American model allows for the fierce assertion of cross-cutting identities, with each version triggering its own blowback: race with racism, nationality with xenophobia, ethnicity with bigotry, religion with intolerance, gender with misogyny, sexual orientation with homophobia, and so on. We cannot have the mixing without the friction, but suffering the friction does not invalidate the mixing. The grand sweep of history demonstrates there is great progress to be found in tolerating diversity—however challenging it sometimes becomes.

Our Union's vast panoply of tribes offers individuals infinite opportunities for blended identities, yet we remain distinctly tribal in how we choose to live those identities. Rather than giving lie to the notion of a melting pot, this enduring dynamic only indicates just what a perfect avatar America continues to be for globalization's future: not one of soul-crushing homogenization but vibrant, life-unleashing heterogeneity—not some tasteless gruel but a mouth-watering smorgasbord. We have earned, and continue to earn, our right to lead in this manner, not because our Union is perfect but because we never stop endeavoring to form a more perfect Union.

Nonetheless, the Big Sort's political fallout is profound: by concentrating ideological like-mindedness, both national parties have grown safer in their seats, more extreme in their positions, and less willing to reach across the aisle. By embracing Donald Trump's ethno-nationalism, the GOP adopts an authoritarian ethos by ignoring, strong-arming, and destroying long-standing political norms—most damagingly with the Big Lie about the 2020 national election and its transparently fascistic "election integrity" campaign.

The Right's ethno-nationalism now openly embraces self-segregation as a godsend because of the electoral advantages it provides to a minority party that depends on the unequal representation found in the US Senate, where tiny Wyoming cancels the vote of a California sixty-seven times its size in population.

Nationhood is shared identity. When national identity is fractured and separated into opposing camps, that *apartness* congeals into an *apart-hood* of unequal citizenship recalling *apartheid* South Africa. That regime's laws banned mixed-race marriages, restricted Blacks' access to unions and certain public spaces, and limited Blacks' ability to travel or reside within the country—an institutionalized racism highly reminiscent of the American South's lengthy Jim

Crow era (1870s–1960s). During apartheid, South African Blacks essentially forfeited all their political rights whenever they stepped out of their designated homelands—a geo-locational form of restricted or partitioned citizenship.

In apartheid South Africa's authoritarian regime, inequality before the law was based on race. In America today, that inequality—long institutionalized against people of color—finds renewed expression along identity lines (e.g., gender, sexual orientation, religiosity [or lack thereof], ideology), fostering sharp inequalities in voting rights, reproductive care, education, healthcare, law enforcement, incarceration rates, and so on.

Increasingly, our rights as Americans vary by geo-location, meaning rights we enjoy in one state disappear the second we cross over to another state—like abortion rights today. Now, right-wing extremists plot to tag red states' citizens with legal restrictions designed to travel with them—ball-and-chain-like—whenever they step out of their designated home states. Replace bounty-hunting slavers with bounty-hunting forced-birthers and today we can say that Mrs. Dred Scott is alive and at risk if she is living in the wrong state.

As we citizens are trackable in real time, thanks to our smartphones, we are at risk of being subjected to overlapping, apartheid-enabling regulatory regimes that give lie to the notion that all stand equal before the law.

Americans live in an era of minority rule, when presidents can be unpopularly elected (2000, 2016) and state legislatures rigged for domination by the far smaller of the two parties' bases. This structural imbalance reshaped the Supreme Court into a conservative supermajority despite GOP presidential candidates losing the popular vote in seven of the last eight national elections. With the Senate filibuster allowing forty members to torpedo any bill, GOP senators representing a mere 19 percent of the US electorate regularly wield that veto. During South Africa's apartheid era, ruling Whites made up 19 percent of the population, demonstrating that such suppression of the popular will can be maintained for some time, providing you are willing to apply enough state-sponsored political violence to enforce order.

Political apartheid is but one of many signs of a democracy's growing illiberalism—or slide toward authoritarianism. America currently displays a number of these signs, the most frustrating to this political scientist being the absolute decline of Congress's legislative activity. This not only forces judicial activism—politicizing the courts—but it also reflects the purely performative nature of being a politician today: one holds office to *be someone* (i.e., not *them*), not to *do something* (accomplished now by simply preventing *their* rule).

Such political stalemating conforms to the alt-right's strategy of accelerationism: political violence designed to trigger a "cleansing" civil war and a revolution reestablishing "real" (read, White Christian) American civilization. Fortunately, history shows that highly fractionalized political systems are no more prone to civil war than homogenous ones.

That record should give the alt-right's opponents the confidence to fight that "fire" with some of their own—namely, accelerating Whites' transition to majority-minority status. If the days of White privilege are numbered, then speeding that countdown changes nothing except the duration of the social pain we must collectively endure. Indeed, with the extreme Right working so openly to slow that countdown through various electoral, legislative, regulatory, and judicial schemes—many of which pervert the spirit of our laws and hollow out our democracy—such an effort arguably restores balance to competing political movements.

Putting aside promoting higher birth rates, which never works in modern societies, an anti-alt-right accelerationism is best accomplished inorganically, either on a wholesale basis through higher immigration (too politically hard) or through a targeted mergers-and-acquisitions (M&A) approach of accepting new Union members—a less inconceivable notion when Latinos expand to one-third of your electorate by midcentury.

The M&A approach has the added benefit of directly addressing the electoral imbalance distorting American politics. In contrast to expanding the House of Representatives, abolishing the Electoral College, or nullifying its operation through the proposed National Popular Vote Interstate Compact, all of which directly attack the Republicans' current structural advantage, admitting new states creates a more competitive playing field—despite what Great Replacement fearmongers proclaim.

As Republicans boost their appeal to Latinos—hardly a monolithic voting bloc—there is little reason to assume that the growth of non-White voters favors Democrats only. Given Latin America's long history of veering between rightist and leftist governments, it is fair to say that Latino voters are neither natural Democrats nor natural Republicans. Thus, when we grow our Union, the GOP is logically encouraged to shift back to its traditional pro-business, pro-military roots versus its current fixation on, and capture by, a narrow base of White Christian nationalism. America needs to get back to a political landscape in which both major parties work to craft ruling majorities that attract a genuine national majority of voters.

In the end, what expands our Union improves our Union, just as what expands globalization improves globalization. The corrective discord triggered by each process is both the price and the proof of our collective progress—no risk, no reward. Our destiny thus manifested, we are entirely incentivized—even compelled—to move forward to mutually beneficial outcomes that restore America's global leadership.

America does face existential threats. The first is a national evolution unreflective of our history-bending journey as a globalization-in-miniature. The second is a global future unreflective of our history-bending journey as globalization's progenitor. Our Union will not survive as a White Christian nationalist state, nor will it survive in a world of China's uncontested making.

America's fate is inextricably intertwined with that of globalization. Per American poet Robert Frost, "The best way out is always through."

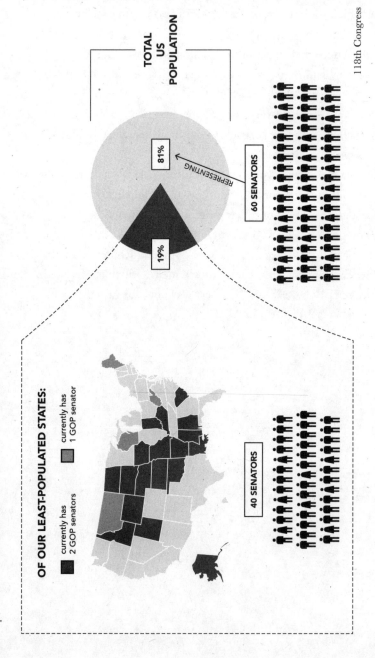

Fig. 24 | Forty GOP senators can prevent the Senate from moving legislation forward.

OF OUR LEAST-POPULATED STATES:

currently has
2 GOP senators

currently has
1 GOP senator

40 SENATORS

TOTAL
US
POPULATION

81%

19%

REPRESENTING

60 SENATORS

118th Congress

45 *Synthesis:* Mil Millones de Americanos

Climate change forces a shotgun wedding between Anglo and Latin Americas. The way to make it work is not by mass immigration but state assimilation into a larger American Union.

In his 2020 book, US liberal journalist Matthew Yglesias made the case for *One Billion Americans* through (a) more vigorous public- and private-sector support for larger families, and (b) reform of the US immigration system to accommodate a far larger inbound flow. Aggressively expanding the US population, he argued, would help us keep up with rising China—a country our equal in territory.

Right instinct, wrong path.

We do not need to overstuff America to match China and India's economic demand signal; we simply need to grow these United States—a political process that is, on paper, surprisingly easy and straightforward. Per the US Constitution (Article IV, section 3, clause 1), all it takes is the applying political entity to hold a popular referendum, typically triggering Congress's request for that entity to draw up an acceptable constitution. Once both sides approve the devised ruleset, Congress passes a resolution thereupon signed by the president, who proclaims the new state and orders an updated flag for the next Fourth of July. The reason our ruleset is so simple is that we spent most of our history rapidly admitting members. It is how we built the United States and what it is built for.

The Western Hemisphere holds one billion souls *now*. We do not need to invite more people in; we just need to actualize what we already share—two resource-blessed continents and a blended hemispheric culture decidedly advantaged for the tumultuous, transformative, and trying decades ahead. Eventual statehood is the lure, but anything short of that still places us collectively on a path that is a soft-power success unto itself. The journey is everything, so long as we engage this process with open hearts and minds.

Understand, this is not a path where America simply gets what it wants, but one in which the rest of the Americas get what they deserve—namely, the preservation and expansion of the hemisphere's burgeoning-but-vulnerable middle class amidst climate change's tectonic reshaping of our shared environment. Democracies live or die with their middle class. The same will be true of this expanding American Experiment: America wins or loses in concert with our hemisphere.

Likewise understand that this is primarily a defensive US grand strategy. America's superpower competitors will similarly experiment in ways that— from today's immediate perspective—are inconceivable. But climate change already redefines our sense of what is conceivable and inconceivable within our lifetimes. The Anthropocene beckons. We should pay attention less out of the threat generated than out of the opportunities afforded, because we will live in a far different world located on the far side of this transformation.

Powers both great and small will be forced to try all sorts of economic, security, and political schemes to avoid, or at least mitigate, Middle Earth's depopulation over this century. If Northern states want to avoid uncontrollable migrant flows, then we need to construct and extend channels of aid and investment designed to expand social resiliency across Middle Earth. We can attempt that primarily as intervening external powers, but that limits our ability to make sure money and resources are well spent, yielding downstream success—and profits. We are likely to do better when we formally link those capacity-building efforts with those states' progress toward deeper membership in shared economic and political unions. That promised extension of economic security by superpowers will constitute the twenty-first-century equivalent of a nuclear umbrella—as in, *step under our protection and plan your economic future with confidence.* This is essentially the EU's "carrot" of accession and what China promises with its Belt and Road Initiative, which, despite Western criticism, consistently delivers local economic growth among its lower-income partner states.

America cannot compete without a similar offering, meaning we picked the worst possible moment to go all nativist. The fact that the UK picked a similar moment to do the same only proves just how mistaken we are to continue that "special relationship." London's days of mentoring anybody are long gone.

In all these arguments, I do not ask you to consider this pathway because it is progressive, cool, or visionary; I am telling you that America will inevitably attempt such integrating schemes out of necessity and even desperation.

That being the case, we need to start this conversation now. Americans have long argued that it would be better not to burden our military with so much of our foreign policy agenda. This would be a path of lightening that load, de-militarizing our foreign policy, and enlisting a truly Whole of Government approach to our long-ignored hemisphere. It would also represent a US grand strategy far more likely to engage our younger generations.

Finally, we need to gain some perspective on the challenges ahead, as there are crucial questions yet to be systematically addressed:

- ★ How many people across Middle Earth will be put on the move?
- ★ How many can we in the North practically hope to maintain in place?
- ★ Of those put on the move, how many can and should Northern states accommodate?
- ★ How many Middle Earth nations will suffer state failure?
- ★ Of those that do, how many will be salvageable with outside help or extended forms of belonging in larger unions?
- ★ How many will be unsalvageable, and what should we do with them?

The list goes on and on.

America's foreign policy establishment will invariably scoff at the notion of preemptively engaging Latin America along these ambitious lines, citing those regions' long-standing back-burner status. Within the national security community, there will always be some overseas crisis deemed more worthy of our focused attention. That is because too many of them still think of the United States as a peerless global hegemon facing a handful of "near-peer competitors," when the truth is, America itself has slipped into the near-peer ranks in most domains—save hard military power and soft brand power.

In response, I am again compelled to inquire: If not the Western Hemisphere, then where better to lock in our status as the regionally integrating force of note? Is anyone under the impression that America can steer Asia's future integration *more* than China? Manage Russia's long-term relationship with Europe *more* than Europe itself? Ensure the Middle East's stability *more* than primary customers China and India? Or even regional hegemons Israel and Saudi Arabia? Finance Africa's massive urbanization processes *more* than that continent's de facto World Bank, China?

It is not pie in the sky to advocate that the United States concentrate on leading its hemisphere's economic and political integration. Rather, it is all that is left on our plate in terms of realistically pooled sovereignty. It will not get any better than that, and nothing beyond is feasible until we achieve it. America can most definitely say no to this ambition, but none other is in the offing—nor even remotely on target for the threats, crises, and opportunities that will dominate our nation's future. Moreover, the longer we delay action, the more inevitable this task becomes in the face of our competitors' encroachment. We can neither run nor hide away from this future. It is already baked in, much like climate change.

Consider the choice from the opposite angle: Is there anything in the global scenarios presented here that suggests it will be better—or more realistic—for less-developed and emerging economies to navigate these turbulent decades by going it alone *versus* pooling their sovereignty (and risk) within multinational unions anchored by a like-minded superpower? Channeling the fictional detective Sherlock Holmes, *when you have examined the inevitable, then whatever is revealed, however inconceivable, must be the truth.* The truth here is that the supreme collision of climate change, an ascendant global middle class, and demographic collapse compels governments—North and South—to seek expanded and accelerated integration as a means for state survival and advancement across this century, the most structurally transformative period our world system has yet encountered.

To reject this challenge is to condemn your state to one or more forms of sovereign bankruptcy—political, economic, or security. This truth should shock no one in our United States, as none of our members would today enjoy more than a fraction of the wealth, power, and freedom afforded by our Union if they, in a fit of pique, were to exit. Without the logic and benefits of integration, our Union does not exist, which is why a grand strategy centered on that purpose is self-evidently—and entirely—American in nature. It is simply who we are.

The baseline economic arguments for undertaking this grand strategy are straightforward: Latin America and the Caribbean suffer from low levels of regional economic integration, as does the Western Hemisphere as a whole.

There is good money to be made there, particularly as our business community instinctively turns toward nearshoring strategies in response to the global economy's recent and ongoing tumults.

Latin America possesses the natural and human resources but often lacks sufficiently developed economic, political, and legal infrastructures, the upgrading of which should comprise the bulk of our Union's accession-credentialing process. As the editorial board of the *Washington Post* recently noted, the United States "must understand that the institutional challenges facing Latin America are not altogether unlike the ones confronting this country, with its own growing distrust of elites and multiple threats to democratic stability." Point being our nation-building journeys presently overlap—just as they often have.

Right now, the Chinese offer Latin America and the Caribbean hard infrastructure at low cost in return for management leases on the resulting facilities, along with attached sales of their social control technologies. If your country is lucky, the Chinese will not get too pushy as your government falls deeper in their debt (consider, for example, Ecuador), but there is no path forward to a stabilizing, empowering, or liberalizing membership in a larger China-led economic or political structure. China's dream is its own; your state can contribute to it but cannot partake of it.

A good example of this lopsided negotiating is Beijing's 2022 security agreement with the Solomon Islands—a deal that "allows both sides to maintain social order and protect lives and property in the South Pacific archipelago." Nice hegemony if you can get it, and a real shocker to the United States and its local allies.

Now imagine something more shocking but in the other direction, such as Washington and Manila initiating negotiations over the Philippines's multiple candidacies for US statehood. Inconceivable for a former US colony with a population of 100 million and an economy the size of Wisconsin? From today's perspective yes, and yet, contemplate how nations around the world might play that diplomatic card against an increasingly assertive China in the decades ahead. All we have to do is shuffle the deck and start dealing.

Emerging markets represent globalization's frontier, as in, economies that need to become firmly settled in global value chains—whatever their practical length. America's history of growth is one of integrating frontier economies, whether it was our Wild West, the nascent post–World War II West, or today's rapidly privatized space industry. Our model for such integration is so powerful that its major aspects now define globalization's core processes, making it the most impactful soft power we wield.

What is most challenging for US foreign policy right now is coming to grips with the reality that, in the superpower brand wars of this era's globalization, our integration offering is inferior to those of our prime competition—today, China and the EU in the economic and political realms, respectively. That reality can trigger a crisis of confidence; it can also feed our growing existential dread.

What it *should* do is humble us sufficiently to conceive of a better way forward, one in which we boost our attractiveness to other states, solicit their free association, financially incentivize their emulation, and accept their application for new membership in our growing and still-history-bending Union.

Our message to the world—but especially our hemispheric neighbors—must be: *Let us go forward in union.*

An Americas-First Grand Strategy: Crowdsourcing the Right Story, Choosing the Right Paths

CODA

Global trends support North-South integration in our hemisphere. To succeed, America must dictate less and listen more. The right story is out there, awaiting our joint articulation.

Globalization is a story that needs a happy ending, not a hopeful outcome to await but a future we feel compelled to create. In this time of troubles, I seek not to pander to your strongest emotions but to appeal to your enduring ambitions as Americans. Our patriotism traditionally—and uniquely—leans *forward*, anticipating achievements over harboring grievances. That enduring optimism is America's softest power, attracting talent and imitation the world over. Now, more than ever, we must re-harness it for the journey ahead.

For more than a decade, the world has witnessed America's slow retreat from global leadership while the power of the US presidency has withered at home and abroad. As fears of our decline proliferate, Americans grow addicted to today's opioid of the masses: elite-funded populism yielding angry-but-ineffectual political leaders given to polarizing strategies, disinformation operations, and scorched-earth tactics. Slouching toward Armageddon, we seem hell-bent on channeling George Orwell through George Floyd: *If you want a picture of the future, imagine a knee pressing on a human neck—forever.*

This is not who we are, or what we can be in this world.

I believe in America looking out for itself—first and foremost; I just think we too narrowly define its present and potential. We spend far too much energy debating our nation's past—an unreachable place to which today's unreasonable fears herd us. Unions evolve and expand, or they stagnate and shrink—just like globalization. We either grow with our creation or history strands us.

These United States are the greatest integrating force the world has ever seen. We are not an island nation given to self-preserving retreat. We are a continental power in an age of continental powers, and we have it within ourselves to anchor a truly hemispheric power in a future marked by South-North integration.

All I ask of you as an American citizen is to acknowledge our nation's world-shaping accomplishments, recognize our Union's history-bending trajectory, and accept the strategic challenge lying before us. America's greatness is undisputed: our model of security, economic, and political integration has unleashed more worldwide wealth creation and poverty reduction in the last seven decades than our European predecessors accomplished in five centuries. Our world is more peaceful now than it has ever been, and we enjoy a super-abundance of goods and services previously unknown in human history.

The price for those accomplishments is equally clear: we have remade our planet and must now reconfigure our maps, our nations, and our flags to accommodate the accelerating velocity of climate change. As globalization consolidates along latitudinal lines, there will be winners and losers. I want the United States to win that competition and believe that my fellow citizens—particularly younger generations—prefer the same over self-debasing alternatives.

The Pentagon recently asked the RAND Corporation to define the primary determinants of national competitiveness in the twenty-first century. The study identified seven indicators: a driving national ambition; widely shared opportunities for citizens; a coherent national identity not built on race; an active state; effective social institutions; an emphasis on learning and adaptation; and significant diversity and pluralism. As Michael J. Mazarr, who led the study, argues, "Countries with too little ambition, diversity, or willingness to adapt risk spiraling into decline." Point being that decline is *not* about other nations rising but your nation simply giving up and retreating into ethno-nationalism. Our choice is clear: we either build the future we want to see or content ourselves with living in a world defined by others.

The Americas-First grand strategy outlined here checks all seven of RAND's boxes simply by reconnecting our Union to its original animating impulses. Abraham Lincoln, our greatest leader, did much the same by front-loading America's post–Civil War Reconstruction with westward integrating impulses, for he realized that period's intense divisions were best overcome by a larger unifying process: not North punishing South but East integrating West. We need the same dynamic today, repairing our Union by expanding our Union.

I have chosen not to present any detailed plan for executing the grand strategy here proposed. That is an admission of both how early we are in any such campaign—despite the clear strategic urgency—and the great complexity awaiting our future engagement. It is also my recognition that plenty of models exist out there for our examination, comparison, and reconfiguring—a task beyond any one book and arguably only achievable through listening to, and dialogue with, those hemispheric neighbors we deem most suitable for pioneering this path. Finally, I did not wish to impart the impression of this vision being somehow limited, in any application, to a small number of US government offices and agencies. As with all things globalization, I think our government enables while our business community creates and thereby leads.

My goal here has been to prepare you, the reader, for the inevitabilities lying ahead, along with opening your mind to possible solution sets that will invariably strike many of you as inconceivable from today's fixed perspective.

I realize my arguments represent a bold leap for many of us who, just a few years ago, elected a president whose foreign policy mantra was to "build that wall." But it is exactly in times like this that *inconceivables* succumb to *inevitabilities*. Better to bull-rush a looming problem than cower in waiting.

In his autobiography, *My Early Life*, Winston Churchill observed, "Scarcely anything material or established which I was brought up to believe was permanent or vital, has lasted. Everything I was sure or taught to be sure was impossible, has happened." We must embrace such humility for the task ahead.

Like that Greatest Generation and the world they worked so hard to bestow on us, Americans must summon the courage to navigate an equally transformative journey into a future worth creating and entirely within our grasp.

I am certain that it will be America's most glorious adventure yet.

ACKNOWLEDGMENTS

I never expected to write this book. Not because of a lack of desire to, but because I did not see myself joining a firm capable of providing me the vision, time, resources, and collaborators necessary to pull off something of this scope. One of the smartest things I have ever done was to respond to—in the middle of the COVID pandemic—an out-of-the-blue LinkedIn message from Throughline's founder, Scott Williams, politely inquiring about my thoughts on the US military's rapid pull-out from Afghanistan.

In just a few short months, that conversation led to both this book and my joining Throughline, a genuine dream come true for an analyst who has long sought a proper work environment for what I do best: crafting and sharing compelling stories about the future of our world, along with ideas on America's role in shaping it. This book constitutes the greatest creative experience of my career, and I owe it all to Scott. I remain forever in his debt for his decision to seek out and orchestrate our collaboration.

Beyond the impresario Scott and his successor CEO, Brandon Jones, I owe a debt of gratitude to several immensely talented professionals at Throughline for their contributions to, and collaboration with me on, this text. First and foremost is my very own Yoda, vice president for enterprise design Julie Anixter, who brought a wealth of wisdom and experience as she coached me throughout the writing of this book. She is a muse of the first order and now a guiding force in my career. Second is director of graphic recording Jim Nuttle, who, along with daughter Sara Nuttle, is responsible for the brilliant illustrations throughout the volume. Collaborating with both was a blast—a creative luxury I never imagined I would enjoy. Third is senior business strategist Tom Zorc, who expertly captained this unprecedented initiative from launch to landing. His keen judgment is reflected throughout the book and, as such, I focused my efforts on impressing him as the target reader.

Just outside that inner circle are senior content strategist Liz Gaither and associate business strategist Maura Collins, who expertly managed all manner of processes surrounding this book's creation and marketing efforts. If our enterprise was a naval ship, Liz was our XO, while Maura was my go-to right-hand throughout. In combination, their sharing the load made this intense effort a true joy for this author.

A special thanks goes to Throughline's creative director, Julia Tylor, for her design of the cover, which was a fascinatingly iterative collaboration overseen by BenBella's art director, Sarah Avinger. Enterprise design firms like ours live and die with leaders like Julia, and it was a great privilege to work with such a singular, Don Draper–like talent. Behind Julia stood both senior creative advisor Rebecca Williams and art director Jeff Bade, whose creative inputs are likewise reflected throughout this book.

As for the two dozen brilliantly executed data visualizations sprinkled throughout the volume, there the credit lies completely with principal designers Juraj Mihalik and Tom Zorc and senior designer Will Simms. The care and creativity all three brought to this effort were outstanding.

Throughline's executives are experts at managing creative talent and throughout this intense effort I greatly benefited from the combined efforts of strategy principal Shaun Budnik, senior advisor Erica Rossi, and my executive sponsor, Trevor Brown. Even after three decades in this business, they each taught me plenty about the work and my proper role in it.

Finally, at Throughline, I must extend my thanks to senior content strategists Myrthe Doedens and Andi Martin for their red team review of the book's illustrations, as well as to principal content strategist Amanda Sadler for her scrutiny of the data visualizations. Their keen feedback moved that needle.

Shifting to our publisher, BenBella, there are an equal number of talented professionals to acknowledge. First, of course, is publisher and CEO Glenn Yeffeth, who immediately understood our ambitions and intentions—and fears—with this book. Glenn's initial thirty-page (!) editorial feedback on the first draft was something I will never forget. By following his proposed reordering of the content, I finally and completely understood what I was trying to say with this book. It was a great gift on his part, and the effort I had to put in to satisfy his vision of the book was the creative peak of this journey.

Editor Rachel Phares was everything an author could ask for, eliminating any and all concerns on flow, tone, and accessibility. Her guidance and calm presence throughout effectively balanced this author's consistent lurching between fear and fortitude, and for that I am most grateful. Drilling down, I also gratefully acknowledge the efforts of copy editor Judy Gelman Myers and proofreaders Lisa Story and Michael Fedison.

Having previously worked with a major publishing house, I have to say that I was completely blown away by the energy, creativity, and customized care that everyone at BenBella brought to this collective effort. Production editor Kim Broderick and production assistant Isabelle Rubio expertly managed the book's physical and electronic transformations, while senior marketing director Jennifer Canzoneri oversaw an innovative media campaign with the support of marketing assistants Kellie Doherty, Jenny Rosen, and Amy Preston. COO Adrienne Lang managed the book's strategic packaging and positioning, ably assisted by vendor content manager Alicia Kania, senior publishing associate Susan Welte, publishing assistant Madeline Grigg, and customer service representative Raquel Moreno. On the administrative side, I gratefully acknowledge CFO Aida Herrera and her team of Lise Engel, Debbie Petersen, and Mallory Frost. BenBella's reputation as an author-friendly publishing house is totally deserved and I look forward to working with their entire crew in the years ahead.

Finally, I want to acknowledge the forbearance of my immediate family. Writing a book is a supremely selfish and self-centered endeavor, and my spouse, Vonne, and still (then) at-home kids, Jerry, Vonne Mei, Metsu, and Abebu, were generously accommodating of my needs and habits across the generation and assembly of this material. Their collective moral support, along with that of eldest offspring, Emily and Kevin—plus daughter-in-law Ana—remains my primary motivation as an author, husband, and father. They are my tribe, and our love for one another means everything to me.

ENDNOTES

Preface—Globalization's Throughlines: Restoring US Global
Leadership in a Turbulent Era

1   *America was fantastically . . . previous five centuries.* Max Roser, "Extreme Poverty:
    How Far Have We Come, How Far Do We Still Have to Go?" Our World
    in Data Web Page, November 2021, retrieved from https://ourworldindata.org
    /extreme-poverty-in-brief; and Roser, "World GDP over the Last Two Millen-
    nia," in "Economic Growth," Our World in Data Web Page, 2017, retrieved from
    https://ourworldindata.org/economic-growth.

2   *Even in the . . . long thought impossible.* Homi Kharas and Kristopher Hamel,
    "A Global Tipping Point: Half the World Is Now Middle Class or Wealthier,"
    Brookings (blog), September 27, 2018, retrieved from https://www.brookings.edu
    /blog/future-development/2018/09/27/a-global-tipping-point-half-the-world-is
    -now-middle-class-or-wealthier/.

3   *Russia's Vladimir Putin . . . own new maps.* Gerald F. Seib, "Putin and Xi's Bet
    on the Global South: As Their Relations with the West Deteriorate, Russia and
    China Are Seeking to Rewire Global Power Flows in Way That Will Work to
    Their Advantage for Years to Come," *Wall Street Journal*, July 15, 2022, retrieved
    from https://www.wsj.com/articles/putin-and-xis-bet-on-the-global-south
    -11657897521.

3   *India's minister of . . . and economic development.* "India's Duty to Become Voice
    of Global South: Jaishankar," India Today Web Page, January 7, 2023, retrieved
    from https://www.indiatoday.in/india/story/india-duty-voice-global-south
    -world-looking-at-with-high-hopes-s-jaishankar-external-affairs-minister
    -2318481-2023-01-07.

3   *America's economic future . . . change's destabilizing impact.* Karen Ward and Fred-
     eric Neumann, "Consumer in 2050: The Rise of the EM Middle Class," *HSBC
     Global Research*, October 2012, retrieved from https://www.lampadia.com/assets
     /uploads_documentos/0abb2-hsbc_report_consumer_in_2050_en.pdf.

Frankenstein's Monster: Coming to Grips with Our Most Powerful Creation (Throughline One)

9   *By the early . . . global economic activity.* "GDP—Gross Domestic Product," country
     economy.com Web Page, retrieved February 22, 2023, from countryeconomy
     .com/gdp?year=1980.

11   *When global institutions . . . its wealth-creating whirlwind.* On this evolution,
     see Michael N. Barnett, Jon C. W. Pevehouse, and Kal Raustiala, eds., *Global
     Governance in a World of Change,* Cambridge, UK: Cambridge University Press,
     retrieved from https://www.cambridge.org/core/services/aop-cambridge-core
     /content/view/C0DC56A9BFB9580143D001A373113501/9781108843232AR
     .pdf/Global_Governance_in_a_World_of_Change.pdf.

12   *Our nation needs . . . artificial intelligence (AI).* My thanks to Stephen F. DeAnge-
     lis, president and CEO of Enterra Solutions LLC and Massive Dynamics LLC,
     for this analysis.

The Empty Throne: Globalization Comes with Rules but No Ruler (Thread 1)

15   *Pre-nineteenth-century globalization . . . the mid-50s since.* Esteban Ortiz-Ospina
     and Diana Beltekian, "Globalization over Five Centuries" in "Trade and Global-
     ization," Our World in Data Web Page, October 2018, retrieved from https://
     ourworldindata.org/trade-and-globalization.

15   *Despite the flatlining . . . unlike big-market superpowers.* "Trade Openness—
     Country Rankings," theGlobalEconomy.com Web Page, retrieved February 22,
     2023, from https://www.theglobaleconomy.com/rankings/trade_openness/.

16   *That post-WWII, US-led . . . pre–World War I peak.* Ortiz-Ospina and Beltekian,
     "Growth of Global Exports" in "Trade and Globalization."

16   *In doing so . . . imperial rule ($8.5T).* Roser, "World GDP over the Last Two
     Millennia."

16   *Even adding in . . . world-spanning colonial empire.* Roser, "GDP Per Capita, 1820
     to 2018" in "Economic Growth."

16 *No matter how . . . global population today.* Roser, "Extreme Poverty."

17 *Headquartered in Geneva . . . and dispute resolution.* "WTO in Brief," World Trade Organization, retrieved February 22, 2023, from www.wto.org/english/thewto _e/whatis_e/inbrief_e/inbr_e.htm.

17 *Moreover, these preferential . . . into their texts.* Todd Allee, Manfred Elsig, and Andrew Lugg, "The Ties Between the World Trade Organization and Preferential Trade Agreements: A Textual Analysis," *Journal of International Economic Law* 20, no. 2 (2017), retrieved from doi.org/10.1093/jiel/jgx009.

17 *After first appearing . . . in force worldwide.* "Integrated Database," World Trade Organization Web Page, retrieved February 22, 2023, from https://www.wto.org /english/tratop_e/region_e/region_e.htm.

17 *More importantly, most . . . among developing economies.* World Trade Organization, *World Trade Report 2011*, 55, retrieved from https://www.wto.org/english /res_e/booksp_e/anrep_e/world_trade_report11_e.pdf.

17 *When we add . . . of some sort.* Ortiz-Ospina and Beltekian, "Share of Bilateral and Unilateral Trade Partnerships Around the World" in "Trade and Globalization."

17 *Trade among rich . . . hugely positive legacy.* Ortiz-Ospina and Beltekian, "Share of Global Exports by Income Level of the Trade Partners" in "Trade and Globalization."

17 *Abundant historical data . . . technologies created elsewhere.* Esteban Ortiz-Ospina, "Does Trade Cause Growth?" Our World in Data Web Page, October 22, 2018, retrieved from https://ourworldindata.org/trade-and-econ-growth.

The Eye-of-the-Storm Fallacy: Americans' Poor Understanding of Globalization (Thread 2)

22 *While Americans constitute . . . to five times).* Jean-Paul Rodrigue, "Share of the World Commodity Consumption, China and the United States, c2020," from *The Geography of Transport Systems* (New York: Routledge, 2020) and retrieved from https://transportgeography.org/contents/chapter7/freight-transportation -value-chains/usa-china-commodity-consumption/.

22 *A good example: . . . China's vast audience.* Shirley Li, "How Hollywood Sold Out to China: A Culture of Acquiescing to Beijing's Censors Is Now the Norm, and There's Little Sign of it Changing," *The Atlantic*, September 10, 2021, retrieved from https://www.theatlantic.com/culture/archive/2021/09/how-hollywood -sold-out-to-china/620021/.

The World at War: Our Successful Downsizing of Conflict over the Years (Thread 3)

25   *We are a . . . time in history.* Steven Pinker, *The Better Angels of Our Nature: Why Violence Has Declined* (New York: Viking Press, 2011).

25   *To put that . . . world at war.* The low-end estimate of 60 million dead (15m military and 45m civilian) over eight years (1937–1945) equals 20,000 dead per day; see "Research Starters: Worldwide Deaths in World War II," The National WWII Museum, retrieved February 22, 2023, from www.nationalww2museum .org/students-teachers/student-resources/research-starters/research-starters-world wide-deaths-world-war.

25   *An effective way . . . State, and War.* Kenneth N. Waltz, *Man, the State, and War: A Theoretical Analysis* (New York: Columbia University Press, 1959).

26   *History is clear . . . like climate change.* Max Roser et al., "War and Peace," Our World in Data Web Page, retrieved February 22, 2023, from ourworldindata.org /war-and-peace.

Cold Wars as Comfort Food: The Pentagon's Need for a Near-Peer Competitor (Thread 4)

30   *The best example . . . narrow strategic bet.* Max Boot, "The Top Marine Faces Unprecedented Opposition. He Says That's 'Positive,'" *Washington Post*, July 20, 2022, retrieved from www.washingtonpost.com/opinions/2022/07/20/marine -corps-commandant-reforms-changing-force-role/.

31   *The prime example: . . . expanding middle-class populations.* Jonathan E. Hillman and Maesea McCalpin, "Watching Huawei's 'Safe Cities,'" Center for Strategic & International Studies Web Page, November 4, 2019, retrieved from https:// www.csis.org/analysis/watching-huaweis-safe-cities.

Nuclear Clubbing: America's Obsession with Preventing Proliferation (Thread 5)

33   *However, for every . . . were escorted, away.* For details, see Wikipedia's "List of States with Nuclear Weapons," retrieved February 22, 2023, from en.wikipedia .org/wiki/List_of_states_with_nuclear_weapons; and "Nuclear Proliferation," retrieved February 22, 2023, from en.wikipedia.org/wiki/Nuclear _proliferation.

35   *At the Cold . . . far smaller numbers.* Max Roser, Bastian Herre, and Joe Hasell, "Nuclear Weapons," Our World in Data Web Page (citing Arms Control Association), 2020, retrieved from ourworldindata.org/nuclear-weapons.

35 *China's military continues . . . the United States.* "And Then There Were Three: How Will America Deal with Three-Way Nuclear Deterrence? *The Economist*, November 29, 2022, retrieved from https://www.economist.com/united-states /2022/11/29/how-will-america-deal-with-three-way-nuclear-deterrence.

State-on-State War in the Post–Cold War Era: How America's New Rules Come Back to Haunt Us (Thread 6)

39 *During the Cold . . . one per year.* Roser et al., "War and Peace."

39 *Instead, the rising . . . twelve were internationalized.* Roser et al., "War and Peace."

39 *As for the . . . W. Bush administrations.* Roser et al., "War and Peace"; and Thomas P.M. Barnett, *The Pentagon's New Map: War and Peace in the Twenty-First Century* (New York: G.P. Putnam's Sons, 2004), 138–54.

40 *Unsurprisingly, the combination . . . across the 2010s.* Roser et al., "War and Peace."

41 *Everything Putin said . . . measure"—however brutal.* Darragh Roche, "Vladimir Putin Says He Was Forced to Invade Ukraine: 'No Other Choice,'" *Newsweek*, April 12, 2022, retrieved from www.newsweek.com/vladimir-putin-forced -invade-ukraine-war-russia-no-other-choice-1697208; and "Russia's Military Ops in Ukraine 'Forced Measure'; Don't Intend to 'Damage' Global Eco System: Putin," *Times of India*, February 24, 2022, retrieved from timesofindia .indiatimes.com/world/europe/russias-military-ops-in-ukraine-forced-measure -dont-intend-to-damage-global-eco-system-putin/articleshow/89809519.cms.

41 *As he stated . . . from this system."* (Transcript) "Meeting with Representatives of Russian Business Circles," President of Russia Web Page, February 24, 2022, retrieved from http://www.en.kremlin.ru/events/president/news/67846.

41 *The 97 percent . . . small consumer market.* "Russia's Share of Global GDP," World Economics Web Page, retrieved February 22, 2023, from www.worldeconomics .com/Share-of-Global-GDP/Russia.aspx.

41 *Given sufficient cause . . . for Moscow's oil.* Julian Lee (Bloomberg), "Putin's Few Oil Buyers Demand Deep Discounts," *Washington Post*, November 28, 2022, retrieved from https://www.washingtonpost.com/business/energy/putins-few -oil-buyers-demand-deep-discounts/2022/11/27/0496cf60-6e32-11ed-8619 -0b92f0565592_story.html.

Symmetrizing the Global War on Terror (GWOT): Our Badasses Are Better Than Your Bad Actors (Thread 7)

46 *For those of . . . additional US troops.* Thomas P.M. Barnett, "The Monks of War," *Esquire*, March 2006, retrieved from https://classic.esquire.com/article/2006 /3/1/the-monks-of-war.

46   *To justify America's . . . "pivot" to Asia.* Kenneth G. Lieberthal, "The American Pivot to Asia," Brookings Web Page, December 21, 2011, retrieved from www .brookings.edu/articles/the-american-pivot-to-asia/.

47   *Israel's stubborn GWOT-era . . . significant collateral damage.* Sebastien Roblin, "Mow the Lawn: Israel's Strategy for Perpetual War with the Palestinians," *National Interest* (blog), March 22, 2021, retrieved from nationalinterest.org /blog/buzz/mow-lawn-israel's-strategy-perpetual-war-palestinians-185775.

47   *Donald Trump correctly . . . leaders into "killers."* Peter Beinart, "For Trump, 'We Have a Lot of Killers' Isn't a Criticism," *The Atlantic*, February 6, 2017, retrieved from www.theatlantic.com/politics/archive/2017/02/for-trump-we-have-a-lot -of-killers-isnt-a-criticism/515748/.

America's New Map: Climate Change as Globalization's Next Ordering Principle (Thread 8)

49   *My book* The *. . .* Times *bestseller list.* Thomas P.M. Barnett, "The Pentagon's New Map: It Explains Why We're Going to War, and Why We'll Keep Going to War," *Esquire*, March 2003, retrieved from https://classic.esquire.com/article /2003/3/1/the-pentagons-new-map; and Barnett, *Pentagon's New Map.*

50   *In the last . . . of climate change.* Thomas P.M. Barnett, *Great Powers: America and the World After Bush* (New York: G. P. Putnam's Sons, 2009), 357–68.

Climate Changes Everything: A Horizontal World Made Vertical (Throughline Two)

53   *Ptolemy, the second-century . . . was on top.* Nick Danforth, "How the North Ended Up on Top of the Map," Aljazeera America, February 16, 2014, retrieved from http://america.aljazeera.com/opinions/2014/2/maps-cartographycolonialismnor theurocentricglobe.html.

54   *For example, human . . . than Mother Nature.* Andrew J. Plumptre et al., "Where Might We Find Ecologically Intact Communities?" *Frontiers in Forests and Global Change* 4 (2021), retrieved from https://www.frontiersin.org/articles/10 .3389/ffgc.2021.626635/full; and Bruce H. Wilkinson, "Humans as Geologic Agents: A Deep-Time Perspective," *GeoScience World* 33, no. 3 (2005), retrieved from https://pubs.geoscienceworld.org/gsa/geology/article-abstract/33/3/161 /29518/Humans-as-geologic-agents-A-deep-time-perspective.

54   *We have altered . . . on Earth today."* David Wallace-Wells, interview by Dave Davies, "Our New Climate Reality," *Fresh Air*, National Public Radio, November 10, 2022, retrieved from https://www.npr.org/2022/11/08/1135127652/our -new-climate-reality.

54 *In recognition of . . . detonating nuclear bombs.* "Anthropocene," National Geographic Resource Library Web Page, Encyclopedic Entry, retrieved February 22, 2023, from https://education.nationalgeographic.org/resource/anthropocene.

54 *In seeding and . . . rising surface temperatures.* "Great Acceleration," Welcome to the Anthropocene Web Page, retrieved February 22, 2023, from https://www.anthropocene.info/great-acceleration.php.

55 *The two dynamics . . . climate change denialism.* Ron Brackett, "America Leads Western Nations in Denying Climate Change, According to Poll," Energy Policy Institute at the University of Chicago Web Page, May 9, 2019, retrieved from https://epic.uchicago.edu/news/america-leads-western-nations-in-denying-climate-change-according-to-poll/.

55 *As Gaia Vince . . . have ever experienced."* Gaia Vince, *Nomad Century: How Climate Migration Will Reshape Our World* (New York: Flatiron Books, 2022), 7.

55 *We can hope . . . eventual "species-wide approach."* Vince, *Nomad Century*, xiii.

56 *Vince describes the . . . resources to combat.* Vince, *Nomad Century*, 10–30.

56 *America witnesses their . . . with government aid.* Justin Klawans, "Natural Disasters Displaced More Than 3 Million Americans in 2022, U.S. Census Says," *The Week*, February 12, 2023, retrieved from https://theweek.com/natural-disasters/1020918/natural-disasters-displaced-more-than-3-million-americans-in-2022-us.

56 *Vince points out . . . and fertile land."* Vince, *Nomad Century*, 49.

56 *As Vince declares . . . those receiving them.* Vince, *Nomad Century*, xi.

56 Nomad Century *notes . . . changing the climate."* Vince, *Nomad Century*, 207.

56 *In Vince's judgment . . . race, and ancestry.* Vince, *Nomad Century*, 115–16.

56 *Far from perfect . . . belongs to us."* Vince, *Nomad Century*, xvi.

When Wide Beat Tall: Why Humans See an East-West World (Thread 9)

59 *Since then, humans . . . geography and environment.* Jared Diamond, *Guns, Germs, and Steel: The Fates of Human Societies* (New York: W. W. Norton & Company, 1997), 13–32.

60 *Diamond detailed how . . . vertical (latitudinal) height.* Diamond, *Guns, Germs, and Steel*, 176–77.

60 *Eurasia's primary developmental . . . only minimally required.* Diamond, *Guns, Germs, and Steel*, 176–91.

60 *Per Diamond's telling . . . the above-mentioned developments.* Diamond, *Guns, Germs, and Steel*, 77.

60 *These positive feedback . . . advantaged for conquest.* Diamond, *Guns, Germs, and Steel*, 354–75.

61 *Over time, this . . . long colonial era.* Adam Sneyd, "The New International Economic Order Stumbled Once Before. Will It Succeed a Second Time Around?" The Conversation Web Page, February 15, 2023, retrieved from https://theconversation.com/the-new-international-economic-order-stumbled-once-before-will-it-succeed-a-second-time-around-198969.

Middle Earth Is Doomed! North Integrates South or Faces Its Disintegration! (Thread 10)

63 *Scientists have long . . . a decade later.* International Panel on Climate Change (IPCC), "Climate Change 2021: The Physical Science Basis (Sixth Assessment Report): Summary for Policymakers," retrieved from www.ipcc.ch/report/ar6/wg1/downloads/report/IPCC_AR6_WGI_SPM.pdf; and National Ocean Service, National Oceanic and Atmospheric Administration, US Department of Commerce, "Sea Level Rise Technical Report: Updated Projections Available Through 2150 for All US Coastal Waters," retrieved from oceanservice.noaa.gov/hazards/sealevelrise/sealevelrise-tech-report.html.

63 *The South, except . . . farming for jobs.* "Urban Population (% of Total Population)—Latin America & Caribbean," World Bank Web Page, 2018, retrieved from https://data.worldbank.org/indicator/SP.URB.TOTL.IN.ZS?locations=ZJ.

64 *Development experts increasingly . . . the climate emergency."* UN High Commissioner for Refugees (UNHCR) Filippo Grandi, "Climate Change Is an Emergency for Everyone, Everywhere," UNHCR Web Page, November 5, 2021, retrieved from https://www.unhcr.org/en-us/news/stories/2021/11/618a301d5/climate-change-emergency-everywhere.html.

64 *Today, we measure, . . . in the billions.* Chi Xu et al., "Future of the Human Climate Niche," *Proceedings of the National Academy of Sciences of the United States of America* 117, no. 21 (2020), 11350–55, retrieved from www.pnas.org/doi/10.1073/pnas.1910114117.

64 *Today, less than . . . a continuous basis.* Zohra Bensemra, "Three Billion People Could Live in Places as Hot as the Sahara by 2070 Unless We Tackle Climate Change," World Economic Forum Web Page, May 13, 2020, retrieved from www.weforum.org/agenda/2020/05/temperature-climate-change-greenhouse-gas-niche-emissions-hot/.

64 *But let us . . . the world average).* As calculated by geographer and earth scientist Laurence C. Smith, *The New North: The World in 2050* (London, Profile Books, 2011), 174 and the associated endnote on 293; and "List of Countries and Dependencies by Population Density," Wikipedia, retrieved February 22, 2023, from https://en.wikipedia.org/wiki/List_of_countries_and_dependencies_by_population_density.

65 *As Gaia Vince . . . what will occur,"* Vince, *Nomad Century,* 64-65.

65 *Canada, America, and . . . and the Middle East).* Food and Agriculture Organization (FAO), United Nations, "The State of Agricultural Commodity Markets: Agricultural Trade, Climate Change and Food Security," 2018, retrieved from www.fao.org/3/I9542EN/i9542en.pdf; and FAO, "Climate Change Will Depress Agricultural Yields in Most Countries in 2050, Given Current Agricultural Practices and Crop Varieties," retrieved February 22, 2023, from www .fao.org/fileadmin/templates/cpesap/C-RESAP_Info_package/Links/Module _1/reduction_yields_wb.pdf.

65 *As a result . . . extreme ecological threats."* Institute for Economics & Peace (IEP), "Ecological Threat Report 2021: Understanding Ecological Threats, Resilience and Peace," October 2021, IEP Web Page, retrieved from https://www .visionofhumanity.org/ecological-threat-report-2021-summary-and-key-findings/.

65 *For some time . . . and El Salvador.* Paul J. Angelo, "Why Central American Migrants Are Arriving at the US Border," Council on Foreign Relations Web Page, March 22, 2021, retrieved from www.cfr.org/in-brief/why-central -american-migrants-are-arriving-us-border.

65 *Across that region's . . . years of drought."* Elizabeth Courtney, "Hidden in Plain Sight: How Stories of Central American Climate Displacement Were Buried Under a Border Crisis," Open Americas Web Page, September 4, 2020, retrieved from https://openamericas.org/2020/09/04/hidden-in-plain-sight-how-stories -of-central-american-climate-displacement-were-buried-under-a-border-crisis/; and "Erratic Weather Patterns in the Central American Dry Corridor Leave 1.4 Million People in Urgent Need of Food Assistance," World Food Programme Web Page, April 25, 2019, retrieved from https://www.wfp.org/news/erratic -weather-patterns-central-american-dry-corridor-leave-14-million-people -urgent-need.

66 *Come midcentury, climate . . . the US impact.* Economist Intelligence Unit, "Global Economy Will Be 3 Percent Smaller by 2050 Due to Lack of Climate Resilience," November 20, 2019, retrieved from www.eiu.com/n/global-economy-will -be-3-percent-smaller-by-2050-due-to-lack-of-climate-resilience/.

66 *A grim scenario . . . farmers, and herders.* Ben Adler, "Climate Change Is Fueling New Violent Conflict in Africa, U.N. Says," Yahoo! News, December 16, 2021, retrieved from news.yahoo.com/climate-change-is-fueling-new-violent-conflict -in-africa-un-says-100039934.html.

66 *In extremis, we . . . Mexico's criminal elements.* Amber Phillips, "'They're Rapists.' President Trump's Campaign Launch Speech Two Years Later, Annotated," *Washington Post,* July 16, 2017, retrieved from www.washingtonpost.com/news /the-fix/wp/2017/06/16/theyre-rapists-presidents-trump-campaign-launch -speech-two-years-later-annotated/.

Poleward Bound (I Wish I Were . . .): Climate Change Puts Every Species on the Move (Thread 11)

69   *Thanks to climate . . . turbocharging their precipitation.* Joel R. Norris et al., "Evidence for Climate Change in the Satellite Cloud Record," *Nature* 536 (2016), retrieved from www.nature.com/articles/nature18273; and George Tselioudis et al., "Midlatitude Cloud Shifts, Their Primary Link to the Hadley Cell, and Their Diverse Radiative Effects," *Geophysical Research Letters* 43, no. 9 (2016), retrieved from https://agupubs.onlinelibrary.wiley.com/doi/full/10.1002/2016GL068242.

70   *Scientists project that . . . Canada and Russia.* Myron King et al., "Northward Shift of the Agricultural Climate Zone Under 21st-Century Global Climate Change," *Scientific Reports* 8, no. 7904 (2018), retrieved from www.nature.com/articles /s41598-018-26321-8/.

70   *Asking animals and . . . nonstarter for most.* "Rates of Projected Climate Change Dramatically Exceed Past Rates of Climatic Niche Evolution Among Vertebrate Species," *Ecology Letters* 16 (2013), retrieved from https://www.wienslab.com /Publications_files/Quintero%26Wiens_Ecol_Lett_2013.pdf.

70   *That means a . . . to human activity.* Geraldo Ceballos, Paul R. Ehrlich, and Rodolfo Dirzo, "Biological Annihilation via the Ongoing Sixth Mass Extinction Signaled by Vertebrate Population Losses and Declines," *Proceedings of the National Academy of Sciences* 114, no. 30 (2017), retrieved from https://www.pnas .org/doi/full/10.1073/pnas.1704949114.

70   *Thousands of studies . . . climate change curve.* For example, see the following study examining data gathered on over 2,000 species: Joanne M. Bennett et al., "The Evolution of Critical Thermal Limits of Life on Earth," *Nature Communications* 12, no. 1198 (2021), retrieved from https://www.nature.com/articles/s41467-021 -21263-8.

70   *Shifting the timing . . . far more difficult.* Helen Thompson, "Ten Species That Are Evolving Due to the Changing Climate," *Smithsonian Magazine* (2014), retrieved from www.smithsonianmag.com/science-nature/ten-species-are-evolving-due -changing-climate-180953133/.

70   *In general, species . . . larger, longer-lived species.* Renee Cho, "What Helps Animals Adapt (or Not) to Climate Change?" Columbia Climate School Web Page, March 30, 2018, retrieved from news.climate.columbia.edu/2018/03/30/helps -animals-adapt-not-climate-change/.

70   *That means climate . . . of human disease.* Susan Cosier, "Diseases on the Move," Natural Resources Defense Council Web page, March 18, 2015, retrieved from www.nrdc.org/onearth/diseases-move.

70   *Even scarier is . . . or Siberia's permafrost.* Ulisses E. C. Confalonieri, Carina Margonari, and Ana Flavia Quintao, "Environmental Change and the Dynamics of

Parasitic Diseases in the Amazon, *Acta Tropica* 129 (2014), retrieved from www
.sciencedirect.com/science/article/pii/S0001706X13002489; and "New Viruses
Unknown to Humanity Could Emerge from Siberia's Melting Permafrost—
Nobel Laureate," *Moscow Times*, October 12, 2021, retrieved from www
.themoscowtimes.com/2021/10/12/new-viruses-unknown-to-humanity-could
-emerge-from-siberias-melting-permafrost-nobel-laureate-a75264.

71   *For decades, species . . . the normal pace.* I-Ching Chen et al., "Rapid Range Shifts
of Species Associated with High Levels of Climate Warming," *Science* 333, no.
6405 (2011), retrieved from www.science.org/doi/10.1126/science.1206432.

71   *Over the next . . . and become self-perpetuating.* Mika Rantanen et al., "The Arctic
Has Warmed Nearly Four Times Faster Than the Globe Since 1979," *Communications Earth and Environment* 3, no. 168 (2022), retrieved from www.nature
.com/articles/s43247-022-00498-3; Sarah Kaplan, "Satellited Images Show the
Amazon Rainforest Is Hurtling Toward a 'Tipping Point,'" *Washington Post*,
March 7, 2022, retrieved from www.washingtonpost.com/climate-environment
/2022/03/07/amazon-rainforest-tipping-point-climate/; Joshua Yaffa, "The
Great Siberian Thaw," *New Yorker*, January 17, 2022, retrieved from www.new
yorker.com/magazine/2022/01/17/the-great-siberian-thaw; and Michael Birnbaum and Ellen Francis, "'Zombie' Viruses Are Thawing in Melting Permafrost Because of Climate Change: Ancient Viruses Are Locked in Russia's
Permafrost. We May Soon Get a Peek," *Washington Post*, December 2, 2022,
retrieved from https://www.washingtonpost.com/climate-environment/2022/12
/02/zombie-virus-russia-permafrost-thaw/.

Go North, Young Man! The Geopolitical Upside of Climate Change (Thread 12)

75   *Framed by the . . . (14 million km²).* Smith, *New North*, 174 and the associated
endnote on 293.

75   *Humanity swaps one . . . "the New North."* Smith, *New North*, 6–7.

75   *Recall Abraham Lincoln's . . . wartime food production.* Carl Sandburg, *Abraham
Lincoln: The Prairie Years and the War Years* (New York: Harcourt Brace, 1954),
300.

75   *If Canada once . . . North with Latinos?* Eli Yarhi and T. D. Regehr, "Dominion
Lands Act," The Canadian Encyclopedia Web Page, January 30, 2020, retrieved
from www.thecanadianencyclopedia.ca/en/article/dominion-lands-policy.

75   *In recent years, . . . like North Dakota.* Renee Stepler and Mark Hugo Lopez, "US
Latino Population Growth and Dispersion Has Slowed Since Onset of the Great
Recession: South Still Leads Nation in Growth Overall, but Three Counties in
North Dakota Top List of Fastest-Growing," Pew Research Center Web Page,

September 8, 2016, retrieved from https://www.pewresearch.org/hispanic/2016
/09/08/latino-population-growth-and-dispersion-has-slowed-since-the-onset
-of-the-great-recession/.

76 *While many security . . . without great-power conflict.* Kris Osborn, "Is the US Military Ready for a War in the Arctic?" *National Interest* (blog), December 8, 2020, retrieved from nationalinterest.org/blog/buzz/us-military-ready-war-arctic -174028.

76 *There are, for . . . fingers crossed post–Ukraine.* Smith, *New North*, 152.

76 *Thirty percent of . . . Beijing's determined attention.* Arnfinn Jorgensen-Dahl, "Arctic Oil and Gas," Arctis Knowledge Hub Web Page, 2010, retrieved from http:// www.arctis-search.com/Arctic+Oil+and+Gas.

76 *Granted observer status . . . Iceland, and Finland.* Erik Matzen, "Denmark Spurned Chinese Offer for Greenland Base Over Security: Sources," Reuters, April 6, 2017, retrieved from www.reuters.com/article/us-denmark-china-greenland -base-idUSKBN1782EE; Arthur Guschin, "China, Iceland and the Arctic," *The Diplomat*, May 20, 2015, retrieved from thediplomat.com/2015/05/china -iceland-and-the-arctic/; and Matti Puranen and Jukka Aukia, "Finland's China Shift," *The Diplomat*, February 8, 2022, retrieved from thediplomat.com/2022 /02/finlands-china-shift/.

76 *Beijing finances Russia's . . . outposts, and ports.* John Grady, "Russia Wants to Keep Status as Arctic Superpower, Says Expert," USNI News, November 5, 2021, retrieved from news.usni.org/2021/11/05/russia-wants-to-keep-status-as-arctic -superpower-says-expert.

76 *Still, with most . . . to be had.* Jorgensen-Dahl, "Arctic Oil and Gas."

77 *As usual, the . . . "polar great power."* Bonnie S. Glaser and Elizabeth Buchanan, "China in the Arctic: Ambitions and Strategy," German Marshall Fund Web Page, March 8, 2022, retrieved from www.gmfus.org/news/china-arctic -ambitions-and-strategy.

77 *Today, Native Alaska–owned . . . vast northern territories.* Smith, *New North*, 213.

77 *In contrast, Europe . . . their developmental destiny.* Smith, *New North*, 219.

77 *Still, there is . . . or North America.* Abrahm Lustgarten, "How Russia Wins the Climate Crisis," *New York Times Magazine*, December 16, 2020, retrieved from https://www.nytimes.com/interactive/2020/12/16/magazine/russia-climate -migration-crisis.html.

78 *Canadian journalist Diane . . . important Arctic region.* Diane Francis, *Merger of the Century: Why Canada and America Should Become One Country* (Toronto: Harper Collins, 2013); and Francis, "Why the U.S. Should Merge with Canada," *Politico*, April 10, 2014, retrieved from https://www.politico.com/magazine /story/2014/04/why-the-us-should-merge-with-canada-105610/.

78   *Canada plus America . . . jurisdiction on Earth."* Francis, "Why the U.S. Should Merge with Canada."

78   *A straight-up business . . . and West Germany.* Francis, *Merger of the Century,* 215–27.

Destiny's Child: How Demographics Determine Globalization's Winners, Losers, and Future (Throughline Three)

84   *With the birth . . . stunningly rapid rate.* Rong Chen et al., "China Has Faster Pace Than Japan in Population Aging in Next 25 Years," *BioScience Trends* 13, no. 4 (2019), retrieved from www.jstage.jst.go.jp/article/bst/13/4/13_2019.01213 /_article.

84   *China recently rescinded . . . of breathtaking speed.* Trevor Lloyd, "Ending the One-Child Policy in China Shows Continued Imbalance," *Borgen Magazine,* October 29, 2021, retrieved from www.borgenmagazine.com/one-child-policy/.

The Golden Ticket: Cashing In a Demographic Dividend Is Hardly Guaranteed (Thread 13)

87   *China is the . . . in half (<2:5).* "China: Age Dependency Ratio," The Global Economy Web Page, retrieved February 22, 2023, from www.theglobaleconomy.com /China/Age_dependency_ratio/.

87   *It took America . . . promoting the opposite.* Max Roser, "Fertility Rate," Our World in Data Web Page, December 2, 2017, retrieved from ourworldindata.org /fertility-rate.

88   *Fertility is primarily . . . an economic win-win.* Roser, "Fertility Rate."

88   *Over the period . . . doubled its output.* "Demographic Dividend," United Nations Population Fund Web Page, retrieved February 22, 2023, from www.unfpa.org /demographic-dividend.

88   *The whole point . . . has already begun.* Albee Zhang and Farah Master, "China's First Population Drop in Six Decades Sounds Alarm on Demographic Crisis," Reuters, January 17, 2023, retrieved from https://www.reuters.com/world/china /chinas-population-shrinks-first-time-since-1961-2023-01-17/.

89   *This is the . . . next two centuries.* Thomas Malthus, *An Essay on the Principle of Population* (London: St. Paul's Church-Yard, 1798), retrieved from http://www .esp.org/books/malthus/population/malthus.pdf.

89   *Absent climate change . . . productivity inexorably rises.* Anthony Cilluffo and Neil G. Ruiz, "World's Population Is Projected to Nearly Stop Growing by the End of the Century," Pew Research Center Web Page, June 17, 2019, retrieved from

www.pewresearch.org/fact-tank/2019/06/17/worlds-population-is-projected-to
-nearly-stop-growing-by-the-end-of-the-century/.

89   *Middle Earth still . . . expand through midcentury.* Population Division, Department of Economic and Social Affairs, "Youth Population Trends and Sustainable Development," United Nations Web Page, May 2015, retrieved from www.un
.org/esa/socdev/documents/youth/fact-sheets/YouthPOP.pdf.

The Secret History of Globalization: Follow the Demographic Dividend (Thread 14)

94   *Taking advantage of . . . its rapid aging.* "Japan Population 1950–2023," Macrotrends Web Page, retrieved February 22, 2023, from https://www.macrotrends
.net/countries/JPN/japan/population.

94   *China's own demographic . . . workers by 2050.* "China: Age Dependency Ratio," The Global Economy Web Page; and Joe Myers, "China's Working-Age Population Will Fall 23% by 2050," World Economic Forum Web Page, July 25, 2016, retrieved from www.weforum.org/agenda/2016/07/china-working-ageing-population/.

94   *But Southeast Asia's . . . one billion workers.* Richard Jackson and Neil Howe, *The Graying of the Great Powers: Demography and Geopolitics in the 21st Century* (Washington, DC: Center for Strategic and International Studies, 2008), 163–74.

95   *A good example: . . . billion in 2013.* "China Foreign Direct Investment 1979–2023," Macrotrends Web Page, retrieved February 22, 2023, from www.macrotrends
.net/countries/CHN/china/foreign-direct-investment.

95   *China recently achieved . . . worn by America.* Ros Krasney and Bloomberg, "China Passes US as Top Spot for New Foreign Investment," *Fortune*, January 25, 2021, retrieved from fortune.com/2021/01/25/china-us-foreign-direct-investment-fdi
-2020/; and "China Ranks No. 1 Globally in Outward FDI for the First Time," *Global Times*, September 29, 2021, retrieved from https://www.globaltimes.cn
/page/202109/1235451.shtml.

95   *Tellingly, India now . . . billion in 2021.* "India Foreign Direct Investment 1970–2023," Macrotrends Web Page, retrieved February 22, 2023, from www
.macrotrends.net/countries/IND/india/foreign-direct-investment; and "FDI Inflow to India Fell to $74.01 Billion in 2021," NDTV Web Page, March 23, 2022, retrieved from www.ndtv.com/business/fdi-inflow-to-india-declines-to
-74-01-billion-in-2021-2838965.

95   *In 2020, amidst . . . is to come.* "Global Foreign Direct Investment Fell by 42% in 2020, Outlook Remains Weak," UNCTAD Web Page, January 24, 2021, retrieved from unctad.org/news/global-foreign-direct-investment-fell-42-2020
-outlook-remains-weak.

95 *In 1960, the . . . larger in size.* "List of Countries by Motor Vehicle Production," Wikipedia, retrieved February 22, 2023, from en.wikipedia.org/wiki/List_of _countries_by_motor_vehicle_production.

Globalization's Prime Directive: Accommodate Peacefully Rising Economic Pillars (Thread 15)

100 *A generation ago . . . of those nations.* Roland Rajah and Alyssa Leng, "The U.S.-China Trade War: Who Dominates Global Trade?" Lowy Institute Web Page, retrieved February 22, 2023, from https://interactives.lowyinstitute.org/charts /china-us-trade-dominance/us-china-competition/.

100 *That is why . . . but entirely logical.* On why China's larger naval fleet matters, see Capt. Sam J. Tangredi, USN (ret.), "Bigger Fleets Win: In Naval Warfare, a Smaller Fleet of Superior Quality Ships Is Not a Way to Victory. The Side with the Most Ships Almost Always Wins." *Proceedings of the US Naval Institute* 149, no. 1, retrieved from https://www.usni.org/magazines/proceedings/2023 /january/bigger-fleets-win.

100 *This is the . . . of "national rejuvenation."* Zinnia Lee, "China Congress: Xi Outlines Superpower Ambitions Amid Tensions with US and Economic Woes," *Forbes*, October 17, 2022, retrieved from https://www.forbes.com/sites/zinnialee /2022/10/17/china-congress-xi-outlines-superpower-ambitions-amid-tensions -with-us-and-economic-woes/.

100 *Today, China's petty . . . for our forces.* See, for example, "Japan Defence: China Threat Prompts Plan to Double Military Spending," BBC Web Page, December 16, 2022, retrieved from https://www.bbc.com/news/world-asia-64001554; and Rupert Wingfield-Hayes, "US Secures Deal on Philippines Bases to Complete Arc Around China," BBC News Web Page, February 2, 2023, retrieved from https://www.bbc.com/news/world-asia-64479712.

102 *India is already . . . the Global South.* Adam Schrader, "Indian PM Narendra Modi Vows 'Developed India' in 25 Years," UPI Web Page, August 15, 2022, retrieved from www.upi.com/Top_News/World-News/2022/08/15/modi-vows -developed-india-25-years-indpendence-day-speech/4671660569230/.

The Dorian Gray of Great Powers: By Staying Young(ish), America Stays Relevant (Thread 16)

107 *In 1900, global . . . the year 2000.* Max Roser, Esteban Ortiz-Ospina, and Hannah Ritchie, "Life Expectancy," Our World in Data Web Page, October 2019, retrieved from ourworldindata.org/life-expectancy.

107   *That stunning achievement . . . in early childhood.* Rino Rappuoli, "Vaccines: Science, Health, Longevity, and Wealth," *Proceedings of the National Academy of Sciences* (2014), retrieved from https://www.pnas.org/doi/10.1073/pnas.1413559111.

107   *One of the . . . the death rate.* Roser, "Fertility Rate."

107   *The UN defines . . . children in America.* Yoshio Tahara, "Cardiopulmonary Resuscitation in a Super-Aging Society," *Circulation Journal*, 2016, retrieved from www.jstage.jst.go.jp/article/circj/80/5/80_CJ-16-0307/_html; and "Older People Projected to Outnumber Children for First Time in US History," US Census Bureau, March 13, 2018, retrieved from www.census.gov/newsroom/press-releases/2018/cb18-41-population-projections.html.

108   *Between now and . . . after we do.* Roser, "Fertility Rate."

108   *In 2050, China's . . . zoom past ours.* "China's Elderly Population to Reach 487m Around 2050," The State Council of the People's Republic of China, October 9, 2019, retrieved from english.www.gov.cn/statecouncil/ministries/201910/09/content_WS5d9dc831c6d0bcf8c4c14c66.html.

108   *Come midcentury, India . . . age of thirty-seven.* "Attitudes About Aging: A Global Perspective—Chapter 2. Aging in the US and Other Countries, 2010 to 2050," Pew Research Center, January 30, 2014, retrieved from www.pewresearch.org/global/2014/01/30/chapter-2-aging-in-the-u-s-and-other-countries-2010-to-2050/.

108   *Russia will keep . . . suffers this century.* "Russia: Median Age of the Population From 1950 to 2100," Statista Web Page, July 2019, retrieved from www.statista.com/statistics/275400/median-age-of-the-population-in-russia/; "Life Expectancy by Country 2023," World Population Review Web Page (citing UN), retrieved February 22, 2023, from worldpopulationreview.com/countries/life-expectancy; and "Population of Russia," Statistics Times Web Page (citing UN), August 23, 2021, retrieved from statisticstimes.com/demographics/country/russia-population.php.

108   *America will be . . . the EU (forty-seven).* Pew Research Center, "Attitudes About Aging"; and "Median Age Over 43 Years in the EU," Eurostat Web Page, May 11, 2019, retrieved from ec.europa.eu/eurostat/web/products-eurostat-news/-/DDN-20191105-1#.

108   *Elders need help . . . change's ravaging effects.* Jackson and Howe, *Graying of the Great Powers*, 93–122.

108   *As US demographers . . . over the young."* Jackson and Howe, *Graying of the Great Powers*, 131.

108   *There is a . . . median age (thirty-eight).* Eric Schaal, "How Old Is the Average Fox News Viewer in America?" Showbiz CheatSheet Web Page, January 10, 2019, retrieved from www.cheatsheet.com/entertainment/how-old-is-the-average-fox-news-viewer-in-america.html/; and David Smith, "Gerontocracy: The

Exceptionally Old Political Class That Governs the US," *The Guardian*, February 19, 2023, retrieved from https://www.theguardian.com/us-news/2023/feb/19/us-congress-presidency-gerontocracy.

109 *The danger we . . . own privileged hegemony."* Jackson and Howe, *Graying of the Great Powers*, 4.

109 *The vast bulk . . . children per woman.* Steven A. Camarota and Karen Zeigler, "Immigrants Coming to America at Older Ages: A Look at Age at Arrival Among New Immigrants, 2000 to 2019," Center for Immigration Studies Web Page, March 29, 2021, retrieved from https://cis.org/Report/Immigrants-Coming-America-Older-Ages; and Camarota and Zeigler, "Fertility Among Immigrants and Native-Born Americans: Difference Between the Foreign-Born and the Native-Born Continues to Narrow," Center for Immigration Studies Web Page, February 16, 2021, retrieved from https://cis.org/Report/Fertility-Among-Immigrants-and-NativeBorn-Americans.

109 *The United States . . . younger than America."* Pew Research Center, "Attitudes About Aging"; and Eurostat, "Median Age."

109 *As Russia depopulates . . . forty-two in 2050.* "Russian Federation," Population Pyramid.net Web Page, retrieved February 22, 2023, from www.populationpyramid.net/russian-federation/2050/; and "Russia: Median Age of the Population from 1950 to 2100," Statista Web Page.

America's 50/50/50 Journey: From 1950 to 2050, Whites Fall to Less Than 50 Percent of Population (Thread 17)

113 *A 1970 book . . . survive until 1984?"* Andrei Amalrik, *Will the Soviet Union Survive Until 1984?* (New York: HarperCollins, 1981).

113 *Amalrik doubted the . . . the total population."* Amalrik, *Soviet Union Survive*, 38.

113 *The coup de . . . empire's violent "deimperialization."* Amalrik, *Soviet Union Survive*, 64.

113 *Swap in an . . . like the rest.* William H. Frey, "The US Will Become 'Minority White' in 2045, Census Project," *Brookings* (blog) March 14, 2018, retrieved from www.brookings.edu/blog/the-avenue/2018/03/14/the-us-will-become-minority-white-in-2045-census-projects/.

113 *American documentarian Ken . . . the American story."* Dustin Waters, "Filmmaker Ken Burns Talks About His New Documentary and Continuing Charleston's Discussion of Race," *Charleston City Paper*, December 16, 2015, retrieved from charlestoncitypaper.com/filmmaker-ken-burns-talks-about-his-new-documentary-and-continuing-charlestons-discussion-of-race/.

113 *America was 81 . . . the twentieth century.* "White Americans," Wikipedia (citing US Census Bureau), retrieved February 22, 2023, from en.wikipedia.org/wiki/White_Americans.

114   *In 2050, Whites . . . 1950 high point.* Jeffrey S. Passel and D'Vera Cohn, "US Population Projections: 2005–2050," Pew Research Center Web Page, February 11, 2008, retrieved from https://www.pewresearch.org/social-trends/2008/02/11/us -population-projections-2005-2050/.

114   *America's current path . . . of our Union.* Currently, both North and South America feature a White percentage share in the mid-40s. See Wikipedia entries "White People," retrieved February 22, 2023, from en.wikipedia.org/wiki/White _people; and "Demographics of South America," retrieved February 22, 2023, from en.wikipedia.org/wiki/Demographics_of_South_America.

115   *America already has . . . nation's major metropolises.* "Majority Minority in the United States," Wikipedia (citing US Census Bureau), retrieved February 22, 2023, from en.wikipedia.org/wiki/Majority_minority_in_the_United_States.

115   *None of these . . . of polled Americans.* Garen J. Wintemute et al., "Views of American Democracy and Society and Support for Political Violence: First Report from a Nationwide Population-Representative Survey," University of California, Davis, preprint retrieved February 22, 2023, from www.medrxiv.org/content /10.1101/2022.07.15.22277693v1.full-text.

115   *Most Americans first . . . not replace us."* Jonathan Sarna, "The Long, Ugly Antisemitic History of 'Jews Will Not Replace Us,'" Brandeis University Web Page, November 19, 2021, retrieved from www.brandeis.edu/jewish-experience/jewish -america/2021/november/replacement-antisemitism-sarna.html.

116   *A fellow traveler of . . . (often still Jews).* "(Backgrounder) 'The Great Replacement': An Explainer," Anti-Defamation League Web Page, April 19, 2021, retrieved at https://www.adl.org/resources/backgrounders/the-great-replacement-an -explainer.

116   *Primary authorship of . . . directed from above.* Renaud Camus, *Le Grand Remplacement* (Paris: David Reinharc Editions, 2011).

116   *In America today, . . . globalization's replacist dynamics.* Nicholas Confessore, "How Tucker Carlson Stoked White Fear to Conquer Cable," *New York Times,* April 30, 2022, retrieved from www.nytimes.com/2022/04/30/us/tucker-carlson-gop -republican-party.html,

116   *The related QAnon . . . anti-Trump Democratic "satanists."* See the six-part HBO documentary series by director Cullen Hoback entitled *Q: Into the Storm,* retrieved from www.hbo.com/q-into-the-storm.

116   *This broad reach . . . their collective rage.* DaMareo Cooper, "How the White Replacement Theory Behind the Buffalo Shooting Also Fueled the January 6 Insurrection," Yahoo! News, June 8, 2022, retrieved from news.yahoo.com/white -replacement-theory-behind-buffalo-152511891.html.

116   *GRT is likewise . . . mass shootings, bombings).* Rick Noack, "Christchurch Endures as Extremist Touchstone, as Investigators Probe Suspected El Paso Manifesto,"

Washington Post, August 6, 2019, retrieved from www.washingtonpost.com /world/2019/08/06/christchurch-endures-extremist-touchstone-investigators -probe-suspected-el-paso-manifesto/.

Making America Great Again: Drunk on Nostalgia, We're on a Road to Nowhere (Thread 18)

119   *The US political . . . China, Russia, etc.).* Minxin Pei, "The Paradoxes of American Nationalism," *Foreign Policy*, May–June 2003, retrieved from foreignpolicy.com /2009/11/02/the-paradoxes-of-american-nationalism/.

120   *While Democrats, at . . . 1980s racial profile.* John Gramlich, "What the 2020 Electorate Looks Like by Party, Race and Ethnicity, Age, Education and Religion," Pew Research Center Web Page, October 26, 2020, retrieved from www.pewresearch.org/fact-tank/2020/10/26/what-the-2020-electorate-looks -like-by-party-race-and-ethnicity-age-education-and-religion/; and "Histori- cal Racial and Ethnic Demographics of the United States," Wikipedia (citing US Census Bureau), retrieved February 22, 2023, from en.wikipedia.org/wiki /Historical_racial_and_ethnic_demographics_of_the_United_States.

120   *Trump only fueled . . . at mass rallies.* Eli Watkins and Abby Phillip, "Trump Decries Immigrants from 'Shithole Countries' Coming to US," CNN Web Page, January 12, 2018, retrieved from www.cnn.com/2018/01/11/politics/immigrants -shithole-countries-trump/index.html; and Tyler Moran and Beatriz Lopez, "Trump's Immigration Messaging Is Being Pushed Hard in Swing States. But It's Not Working," NBC News Web Page, October 21, 2020, retrieved from www.nbcnews.com/think/opinion/trump-s-immigration-messaging-being -pushed-hard-swing-states-it-ncna1244063.

120   *In his populist . . . destroying our jobs."* See "FULL TEXT: President Don- ald Trump's Inauguration Speech," ABC News Web Page, January 20, 2017, retrieved from abcnews.go.com/Politics/full-text-president-donald-trumps -inauguration-speech/story?id=44915821.

121   *The 2020 US . . . among US counties.* William H. Frey, "New 2020 Census Results Show Increased Diversity Countering Decade-Long Declines in Amer- ica's White and Youth Populations," Brookings Web Page, August 13, 2021, retrieved from www.brookings.edu/research/new-2020-census-results-show -increased-diversity-countering-decade-long-declines-in-americas-white-and -youth-populations/.

121   *The US political . . . to produce insurrectionists."* Robert A. Pape, "What an Analy- sis of 377 Americans Arrested or Charged in the Capitol Insurrection Tells Us," *Washington Post*, April 6, 2021, retrieved from www.washingtonpost.com /opinions/2021/04/06/capitol-insurrection-arrests-cpost-analysis/.

121   *British prime minister . . . lost the future."* Winston Churchill, Speech in the House of Commons, "War Situation," June 18, 1940, retrieved from https://www.brainyquote.com/quotes/winston_churchill_136286.

Superpower Brand Wars: The Global Middle Seeks Protection from the Future (Throughline Four)

124   *And when many . . . disavow any responsibility?* Hannah Fingerhut and Nuha Dolby, "AP-NORC Poll: Many in US Doubt Their Own Impact on Climate," Associated Press, August 14, 2022, retrieved from cw33.com/news/science-technology/ap-science/ap-norc-poll-many-in-us-doubt-their-own-impact-on-climate/.

125   *A glimpse of . . . locating hurricane victims.* Michael Birnbaum, "Why the US Is Enlisting a Spy Agency During Hurricanes: The National Geospatial-Intelligence Agency Usually Monitors Iranian Protests and North Korean Missiles. It's Now Helping Find Hurricane Victims, Too," *Washington Post*, January 2, 2023, retrieved from https://www.washingtonpost.com/climate-solutions/2022/12/30/spies-intelligence-drones-hurricane-rescue/.

126   *According to noted . . . for push-marketing purposes.* Kim Taipale, "The Surveillance Society," The Center for Advanced Studies in Science and Technology Policy Working Paper, retrieved February 22, 2023, from http://surveillance-society.info/.

127   *India presents the . . . its energy profile.* On the latter point, see Justin Worland, "How India Became the Most Important Country in the Climate Fight," *Time*, January 12, 2023, retrieved from https://time.com/6246057/india-coal-solar-power-climate-fight/.

127   *The immense opportunity . . . its national workforce.* Ramesh Chand and Jaspal Singh, "Workforce Changes and Employment: Some Findings from PLFS Data Series," NITI Aayong, Government of India Web Page, March 1, 2022, retrieved from https://www.niti.gov.in/sites/default/files/2022-04/Discussion_Paper_on_Workforce_05042022.pdf.

127   *But Russia's depopulation . . . a nationalistic backlash.* "Russia's Population Decline Hits Record Rate," *Moscow Times*, July 29, 2022, retrieved from https://www.themoscowtimes.com/2022/07/29/russias-population-decline-hits-record-rate-a78437.

It's Not Personal, It's Strictly Business: Superpowers Compete to Revise Global Rules (Thread 19)

129   *When it did . . . "end of history."* See Francis Fukuyama's controversial *The End of History and the Last Man* (New York: Free Press, 1992).

130 *A good example . . . once-dominant Washington Consensus.* Dustin R. Turin, "The Beijing Consensus: China's Alternative Development Model." *Inquiries* 2, no. 01 (2010), retrieved from http://www.inquiriesjournal.com/a?id=134.

130 *The latter had . . . cruel "shock therapy."* Stephen R. Hurt, "Washington Consensus," *Encyclopedia Britannica*, retrieved February 22, 2023, from https://www.britannica.com/topic/Washington-consensus.

130 *Per a dynamic . . . an Established #1.* Graham Allison, *Destined for War: Can America and China Escape Thucydides' Trap?* (Geneva, IL: Houghton Mifflin Harcourt, 2017).

131 *All these historical . . . US military hardware.* Pieter D. Wezeman, Alexandra Kuimova, and Siemon T. Wezeman, "Trends in International Arms Transfers, 2021," Stockholm International Peace Research Institute Web Page, Fact Sheet, March 2022, retrieved from https://www.sipri.org/sites/default/files/2022-03/fs_2203_at_2021.pdf.

131 *For a longer-term . . . of Great Powers.* Yan Xuetong, *Leadership and the Rise of Great Powers* (Princeton, NJ: Princeton University Press, 2019).

131 *His highly Confucian . . . moral authority abroad.* Xuetong, *Rise of Great Powers*, 3–11.

131 *But what closed . . . a global leader.* Xuetong, *Rise of Great Powers*, 17–23 and 82–87.

132 *In Yan's analysis, . . . US military power).* Xuetong, *Rise of Great Powers*, 37–53.

132 *In time, this . . . trustworthy, and moral.* Xuetong, *Rise of Great Powers*, 54–78 and 165–71.

132 *Steeped in ancient . . . superior political leadership.* Xuetong, *Rise of Great Powers*, xiii–xiv.

132 *By following ancient . . . great global respect.* Xuetong, *Rise of Great Powers*, 150–53.

132 *If, as an . . . not even close.* Xuetong, *Rise of Great Powers*, 7–11.

132 *You may also . . . so desperately need.* Xuetong, *Rise of Great Powers*, 191–92.

National Affiliation Does Not Grow Out of the Barrel of a Gun: Irredentism as Superpower Brand Failure (Thread 20)

135 *Vladimir Putin famously . . . of imperial powers.* Claire Bigg, "Was Soviet Collapse Last Century's Worst Geopolitical Catastrophe?" Radio Free Europe/Radio Liberty Web Page, April 29, 2005, retrieved from www.rferl.org/a/1058688.html; and John J. Xenakis, "Xi Jinping's Speech on 'The Humiliation of the Chinese Nation for Centuries,'" Breitbart Web Page, December 30, 2018, retrieved from www.breitbart.com/national-security/2018/12/30/world-view-xi-jinpings-speech-on-the-humiliation-of-the-chinese-nation-for-centuries/.

135 *Pay attention to . . . Zaporozhye Oblast, 2022.* See the following Wikipedia entries: en.wikipedia.org/wiki/Pridnestrovian_Moldavian_Soviet_Socialist_Republic; en.wikipedia.org/wiki/Union_State; en.wikipedia.org/wiki/South_Ossetia;

en.wikipedia.org/wiki/Abkhazia; en.wikipedia.org/wiki/Republic_of_Crimea; en.wikipedia.org/wiki/2014_pro-Russian_unrest_in_Ukraine#Failed_proposals; en.wikipedia.org/wiki/Donetsk_People%27s_Republic; en.wikipedia.org/wiki /Luhansk_People%27s_Republic; and https://en.wikipedia.org/wiki/Russian _annexation_of_Donetsk,_Kherson,_Luhansk_and_Zaporizhzhia_oblasts—all retrieved February 22, 2023.

136   *Putin's messaging here . . . an advantageous moment.* Jonathan Landay, "Defiant Putin Proclaims Ukrainian Annexation as Military Setback Looms," Reuters, September 30, 2022, retrieved from https://www.reuters.com/world/putin-host -kremlin-ceremony-annexing-parts-ukraine-2022-09-29/.

136   *In the end . . . anywhere outside Russia.* Francesca Ebel and Mary Ilyushina, "Russians Abandon Wartime Russia in Historic Exodus, *Washington Post*, February 13, 2023, retrieved from https://www.washingtonpost.com/world/2023/02/13 /russia-diaspora-war-ukraine/.

137   *In response to . . . its NATO commitment.* "Will Germany Succeed in Transforming its Foreign Policy?" *The Economist Asks* Podcast, December 1, 2022, retrieved from https://www.economist.com/podcasts/2022/12/01/will-germany-succeed -in-transforming-its-foreign-policy.

137   *The Russia-Ukraine war . . . Sweden and Finland.* David Ignatius, "How the War in Ukraine Has Remade Europe," *Washington Post*, October 5, 2022, retrieved from https://www.washingtonpost.com/opinions/2022/10/05/ukraine-war-changed -europe-nato-russia/.

137   *The blame-America-first types . . . a national embarrassment.* Joseph Gedeon, "Trump Calls Putin 'Genius' and 'Savvy' for Ukraine Invasion," *Politico*, February 23, 2022, retrieved from https://www.politico.com/news/2022/02/23/trump -putin-ukraine-invasion-00010923.

Stuck in the Middle with You: When the Middle Class Is Happy, Everybody's Happy (Thread 21)

141   *According to economist . . . in this pattern.* Benjamin M. Friedman, *The Moral Consequences of Economic Growth* (New York: Alfred A. Knopf, 2005).

141   *Friedman argues that . . . dedication to democracy."* Friedman, *Moral Consequences*, 4.

141   *Consider American history . . . overseas military burdens.* Friedman, *Moral Consequences*, 6–8.

142   *Here it is . . . percent of Americans.* Homi Kharas and Kristofer Hamel, "A Global Tipping Point: Half the World Is Now Middle Class or Wealthier," *Brookings* (blog), September 27, 2018, retrieved from www.brookings.edu/blog /future-development/2018/09/27/a-global-tipping-point-half-the-world-is-now -middle-class-or-wealthier/; and Rakesh Kochhar, "How Americans Compare

with the Global Middle Class," Pew Research Center Web Page, July 9, 2015, retrieved from https://www.pewresearch.org/fact-tank/2015/07/09/how-americans -compare-with-the-global-middle-class/.

142 *By that definition . . . of majority status.* Kharas and Hamel, "A Global Tipping Point."

142 *Meanwhile, the US . . . over 50 percent.* Richard V. Reeves, Katherine Guyot, and Eleanor Krause, "Defining the Middle Class: Cash, Credentials, or Culture?" Brookings Web Page, May 7, 2018, retrieved from https://www.brookings.edu /research/defining-the-middle-class-cash-credentials-or-culture/; and "How the American Middle Class Has Changed in the Past Five Decades," Pew Research Center Web Page, September 20, 2022, retrieved from https://www .pewresearch.org/fact-tank/2022/04/20/how-the-american-middle-class-has -changed-in-the-past-five-decades/.

142 *Aspiration and identity . . . the middle class.* Jeffrey B. Wenger and Melanie A. Zaber, "Most Americans Consider Themselves Middle-Class. But Are They?" Rand Corporation *TheRANDBlog* (blog), May 14, 2021, retrieved from www .rand.org/blog/2021/05/most-americans-consider-themselves-middle-class-but .html.

142 *Studies indicate that . . . experiencing rapid automation.* Claire Cain Miller, "The Long-Term Jobs Killer Is Not China. It's Automation," *New York Times*, December 21, 2016, retrieved from www.nytimes.com/2016/12/21/upshot/the-long -term-jobs-killer-is-not-china-its-automation.html.

143 *Joe Biden's attempt . . . pointless culture wars.* Burgess Everett and Olivia Beavers, "Conservatives Gloat as Congress Starts Off with Little to Show," *Politico*, February 13, 2023, retrieved from https://www.politico.com/news/2023/02/13 /conservatives-new-congress-00082405.

143 *With Vladimir Putin . . . to the ridiculous.* Peter Dickinson, "Goodwill Gestures and De-Nazification: Decoding Putin's Ukraine War Lexicon," Atlantic Council *Ukraine Alert* (blog), June 30, 2022, retrieved from https://www.atlanticcouncil .org/blogs/ukrainealert/goodwill-gestures-and-de-nazification-decoding -putins-ukraine-war-lexicon/.

Go, China. Go! Beijing's Methodical Approach to Geopolitics (Thread 22)

147 *Competitors view conflict . . . different playing styles.* The inspiration for this breakdown comes from Crispin Rovere, "Poker, Chess and Go: How the US Should Respond in the South China Sea," Lowy Institute *The Interpreter* (blog), July 21, 2016, retrieved from www.lowyinstitute.org/the-interpreter/poker-chess-and -go-how-us-should-respond-south-china-sea.

One Belt to Rule Them All, One Road to Find Them, One Initiative to Bring Them All and Infrastructure Bind Them (Thread 23)

152 *Beijing altruistically pitches . . . many developing economies.* Jason Zhengrong Lu, "A Simple Way to Close the Multi-Trillion-Dollar Infrastructure Financing Gap," World Bank Web Page, April 15, 2020, retrieved from https://blogs.worldbank .org/ppps/simple-way-close-multi-trillion-dollar-infrastructure-financing-gap.

152 *In financial terms, . . . Xi's ultimate goal.* "Xi Jinping's Bold Plan for China's Next Phase of Innovation," *The Economist*, April 16, 2022, retrieved from https://www .economist.com/finance-and-economics/2022/04/16/xi-jinpings-bold-plan-for -chinas-next-phase-of-innovation.

153 *Researchers estimate that . . . and environmental damage.* Ammar A. Malik et al., "Banking on the Belt and Road: Insights from a New Global Dataset of 13,427 Chinese Development Projects," AIDDATA—A Research Lab at William and Mary, September 29, 2021, retrieved from www.aiddata.org/publications /banking-on-the-belt-and-road.

153 *The biggest advanced-economy . . . Lanka's Hambantota Port).* Umesh Moramu-dali, "The Hambantota Port Deal: Myths and Realities," *The Diplomat*, January 1, 2020, retrieved from thediplomat.com/2020/01/the-hambantota-port-deal -myths-and-realities/.

153 *Already, several dozen . . . their annual GDP.* "What Is China's Belt and Road Initiative (BRI)?" Chatham House Web Page, September 13, 2021, retrieved from www.chathamhouse.org/2021/09/what-chinas-belt-and-road-initiative-bri.

153 *To critics, that . . . collapse in 2022.* Aditya Gowdara Shivamurthy, "The Sri Lankan Crisis: The Curious Case of China's Complicity," Observer Research Foundation Web Page, May 30, 2022, retrieved from www.orfonline.org/expert -speak/the-curious-case-of-chinas-complicity; and "Chinese 'Spy Ship' Cleared to Enter Hambantota Port," *Colombo Gazette*, August 13, 2022, retrieved from colombogazette.com/2022/08/13/chinese-spy-ship-cleared-to-enter -hambantota-port/.

154 *A quartet of . . . of US dollars.* Chatham House, "China's Belt and Road Initiative."

154 *China's BRI experiment . . . a competitive manner.* Jonathan Lemire and Karl Mathiesen, "G7 Unveils $600B Plan to Combat China's Belt and Road," *Politico*, June 26, 2022, retrieved from www.politico.eu/article/g7-unveils-600b-plan-to -combat-chinas-belt-and-road/.

154 *While America should . . . sabotage the BRI.* On debt forgiveness, see Editorial Board, "Huge Debts to China Come Due. Will the World's Poorest Have to Pay?" *Washington Post*, February 22, 2023, retrieved from https://www.washingtonpost .com/opinions/2023/02/22/chinese-debt-crush-world-poorest-countries/.

154 *The more China . . . are already witnessing.* Matt Schrader and J. Michael Cole, "China Hasn't Given Up on the Belt and Road: Beijing's Development Aid Plan Is Less Flashy—But No Less Ambitious," *Foreign Affairs*, February 7, 2023, retrieved from https://www.foreignaffairs.com/china/china-hasnt-given -belt-and-road; and Jevans Nyabiage, "Why Did China's Belt and Road Initiative Funding in Sub-Saharan Africa Fall to Historical Low Last Year?" *South China Morning Post*, February 11, 2023, retrieved from https://www.scmp .com/news/china/diplomacy/article/3209619/why-did-chinas-belt-and-road -initiative-funding-sub-saharan-africa-fall-historical-low-last-year.

155 *China is presently . . . in Latin America.* Julio Armando Guzmán, "China's Latin American Power Play: To Counter Beijing, the West Must Invest in People," *Foreign Affairs*, January 16, 2023, retrieved from https://www.foreignaffairs.com /central-america-caribbean/chinas-latin-american-power-play.

Crouching Tiger, Hidden Dragon: Is Asia Big Enough for Both Rising India and Risen China? (Thread 24)

159 *For now, America . . . while ours narrow.* "Defense Spending by Country 2023," World Population Review Web Page, retrieved February 22, 2023, from worldpopulationreview.com/country-rankings/defense-spending-by-country.

160 *The United States draws . . . and India two-thirds.* "Where Does the United States Import Crude Petroleum From?" (oec.world/en/visualize/tree_map/hs92 /import/usa/show/52709/2020/), "Where Does China Import Crude Petroleum From?" (oec.world/en/visualize/tree_map/hs92/import/chn/show/52709 /2020/), and "Where Does India Import Crude Petroleum From?" (oec.world /en/visualize/tree_map/hs92/import/ind/show/52709/2020/), Observatory of Economic Complexity Web Page—all retrieved February 22, 2023.

160 *For much of . . . to East Asia.* Halford John Mackinder, "The Geographical Pivot of History," *Geographical Journal*, April 1904, retrieved from wikispooks.com /w/images/c/c6/The_Geographical_Pivot_of_History.pdf.

160 *This is why . . . of pearls" strategy.* Virginia Marantidou, "Revisiting China's 'String of Pearls' Strategy: Places 'with Chinese Characteristics' and Their Security Implications," Center for Strategic and International Studies Pacific Forum, June 2014, retrieved from pacforum.org/wp-content/uploads/2019/02/140624 _issuesinsights_vol14no7.pdf.

160 *In reply, India . . . of diamonds" strategy.* Ash Jha, "Necklace of Diamonds vs String of Pearls: India-China Standoff," *Times of India Readers' Blog* (blog), June 23, 2022, retrieved from timesofindia.indiatimes.com/readersblog/youthwrites /necklace-of-diamonds-vs-string-of-pearls-india-china-standoff-43458/.

160   *The US Navy . . . this strategic competition.* Pranshu Verma, "The Military Wants 'Robot Ships' to Replace Sailors in Battle," *Washington Post*, April 14, 2022, retrieved from www.washingtonpost.com/technology/2022/04/14/navy-robot -ships/.

161   *India and China . . . from both sides.* Lisa Curtis and Derek Grossman, "Trouble at the Roof of the World: Why America Can't Afford to Ignore India and China's Border Dispute," *Foreign Affairs*, February 15, 2023, retrieved from https://www .foreignaffairs.com/china/trouble-roof-world.

161   *Mao Zedong famously . . . and Arunachal Pradesh).* Brig Anil Gupta, "Five Fingers Dream of Mao Zedong," *Indian Defence Review*, January 28, 2021, retrieved from http://www.indiandefencereview.com/news/five-fingers-dream-of-mao -zedong/.

161   *If that was . . . increasingly water-insecure China.* Dechen Palmo, "Tibet's Rivers Will Determine Asia's Future," *The Diplomat*, November 1, 2019, retrieved from thediplomat.com/2019/11/tibets-rivers-will-determine-asias-future/.

161   *That is the . . . like China did.* Trinh Nguyen, "India Must Embrace Foreign Financing to Meet Investment Needs: Clearing Path for Overseas Bond Buyers Will Support Infrastructure and Business," *Nikkei Asia*, November 30, 2022, retrieved from https://asia.nikkei.com/Opinion/India-must-embrace-foreign -financing-to-meet-investment-needs.

162   *As the world . . . times America's total.* "List of Countries by Foreign-Exchange Reserves," Wikipedia, retrieved February 22, 2023, from https://en.wikipedia .org/wiki/List_of_countries_by_foreign-exchange_reserves.

162   *For now, China's . . . past regarding Japan).* Naina Bhardwaj and Melissa Cyrill, "India's FDI Policy Stance with China: What We Know," *India Briefing*, March 5, 2021, retrieved from www.india-briefing.com/news/india-fdi-policy-position -china-what-we-know-21824.html/.

162   *Right now, one . . . with Great Britain.* For an articulation of Indian strategy, see K. Subrahmanyam, "India's Grand Strategy," *Indian Express*, February 3, 2012, retrieved from indianexpress.com/article/opinion/columns/indias-grand-strategy/.

Leave the Gun, Take the Biometrics: How China and America Project Power Differently (Thread 25)

167   *Meanwhile, Washington busies . . . with them globally.* Ganesh Sitaraman, "The National Security Case for Breaking Up Big Tech: Reframing the Tech Giants' Role in an Era of Great Power Competition," Knight First Amendment Institute at Columbia University Web Page, January 30, 2020, retrieved from https:// knightcolumbia.org/content/the-national-security-case-for-breaking-up-big-tech.

Pacification by Gamification: Ruling the World One Cowed Citizen at a Time (Thread 26)

172 *Chinese technology companies . . . the Communist Party.* Arjun Kharpal, "Huawei Says It Would Never Hand Data to China's Government. Experts Say It Wouldn't Have a Choice," CNBC Web Page, March 5, 2019, retrieved from www.cnbc.com/2019/03/05/huawei-would-have-to-give-data-to-china-government-if-asked-experts.html; and Isabelle Qian et al., "Four Takeaways from a Times Investigation into China's Expanding Surveillance State," *New York Times*, June 21, 2022, retrieved from www.nytimes.com/2022/06/21/world/asia/china-surveillance-investigation.html.

172 *Pretty soon you . . . with lower scores.* Sue-Lin Wong and Qianer Liu, "Emotion Recognition Is China's New Surveillance Craze," *Financial Times*, November 1, 2019, retrieved from www.ft.com/content/68155560-fbd1-11e9-a354-36acbbb0d9b6; and Nicole Kobie, "The Complicated Truth About China's Social Credit System," *Wired*, July 6, 2019, retrieved from www.wired.co.uk/article/china-social-credit-system-explained.

173 *It is also . . . a global scale.* Cate Cadell, "China Harvests Masses of Data on Western Targets, Documents Show," *Washington Post*, December 31, 2021, retrieved from www.washingtonpost.com/national-security/china-harvests-masses-of-data-on-western-targets-documents-show/2021/12/31/3981ce9c-538e-11ec-8927-c396fa861a71_story.html.

173 *China observers have . . . their pervasive application.* Junhua Zhang, "China's Social Credit System—A New Cultural Revolution," Austrian Economics Center Web Page, October 15, 2021, retrieved from www.austriancenter.com/chinas-social-credit-system-a-new-cultural-revolution/.

Sensor Chip Meets Censorship: China's 5G Telecom Offering Is a Trojan Horse (Thread 27)

177 *If that strikes . . . surveillance system "Skynet."* Bradley A. Thayer and Lianchao Han, "China's Weapon of Mass Surveillance Is a Human Rights Abuse," *The Hill*, May 29, 2019, retrieved from thehill.com/opinion/technology/445726-chinas-weapon-of-mass-surveillance-is-a-human-rights-abuse/.

177 *By massively subsidizing . . . 5G "Trojan horse."* Stuart Lau, "US President Donald Trump Warns Germany Huawei 5G Deals Will Put Intelligence Sharing at Risk," *South China Morning Post*, February 17, 2020, retrieved from www.scmp.com/news/china/diplomacy/article/3050934/us-president-donald-trump-warns-germany-huawei-5g-deals-will.

178   *Fighting back, the . . . other industrial enterprises.* Josh Horwitz, "Sanctions-Hit Huawei Ramps Up Investment in Chinese Tech Sector," Reuters, September 28, 2020, retrieved from www.reuters.com/article/china-huawei-tech-investment-idUSKBN26K0AE; Gordon Corera, "Huawei's Business Damaged by US Sanctions Despite Success at Home," BBC Web Page, March 31, 2021, retrieved from www.bbc.com/news/technology-56590001; Laurens Cerulus and Sarah Wheaton, "How Washington Chased Huawei Out of Europe," *Politico*, November 23, 2022, retrieved from https://www.politico.eu/article/us-china-huawei-europe-market/; and Joe McDonald, "China's Huawei Looks to Ports, Factories to Rebuild Sales," Associated Press, January 25, 2023, retrieved from https://abcnews.go.com/Business/wireStory/chinas-huawei-ports-factories-rebuild-sales-96624566.

178   *With Joe Biden's . . . with non-financial sanctions.* "Rep. Jim Langevin [D-R.I.] and Demitri Alperovitch Join Washington Post Live to Assess the Cyber Threat Landscape for Businesses, the Impact on the National Economy and Ways to Grow the Cyber Workforce," *Washington Post*, October 19, 2022, retrieved from https://twitter.com/i/broadcasts/1yoKMZQYLXYGQ; Ana Swanson, "Biden Administration Clamps Down on China's Access to Chip Technology," *New York Times*, October 7, 2022, retrieved from https://www.nytimes.com/2022/10/07/business/economy/biden-chip-technology.html; and Agatha Demarais, "The End of the Age of Sanctions: How America's Adversaries Shielded Themselves," *Foreign Affairs*, December 27, 2022, retrieved from https://www.foreignaffairs.com/united-states/end-age-sanctions.

178   *In the global . . . adjustments and work-arounds.* Sarah Bauerle Danzman and Emily Kilcrease, "The Illusion of Controls: Unilateral Attempts to Contain China's Technology Ambitions Will Fail," *Foreign Affairs*, December 30, 2022, retrieved from https://www.foreignaffairs.com/united-states/illusion-controls.

178   *For example, the . . . cellular network markets.* Ina Fried, "US to Spend $1.5 Billion to Jumpstart Alternatives to Huawei," Axios Web Page, December 7, 2022, retrieved from https://www.axios.com/2022/12/07/huawei-alternatives-5g-cellural-equipment-oran.

179   *Add it all . . . horse readily accepted.* Thayer and Han, "China's Weapon of Mass Surveillance"; and Jonathan E. Hillman and Maesea McCalpin, "Watching Huawei's 'Safe Cities,'" Center for Strategic & International Studies Web Page, November 4, 2019, retrieved from https://www.csis.org/analysis/watching-huaweis-safe-cities.

179   *In so penetrating . . . relating to Beijing."* Joshua Kurlantzick, *Beijing's Global Media Offensive: China's Uneven Campaign to Influence Asia and the World* (New York: Oxford University Press, 2022), 8.

Globalization's Consolidation Is Hemispheric Integration: America's Goal of Stable Multipolarity Preordained This Era (Throughline Five)

183   *From the Cold . . . least globalization's stagnation.* Susan Lund et al., "Globaliza-tion in Transition: The Future of Trade and Value Chains," McKinsey Global Institute Report, January 16, 2019, retrieved from www.mckinsey.com/featured -insights/innovation-and-growth/globalization-in-transition-the-future-of -trade-and-value-chains.

184   *Second, any slowdown . . . inputs or labor.* "Slowbalization: The Steam Has Gone Out of Globalisation," *The Economist*, January 24, 2019, retrieved from https://www.economist.com/leaders/2019/01/24/the-steam-has-gone-out-of -globalisation.

184   *China is way . . . re-shoring manufacturing jobs.* Dion Rabouin, "US Companies on Pace to Bring Home Record Number of Overseas Jobs: After COVID-19 Pandemic Upended Supply Chains, American Companies Are Shifting Jobs and Processes to the US," *Wall Street Journal*, August 23, 2022, retrieved from https://www.wsj.com/articles/u-s-companies-on-pace-to-bring-home-record -number-of-overseas-jobs-11660968061.

184   *Finally, there is . . . suffered across manufacturing.* James Manyika et al., "Digital Globalization: The New Era of Global Flows," McKinsey Global Institute Web Page, February 24, 2016, retrieved from www.mckinsey.com/business-functions /mckinsey-digital/our-insights/digital-globalization-the-new-era-of-global -flows.

184   *You might think . . . domestic political control.* David Ignatius, "Will Deterrence Have a Role in the Cyberspace 'Forever War'?" *Washington Post*, September 15, 2022, retrieved from https://www.washingtonpost.com/opinions/2022/09/15 /deterrence-cyberspace-conflict-new-strategy/.

185   *The South is . . . most environmental stress.* "Emerging Markets: Will the Economic Catch-Up Continue?" *The Economist*, October 12, 2022, retrieved from https:// www.eiu.com/n/emerging-markets-will-the-economic-catch-up-continue/.

Nations in the Cloud: Globalization's Digitalization Meets Cyber Sovereignty (Thread 28)

189   *Globalization now includes . . . Russia-v-Ukraine.* "List of Most Streamed Songs on Spotify," Wikipedia (citing Spotify), retrieved February 22, 2023, retrieved from en.wikipedia.org/wiki/List_of_most_streamed_songs_on_Spotify; and Kyle Chayka, "Watching the World's 'First Tik Tok War,'" *The New Yorker*, March 3,

2022, retrieved from www.newyorker.com/culture/infinite-scroll/watching-the -worlds-first-tiktok-war.

189 *Global data flows . . . digitalization of globalization.* Manyika et al., "Digital Globalization."

189 *In the decade . . . jumped forty-five-fold.* Manyika et al., "Digital Globalization."

190 *The driver here . . . less for export.* Lund et al., "Globalization in Transition," Chapter 3, "Shifting Global Demand and the New China Effect."

190 *The EU, for . . . China's demand signal.* "China Trade to GDP Ratio 1960–2023," Macrotrends Web Page, retrieved February 22, 2023, from www.macrotrends.net /countries/CHN/china/trade-gdp-ratio; "US Trade to GDP Ratio, 1970–2023," Macrotrends Web Page, retrieved February 22, 2023, from www.macrotrends .net/countries/USA/united-states/trade-gdp-ratio; and "The EU in the World— International Trade," Eurostat Statistics Explained Web Page, February 2020, retrieved from ec.europa.eu/eurostat/statistics-explained/index.php?title=The _EU_in_the_world_-_international_trade.

191 *On that, see . . . the cyber realm.* For example, see "Facebook Hearings Cold Open— SNL," YouTube video, posted by Saturday Night Live, October 10, 2021, https:// www.youtube.com/watch?v=KwUkFly-xQU.

191 *For example, Russia . . . ensure government access.* Yuxi Wei, "Chinese Data Localization Law: Comprehensive but Ambiguous," Henry M. Jackson School of International Studies Web Page, February 7, 2018, retrieved from jsis.washington .edu/news/chinese-data-localization-law-comprehensive-ambiguous/.

The World in Three Vertical Slices: Why America Should Choose the Door Marked "West" (Thread 29)

196 *Preemptively performing the . . . the Biden administration.* Edward Wong and John Ismay, "US Aims to Turn Taiwan into Giant Weapons Depot: Officials Say Taiwan Needs to Become a 'Porcupine' with Enough Weapons to Hold Out if the Chinese Military Blockades and Invades It, Even if Washington Decides to Send Troops," *New York Times*, October 5, 2022, retrieved from https://www .nytimes.com/2022/10/05/us/politics/taiwan-biden-weapons-china.html.

197 *Given Europe's colonial . . . barn long ago.* See "Africa's Biggest Official Lender: China or the World Bank?" *Africa Press*, March 36, 2022, retrieved from www .africa-press.net/lesotho/all-news/africas-biggest-official-lender-china-or-the -world-bank.

In Globalization, Demand—Not Supply—Is Power: So, the Biggest Markets Command the Most Power (Thread 30)

201 *The business world . . . of discretionary spending.* C.K. Prahalad, *The Fortune at the Bottom of the Pyramid: Eradicating Poverty Through Profits* (Philadelphia: Wharton School Publishing, 2004).

202 *On the dark . . . nation's gender imbalance.* Brook Larmer, "China's Mixed Messages on the Global Trade in Endangered-Animal Parts," *New York Times Magazine*, November 27, 2018, retrieved from www.nationalgeographic.com/animals /article/china-bans-wildlife-trade-after-coronavirus-outbreak; Natasha Daly, "Chinese Citizens Push to Abolish Wildlife Trade as Coronavirus Persists," National Geographic Web Page (2020), retrieved from www.nationalgeographic .com/animals/article/china-bans-wildlife-trade-after-coronavirus-outbreak; Michael Standaert, "How Effective Are China's Attempts to Reduce the Risk of Wildlife Spreading Disease to Humans?" Ensia Web Page (University of Minnesota's Institute on the Environment), November 5, 2020, retrieved from https:// ensia.com/features/farmed-wildlife-zoonotic-disease-china/; and Heather Barr, "China's Bride Trafficking Problem," *The Diplomat*, October 30, 2019, retrieved from thediplomat.com/2019/10/chinas-bride-trafficking-problem/.

202 *More benign: China's . . . US nut exports.* Steve Hargreaves, "China's Latest Investment Craze: US Pecans," CNN Web Page, January 31, 2013, retrieved from money.cnn.com/2013/01/31/news/economy/china-pecan-exports/index.html.

202 *Most impactful and . . . sales by 2030.* Nancy W. Stauffer, "China's Transition to Electric Vehicles," MIT Energy Initiative Web Page, November 25, 2020, retrieved from energy.mit.edu/news/chinas-transition-to-electric-vehicles/.

202 *Think about how . . . sales after 2035.* Rod Meloni and Dane Kelly, "Big Three Expected to Have 100 Electric Vehicles on the Road Within 5 Years: 'This Is Like the Opening Chapter of a Very Long Book,'" Click on Detroit Web Page, October 21, 2020, retrieved from https://www.clickondetroit.com/news/local/2020 /10/21/big-three-expected-to-have-100-electric-vehicles-on-the-road-within -5-years/; and Adam Taylor, "E.U. Plans for Only Electric New Vehicles by 2035 'Without Precedent,'" *Washington Post*, October 28, 2022, retrieved from https://www.washingtonpost.com/climate-solutions/2022/10/28/eu-electric -cars-2035/.

202 *It is no . . . of the EU.* "Car Sales by Country," F&I Tools Web Page, retrieved February 22, 2023, from https://www.factorywarrantylist.com/car-sales-by -country.html.

Strength in Numbers: America Does Not Stack Up Well Against the Competition (Thread 31)

207   *China and India's . . . to third.* Katharina Buchholz, "Global Purchasing Power Is Moving South," Statista Web Page, July 14, 2020, retrieved from https://www.statista.com/chart/17805/countries-with-the-biggest-purchasing-power/.

207   *For over six . . . per capita GDP.* "Top 20 Country GDP (PPP) History & Projection (1800–2040)," YouTube video, posted by WawamuStats, retrieved February 22, 2023, from https://www.youtube.com/watch?v=4-2nqd6-ZXg; and John Hawksworth, Rob Clarry, and Hannah Audino, "The Long View: How Will the Global Economic Order Change by 2050?" PricewaterhouseCoopers Report, February 2017, retrieved from https://www.pwc.com/gx/en/world-2050/assets/pwc-the-world-in-2050-full-report-feb-2017.pdf.

207   *Come midcentury, the . . . and Indian counterparts.* Ward and Neumann, "Consumer in 2050: The Rise of the EM Middle Class."

207   *Consider: In 2000 . . . and global influence.* "China's Consumers Shake the (Retail) World," *Oxford Economics* (blog), retrieved February 22, 2023, from https://blog.oxfordeconomics.com/chinas-consumers-shake-the-retail-world.

207   *By midcentury, China . . . pool only marginally.* Ward and Neumann," Consumer in 2050: The Rise of the EM Middle Class."

207   *After World War . . . the world's GDP.* "A Short History of America's Economy Since World War II," The Wilson Center Web Page, January 23, 2014, retrieved from https://medium.com/the-worlds-economy-and-the-economys-world/a-short-history-of-americas-economy-since-world-war-ii-37293cdb640.

208   *The Americas are . . . souls (723 million non-US).* "Population by Continent 2023," World Population Review Web Page, retrieved February 22, 2023, from https://worldpopulationreview.com/continents.

208   *Add those states' . . . India's $33 trillion.* Hawksworth, Clarry, and Audino, "The Long View."

208   *Based on the . . . colonial roster there.* "Mercosur," European Commission Web Page, retrieved February 22, 2023, from policy.trade.ec.europa.eu/eu-trade-relationships-country-and-region/countries-and-regions/mercosur_en.

208   *Based on the . . . China and India.* Greg Charnock, "Free Trade Area of the Americas: Proposed Free-Trade Zone," *Encyclopedia Britannica*, May 1, 2016, retrieved from www.britannica.com/topic/Free-Trade-Area-of-the-Americas.

209   *The World Bank . . . global value chains."* The World Bank, *Semiannual Report of the Latin America and Caribbean Region: Trade Integration as a Pathway to Development?* The World Bank Web Page, October 2019, retrieved from https://openknowledge.worldbank.org/bitstream/handle/10986/32518/9781464815164.pdf.

209   *Already home to . . . partner is Texas.* "Florida: Gateway to the Americas," Inbound Logistics Web Page, June 2004, retrieved from www.inboundlogistics.com /articles/florida-gateway-to-the-americas/; and Orkun Gonen, "Florida: America's Superstate for Global Trade and Shipping," MoreThanShipping.com Web Page, August 3, 2020, retrieved from www.morethanshipping.com/florida -americas-superstate-for-global-trade-and-shipping/.

You Will Be Assimilated, Resistance Is Futile: America Is Finally Forced to Join Its Own Neighborhood (Thread 32)

211   *Whites of European . . . certain to decline.* This estimate is based on data drawn from the Wikipedia pages "European Emmigration" (https://en.wikipedia.org /wiki/European_emigration), "White People" (https://en.wikipedia.org/wiki /White_people), and "Demographics of the World" (https://en.wikipedia.org /wiki/Demographics_of_the_world)—all retrieved February 22, 2023.

211   *However, these United . . . 45 percent White.* Accepting Mexico's definition of "light-skinned" Mexicans as being equivalent to Whites (or roughly one-half its population), then the total White population of the combined Americas can be estimated at 450 million out of a total population of one billion. See Wikipedia pages "White People" and "White Mexicans" (https://en.wikipedia.org/wiki /White_Mexicans), both retrieved February 22, 2023.

211   *Both are home . . . in the EU).* Data drawn from United Nations Population Division, "International Migrant Stock 2020," retrieved February 22, 2023, from https://www.un.org/development/desa/pd/content/international-migrant-stock.

212   *The United States is . . . sending millions abroad.* "List of Countries and Dependencies by Population Density," Wikipedia (citing UN Department of Economic and Social Affairs, Population Division), retrieved February 22, 2023, from en.wikipedia.org/wiki/List_of_countries_and_dependencies_by_population _density; and Aaron O'Neill, "European Union: Population Density from 2010 to 2020," Statista Web Page, February 23, 2022, retrieved from www.statista .com/statistics/253445/population-density-in-the-european-union-eu/.

212   *In 1960, Europeans . . . of that flow.* Abby Budiman et al., "Facts on US Immigrants, 2018," Pew Research Center Web Page, August 20, 2020, retrieved from www.pewresearch.org/hispanic/2020/08/20/facts-on-u-s-immigrants/.

213   *In the previous . . . and low-tech workers.* Ran Abramitzky and Leah Boustan, "Immigration in American Economic History," *Journal of Economic Literature* (2017), retrieved from www.aeaweb.org/articles?id=10.1257/jel.20151189.

213   *As for assimilation . . . in cultural terms.* Budiman et al., "Facts on US Immigrants, 2018"; and Dylan Matthews, "Hispanic Immigrants Are Assimilating Just as

Quickly as Earlier Groups," *Washington Post*, January 28, 2013, retrieved from www.washingtonpost.com/news/wonk/wp/2013/01/28/hispanic-immigrants are-assimilating-just-as-quickly-as-earlier-groups/.

213 *In any event . . . only for Democrats.* Abramitzky and Boustan, "Immigration in American Economic History."

213 *Persons of color . . . low White fertility.* Frey, "New 2020 Census Results."

213 *As an ethnic . . . by native-born Asians.* Gretchen Livingston and Anna Brown, "Intermarriage in the US 50 Years After Loving v. Virginia: 1) Trends and Patterns in Intermarriage," Pew Research Center Web Page, May 18, 2017, retrieved from www.pewresearch.org/social-trends/2017/05/18/1-trends-and-patterns-in -intermarriage/.

214 *Point being if . . . three American voters.* Jeffrey S. Passel and D'Vera Cohn, "US Population Projections: 2005–2050," Pew Research Center Web Page, February 11, 2008, retrieved from www.pewresearch.org/hispanic/2008/02/11/us -population-projections-2005-2050/.

214 *Better to link . . . manage such spending.* Henry Olsen, "How This Climate Change Fund Could Fuel Populism in Richer Nations," *Washington Post*, November 21, 2022, retrieved from https://www.washingtonpost.com/opinions/2022/11/21 /cop27-fund-backfire-populism-climate-change/.

214 *By signaling such . . . the public sector.* On this point, see the promising ideas surrounding the so-called Bridgetown Initiative in Avinash Persaud, "Opinion: The Bridgetown Initiative," UNCS News Web Page, November 15, 2022, retrieved from https://unclimatesummit.org/opinion-the-bridgetown-initiative/.

The Geopolitics of Belonging: The EU's Model of Political Integration Works (Thread 33)

217 *When polled, Americans . . . of military aid.* Vanessa Williamson, "Americans Overestimate Foreign Aid? Not So Fast," *Brookings* (blog), March 19, 2018, retrieved from https://www.brookings.edu/blog/fixgov/2018/03/19/americans -overestimate-foreign-aid-not-so-fast/.

217 *Now, with China's . . . choice" for humanity.* Christian Shepherd and Lily Kuo, "Xi Presents China as 'New Choice' for Humanity as He Readies for Next Term," *Washington Post*, October 16, 2022, retrieved from https://www.washingtonpost .com/world/2022/10/16/xi-china-communist-party-congress/.

218 *To join the . . . body of law).* "Acquis," EUR-Lex: Access to European Union Law Web Page, retrieved February 22, 2023, from eur-lex.europa.eu/EN/legal -content/glossary/acquis.html.

218 *It helped transform . . . (former Soviet satellites).* Matt Bevington, "How New Member States Join the EU: All You Need to Know," UK in a Changing Europe

(UKICE) Web Page, March 31, 2020, retrieved from ukandeu.ac.uk/explainers/how-new-member-states-join-the-eu-all-you-need-to-know/.

219 *Consider the EU's . . . of utmost importance.* Directorate-General for Communication, "EU Accession Process: Step by Step," European Commission Publications Office Web Page, 2020, retrieved from data.europa.eu/doi/10.2775/88454.

219 *To the EU's . . . Georgia, Azerbaijan, Moldova).* Benjamin Elisha Sawe, "The Copenhagen Criteria: What Makes a Country Eligible to Join the European Union?" WorldAtlas Web Page, September 18, 2017, retrieved from www.worldatlas.com/articles/the-copenhagen-criteria-what-makes-a-country-eligible-to-join-the-european-union.html.

220 *Within the EU . . . negotiations to accession.* Directorate-General for Communication, "EU Accession Process."

220 *Having enlarged from . . . Montenegro, Serbia, Turkey).* Directorate-General for Communication, "EU Accession Process."

220 *Check out the . . . per capita growth.* Adam S. Posen, "The UK and the Global Economy After Brexit," Peterson Institute for International Economics Web Page, April 27, 2022, retrieved from www.piie.com/research/piie-charts/uk-and-global-economy-after-brexit; and Ben van der Merwe, "The UK Economy Has Fallen Far Behind the EU Since Brexit: Britain's GDP Per Head Has Grown Just 3.8 Per Cent Since the Referendum, While the EU's Has Grown by 8.5 Per Cent," *The New Statesman*, June 23, 2022, retrieved from https://www.newstatesman.com/chart-of-the-day/2022/06/uk-economy-fallen-behind-eu-since-brexit.

The West Is the Best: Our Hemisphere Is Advantageously Situated for What Comes Next (Throughline Six)

224 *Blessed with 30 . . . only dream about.* Asia's population density is 95 people per square kilometer, while the Americas feature a mere 22 people per square kilometer. See Victor Kiprop, "Continents by Population Density," World Atlas Web Page, April 17, 2019, retrieved from www.worldatlas.com/articles/continents-by-population-density.html.

224 *As the world's . . . of unmatched biodiversity.* Eight of the top twelve countries for biodiversity are found in the Americas. See Rhett A. Butler, "The Top 10 Most Biodiverse Countries," *Mongabay*, May 21, 2016, retrieved from news.mongabay.com/2016/05/top-10-biodiverse-countries/.

225 *American workers have . . . imports more expensive.* Simeon Djankov et al., "The United States Has Been Disengaging from the Global Economy," Peterson Institute for International Economics Web Page, April 19, 2021, retrieved from https://www.piie.com/research/piie-charts/united-states-has-been-disengaging-global-economy.

226 *Of the top . . . of second-place China (24).* Carmen Ang, "The Top 100 Most Valuable Brands in 2022," Visual Capitalist Web Page, October 27, 2022, retrieved from https://www.visualcapitalist.com/top-100-most-valuable-brands-in-2022/.

Energy Independence Ain't All It's Fracked Up to Be, but It's Why the United States Stopped Obsessing over the Middle East (Thread 34)

229 *While fracking comes . . . half of each.* "Hydraulic Fracturing Accounts for About Half of Current US Crude Oil Production," US Energy Information Agency Web Page, March 15, 2016, retrieved from www.eia.gov/todayinenergy/detail.php?id=25372; and David Bradley, "Fracking Used in Two-Thirds of US Nat Gas Production, EIA Says," Natural Gas Intelligence Web Page, May 5, 2016, retrieved from www.naturalgasintel.com/fracking-used-in-two-thirds-of-u-s-natgas-production-eia-says/.

229 *If we add . . . Saudi Arabia combined.* Jessica Aizarani, "Global Oil Production Share 2021, by Country," Statista Web Page, January 31, 2023, retrieved from https://www.statista.com/statistics/236605/share-of-global-crude-oil-production-of-the-top-15-oil-producing-countries/.

229 *In natural gas, . . . by five times.* Jessica Aizarani, "Natural Gas Production Worldwide in 2021, by Country," Statista Web Page, January 31, 2023, retrieved from https://www.statista.com/statistics/264101/world-natural-gas-production-by-country/.

230 *In the early . . . as we consume.* "Oil and Petroleum Products Explained," US Energy Information Administration Web Page, April 21, 2022, retrieved from www.eia.gov/energyexplained/oil-and-petroleum-products/imports-and-exports.php.

230 *America also now . . . natural gas consumption.* "US Energy Facts Explained," US Energy Information Administration Web Page, June 10, 2022, retrieved from www.eia.gov/energyexplained/us-energy-facts/.

230 *That recently made . . . dependency on Moscow.* "The United States Became the World's Largest LNG Exporter in the First Half of 2022," US Energy Information Administration Web Page, July 25, 2022, retrieved from www.eia.gov/todayinenergy/detail.php?id=53159.

230 *Thanks to hydraulic . . . since the 1950s.* US Energy Information Administration, "US Energy Facts Explained."

230 *In the next . . . to our south.* "North America Can Be Net Energy Exporter by 2025," Reuters, December 11, 2022, retrieved from www.cnbc.com/id/100301519.

230 *This changes the . . . linking their fates.* Dale Aluf, "China's Reliance on Middle East Oil, Gas to Rise Sharply," *Asia Times*, December 30, 2021, retrieved

from https://asiatimes.com/2021/12/china-to-rely-more-on-middle-east-for-oil -and-gas/; and Nidhi Verma, "India Asks Refiners to Cut Reliance on Middle East Oil After OPEC+ Decision," World Energy News Web Page, March 9, 2021, retrieved from www.worldenergynews.com/news/india-asks-refiners-cut -reliance-middle-east-721333.

230 *In combination, the . . . expand through 2050.* See Our World in Data Web Page for "Natural Gas Production by Region" (ourworldindata.org/grapher /natural-gas-production-by-region-terawatt-hours-twh), "Gas Consumption by Region" (ourworldindata.org/grapher/natural-gas-consumption-by-region), "Oil Production by Region" (ourworldindata.org/grapher/oil-production-by -region)—all retrieved February 22, 2023; and DNV GL, "Energy Transition Outlook 2017: Oil and Gas Forecast to 2050," retrieved February 22, 2023, from www.ourenergypolicy.org/wp-content/uploads/2017/09/DNV-GL_Energy -Transistion-Outlook-2017_oil-gas_lowres-single_3108_3.pdf.

230 *Compare that to . . . times more oil.*, "International Energy Outlook 2021," US Energy Information Administration Web Page, October 6, 2021, retrieved from www.eia.gov/outlooks/ieo/tables_side_pdf.php.

230 *Four-fifths of America's . . . exports to Asia.* "Where Does the United States Import Crude Petroleum From? (2020)," Observatory of Economic Complexity Web Page, retrieved from oec.world/en/visualize/tree_map/hs92/import/usa /all/52709/2020/; "Where Does China Import Crude Petroleum From? (2020)," Observatory of Economic Complexity Web Page, retrieved from oec.world/en /visualize/tree_map/hs92/import/chn/all/52709/2020/; and "Where Does Bahrain, Iran, Iraq, Kuwait, Oman, Qatar, Saudi Arabia, and United Arab Emirates Export Crude Petroleum to? (2020)," Observatory of Economic Complexity Web Page, retrieved from https://oec.world/en/visualize/tree_map/hs92/export/bhr .irn.irq.kwt.omn.qat.sau.are/show/52709/2020/—all retrieved February 22, 2023.

231 *The Western Hemisphere's . . . primary energy source.* Natural gas is projected to surpass oil as the world's primary source of energy in the 2040–2045 time frame. See Madhmitha Jaganmohan, "Energy Consumption Worldwide from 2000 to 2019, with a Forecast Until 2050, by Energy Source," Statista Web Page, June 21, 2022, retrieved from www.statista.com/statistics/222066/projected-global -energy-consumption-by-source/.

231 *Global natural gas . . . trillion cubic feet.* "Natural Gas," US Energy Information Administration Web Page, retrieved February 22, 2023, from www.eia.gov /international/data/world/natural-gas/dry-natural-gas-reserves.

231 *But in shale . . . China (1,115 tcf).* "World Shale Resource Assessments," US Energy Information Administration Web Page, September 24, 2015, retrieved from www.eia.gov/analysis/studies/worldshalegas/.

231　*In the United States . . . tied in consumption.* US Energy Information Administration, "US Energy Facts Explained."

231　*The fracking boom . . . to cleaner ones.* A key milestone here being that renewables overtake coal as the world's largest energy source for the generation of electricity in the year 2025. See the Executive Summary of the International Energy Agency's "Renewables 2022" report, December 2022, retrieved from https://www.iea .org/reports/renewables-2022/executive-summary.

Water, Water Everywhere but Not Enough to Drink: Why Tall Now Beats Wide (Thread 35)

235　*On Earth, the . . . remaining single percent.* Jeremiah Castelo, "What Is the Percentage of Drinkable Water on Earth?" World Water Reserve Web Page, December 13, 2021, retrieved from worldwaterreserve.com/percentage-of-drinkable-water -on-earth/.

235　*Per our planet's . . . measured in decades.* John Misachi, "What Is Fossil Water," World Atlas Web Page, August 17, 2018, retrieved from www.worldatlas.com /articles/what-is-fossil-water.html; and Water Science School, "Groundwater Decline and Depletion," US Geological Survey Web Page, June 6, 2018, retrieved from www.usgs.gov/special-topics/water-science-school/science/groundwater -decline-and-depletion.

235　*Global water use . . . pricing it appropriately.* "UN World Water Development Report 2019," United Nations Development Report, March 18, 2019, retrieved from www.unwater.org/publications/world-water-development-report-2019/.

235　*As the water-stressed . . . when suitably incentivized.* Francis Wilkinson, "How California Can Survive Another Historic Drought," *Washington Post*, May 15, 2022, retrieved from https://www.washingtonpost.com/business/how-california -can-survive-another-historic-drought/2022/05/15/be840ef6-d44f-11ec-be17 -286164974c54_story.html.

236　*Of that tiny . . . direct human consumption.* "How We Use Water," United States Environmental Protection Agency Web Page, May 24, 2022, retrieved from www.epa.gov/watersense/how-we-use-water.

236　*Examples of such . . . three decades (27 km/year).* Nicola Jones, "Redrawing the Map: How the World's Climate Zones Are Shifting," *YaleEnvironment 360*, October 23, 2018, retrieved from e360.yale.edu/features/redrawing-the-map-how-the -worlds-climate-zones-are-shifting.

236　*Humans naturally concentrate . . . us remain clustered.* Laurence C. Smith, *Rivers of Power: How a Natural Force Raised Kingdoms, Destroyed Civilizations, and Shapes Our World* (New York: Little, Brown Spark, 2020), 9–44 and 312.

236 *While Europe (10 . . . replenishable freshwater supply.* "Review of World Water Resources by Country," Food and Agriculture Organization of the United Nations, Water Reports 23, 2003, retrieved from www.fao.org/3/Y4473E /y4473e08.htm.

237 *Droughts kill crops . . . 2013 and 2022).* Sam Ro, "Historically Low Mississippi River Water Levels Mean More Barge Congestion," *Insider*, January 30, 2013, retrieved from https://www.businessinsider.com/low-mississippi-river-water-levels-2013-1; and Ray Lombardi, Angela Antipova, and Dorian J. Burnette, "Record Low Water Levels on the Mississippi River in 2022 Show How Climate Change Is Altering Large Rivers," *The Conversation*, December 14, 2022, retrieved from https://theconversation.com/record-low-water-levels-on-the-mississippi-river -in-2022-show-how-climate-change-is-altering-large-rivers-193920.

237 *Recalling that most . . . significant water shortages.* Lund University, "UN Climate Report: How Vulnerable Are We, and How Can We Adapt?" *Phys.Org*, February 25, 2022, retrieved from phys.org/news/2022-02-climate-vulnerable.html.

238 *With sea levels . . . home mortgage window.* National Ocean Service, *2022 Sea Level Rise Technical Report*.

238 *While negotiations concerning . . . Asian—river basins.* On the Colorado River, see Joshua Partlow, "Officials Fear 'Complete Doomsday Scenario' for Drought-Stricken Colorado River," *Washington Post*, December 1, 2022, retrieved from https://www.washingtonpost.com/climate-environment/2022/12/01/drought -colorado-river-lake-powell/.

238 *These situations will . . . charges of "hydro-hegemony."* Joyeeta Gupta, "The Watercourses Convention, Hydro-hegemony and Transboundary Water Issues," *International Spectator* 51, no. 3 (2016), retrieved from https://doi.org/10.1080 /03932729.2016.1198558.

238 *In the Western . . . of our electricity.* Joe Myers, "Which Countries Produce the Most Hydroelectric Power?" World Economic Forum Web Page, October 14, 2015, retrieved from https://www.weforum.org/agenda/2015/10/which -countries-produce-the-most-hydroelectric-power/; and "Hydropower Basics," Office of Energy Efficiency & Renewable Energy, US Department of Energy Web Page, retrieved February 22, 2023, from https://www.energy.gov/eere/water /hydropower-basics.

238 *In South America, . . . suffer a decrease.* Emilio Godoy et al., "The Climate Crisis and Latin American Hydropower," *Dialogo Chino*, July 18, 2022, retrieved from https://dialogochino.net/en/uncategorised/56368-hydropower-latin-america -climate-crisis/.

238 *Meanwhile, ever-wetter Canada, . . . US power generation.* Nia Williams and Allison Lampert, "Canada Plans Hydropower Push as Biden Looks to Clean Up

US Grid," Reuters, February 9, 2021, retrieved from https://www.reuters.com /business/energy/canada-plans-hydropower-push-biden-looks-clean-up-us-grid -2021-02-09/.

238 *Experts fear that . . . another "lost decade."* Will Freeman, "Is Latin America Stuck? Why the Region Could Face a New Lost Decade," *Foreign Affairs*, November 25, 2022, retrieved from https://www.foreignaffairs.com/central-america-caribbean /latin-america-stuck.

The West Feeds the Rest: Climate Change Elevates Food Security to National Security (Thread 36)

241 *In the mid-twentieth . . . increasing food equality.* Max Roser and Hannah Ritchie, "Food Supply," Our World in Data Web Page (citing UN FAO), 2021, retrieved from ourworldindata.org/food-supply.

241 *In global food . . . high-income societies (i.e., obesity).* Michiel van Dijk et al., "A Meta-Analysis of Projected Global Food Demand and Population at Risk of Hunger for the Period 2010–2050," *Nature Food* 2 (2021), retrieved from doi.org /10.1038/s43016-021-00322-9.

242 *The youthful, climate-vulnerable . . . its consumed calories.* Nadine Katkhuda, "Food Security in the Middle East," *EcoMENA*, August 11, 2020, retrieved from www .ecomena.org/food-middle-east/.

242 *The world's primary . . . far more food.* Jeremy Berlin et al., "Five Ways Climate Change Will Affect You: Crop Changes," National Geographic Web Page (2022), from www.nationalgeographic.com/climate-change/how-to-live-with-it /crops.html.

242 *Global agricultural trade . . . such complicating variables.* Susan Reidy, "A Century of Grain Trade," World-Grain.com, May 28, 2021, retrieved from www.world -grain.com/articles/15358-a-century-of-grain-trade.

242 *Keep in mind . . . in the making.* Arif Husain, "The Ukraine War Is Deepening Global Food Insecurity—What Can Be Done?" United States Institute of Peace Web Page, May 16, 2022, retrieved from https://www.usip.org/publications /2022/05/ukraine-war-deepening-global-food-insecurity-what-can-be-done.

242 *Three basic grains . . . of global consumption.* Amber Pariona, "What Are the World's Most Important Staple Foods?" World Atlas Web Page, June 7, 2019, retrieved from www.worldatlas.com/articles/most-important-staple-foods-in-the-world .html.

242 *The top three . . . corn (alongside Japan).* "Corn," Observatory of Economic Complexity Web Page, retrieved February 22, 2023, from oec.world/en/profile/hs /corn.

242 *Tied for second . . . at 33 percent).* "Rice," Observatory of Economic Complexity Web Page, retrieved February 22, 2023, from oec.world/en/profile/hs/rice; and "Wheat," Observatory of Economic Complexity Web Page, retrieved February 22, 2023, from oec.world/en/profile/hs/wheat.

243 *Other commodity markets . . . importer—by far.* "Soybeans," Observatory of Economic Complexity Web Page, retrieved February 22, 2023, from oec.world/en /profile/hs/soybeans; and "Sorghum," Observatory of Economic Complexity Web Page, retrieved February 22, 2023, from oec.world/en/profile/hs/sorghum.

243 *Already the world's . . . in coming decades.* Observatory of Economic Complexity, "Wheat"; and Nicola Jones, "Redrawing the Map."

243 *Russia will be . . . an expanded belt.* Heather A. Conley and Cyrus Newlin, "Climate Change Will Reshape Russia," Center for Strategic and International Studies Web Page, January 13, 2021, retrieved from www.csis.org/analysis/climate -change-will-reshape-russia.

243 *China, as the . . . in that domain.* Prableen Bajpai, "Who Produces the World's Food," Investopedia Web Page, July 28, 2022, retrieved from www.investopedia.com /articles/investing/043015/who-produces-worlds-food.asp; Richard Hoffmann, "The Big Chance for Foreign Food Producers," Ecovis Web Page, retrieved February 22, 2023, from www.ecovis.com/focus-china/big-chance-foreign-food -producers; and Hui Jiang, "China: Evolving Demand in the World's Largest Agricultural Import Market," US Foreign Agricultural Service, US Department of Agriculture Web Page," September 29, 2020, retrieved from www.fas.usda.gov/data /china-evolving-demand-world-s-largest-agricultural-import-market.

243 *Beijing, which clearly . . . recent Five-Year Plan.* Jack Ellis, "Cultivated Meat Included Under China's Five-Year Plan for the First Time," AFN, January 31, 2022, retrieved from agfundernews.com/five-year-plan-cultivated-meat -included-under-china.

243 *Beijing's second track . . . United Arab Emirates.* Ana Swanson, "An Incredible Image Shows How Powerful Countries Are Buying Up Much of the World's Land," *Washington Post*, May 21, 2015, retrieved from www.washingtonpost .com/news/wonk/wp/2015/05/21/rich-countries-are-buying-up-farmland-from -poorer-ones-around-the-world/.

243 *A decade ago, . . . its arable land.* Kristen Butler, "China Buys 5 Percent of Ukraine's Land: China Buys 5 Percent of Ukraine's Total Land—About 9 Percent of its Farmland—to Feed Its Growing Population," UPI.com *Odd News* (blog), September 23, 2013, retrieved from www.upi.com/Odd_News/Blog/2013/09/23 /China-buys-5-percent-of-Ukraines-land/5941379959745/.

244 *Foreigners now control . . . tripling since 2010.* Ryan McCrimmon, "China Is Buying Up American Farms. Washington Wants to Crack Down," *Politico*, July

19, 2021, retrieved from www.politico.com/news/2021/07/19/china-buying-us
-farms-foreign-purchase-499893.

244 *The Americas possess . . . that of Asia.* Food and Agriculture Organization, "Review of World Water Resources by Country."

244 *That reserve capacity . . . feeds the Rest.* Anthony Faiola, "The New Economics of Hunger," *Washington Post*, April 27, 2008, retrieved from www.washington post.com/wp-dyn/content/article/2008/04/26/AR2008042602041.html, with accompanying data chart retrieved from www.infohow.org/business-finance -employment/global-grain-trade/.

Global Value Chains Regionalize Amidst Superpower Brand Wars: America Disregards This at Its Peril (Thread 37)

247 *Thanks to Donald . . . deal ever made."* Andrew Chatzky, James McBride, and Mohammed Aly Sergie, "NAFTA and the USMCA: Weighing the Impact of North American Trade," Council on Foreign Relations Web Page, July 1, 2020, retrieved from https://www.cfr.org/backgrounder/naftas-economic-impact.

247 *It was anything . . . the automobile industry.* Shannon K. O'Neil, *The Globalization Myth: Why Regions Matter* (New Haven, CT: Yale University Press, 2022), 96–97.

247 *The follow-on United States–Mexico–Canada . . . complications as improvements.* O'Neil, *Globalization Myth*, 123.

247 *Thus, America remains, . . . along regional lines.* O'Neil, *Globalization Myth*, 94.

247 *This is how . . . percent in 2021.* O'Neil, *Globalization Myth*, 15; and "US GDP as % of World GDP," YCharts Web Page, retrieved February 22, 2023, from https://ycharts.com/indicators/us_gdp_as_a_percentage_of_world_gdp.

248 *As O'Neil argues: . . . closest to us."* O'Neil, *Globalization Myth*, 16.

248 *Citing the clear . . . in the mid-teens.* O'Neil, *Globalization Myth*, 6–7.

248 *The citizens of . . . sustainable economic future."* "More Than Two-Thirds of Latin Americans Support Integration, Despite the Pandemic," Inter-American Development Bank Web Page, February 18, 2022, retrieved from https:// www.iadb.org/en/news/more-two-thirds-latin-americans-support-integration -despite-pandemic.

248 *Because Latin America . . . colonial-era trade inequalities.* O'Neil, *Globalization Myth*, 12–13.

248 *For America to . . . their own turf."* O'Neil, *Globalization Myth*, 15.

248 *Given that harshly . . . generate "more NAFTAs."* O'Neil, *Globalization Myth*, 155.

249 *While China, in . . . Trump's misguided policies.* O'Neil, *Globalization Myth*, 69; and Pierre Lemieux, "Biden's Protectionism: Trumpism with a Human Face," Cato

Institute Web Page, Fall 2022, retrieved from https://www.cato.org/regulation/fall-2022/bidens-protectionism-trumpism-human-face.

249　*In O'Neil's strict . . . build its own."* O'Neil, *Globalization Myth*, 15.

249　*In that sense, . . . hemispheric trade integration.* "The Destructive New Logic That Threatens Globalisation: America Is Leading a Dangerous Global Slide Towards Subsidies, Export Controls and Protectionism," *The Economist*, January 12, 2023, retrieved from https://www.economist.com/leaders/2023/01/12/the-destructive-new-logic-that-threatens-globalisation.

West Hem Civ 101: Having Outgrown Our Parentage, the Americas Stand Tall (Thread 38)

251　*Across the fifteenth . . . first 150 years).* Alexander Koch and Simon L. Lewis, "Earth System Impacts of the European Arrival and Great Dying in the Americas After 1492," *Quaternary Science Reviews* 207 (2019), retrieved from https://www.sciencedirect.com/science/article/pii/S0277379118307261.

251　*What ensued was . . . major racial groupings.* "Racial Demographics in the Western Hemisphere," Encyclopedia.com, retrieved February 22, 2023, from https://www.encyclopedia.com/social-sciences/encyclopedias-almanacs-transcripts-and-maps/racial-demographics-western-hemisphere.

251　*A telling example: . . . medieval Spanish haciendas.* Lakshmi Gandhi, "How Mexican Vaqueros Inspired the American Cowboy," History.com, September 24, 2021, retrieved from https://www.history.com/news/mexican-vaquero-american-cowboy.

252　*Facilitating our future . . . that, Catholicism (three-fifths).* "These Are the Eight Most Spoken Languages in the Americas," Knowledge Snacks Web Page, retrieved February 22, 2023, from www.knowledgesnacks.com/articles/most-spoken-languages-in-the-americas/; "Christianity by Country" (en.wikipedia.org/wiki/Christianity_by_country) and "Catholic Church by Country" (en.wikipedia.org/wiki/Catholic_Church_by_country), Wikipedia, both retrieved February 22, 2023; and "Global Christianity—A Report on the Size and Distribution of the World's Christian Population," Pew Research Center Web Page, December 19, 2011, retrieved from https://www.pewresearch.org/religion/2011/12/19/global-christianity-exec/.

252　*There, six conservative . . . unconstitutional and anti-democratic.* The six conservative Catholics are Chief Justice John Roberts and Justices Clarence Thomas, Samuel Alito, Neil Gorsuch (raised Catholic, now Episcopalian in practice), Brett Kavanaugh, and Amy Coney Barrett. A seventh Catholic justice is liberal Sonia Sotamayor. On the conservative justices' collective efforts to reshape the legal landscape, see Kimberly Wehle, "The Supreme Court Wants to End the Separation of Church and State: Justice Alito Doesn't Think Society Is Christian Enough. Recent Court Decisions Show How He Intends to Remedy That," *Politico*, August 10, 2022, retrieved from https://www.politico.com/news/magazine /2022/08/10/supreme-court-separation-of-church-and-state-00050571; and William Galston, "What Is Integralism: The Catholic Movement That Wants to Use Government Power in the Name of Public Morality," Persuasion Web Page, November 4, 2022, retrieved from https://www.persuasion.community/p/what -is-integralism.

252 *This growing effort . . . in the 2040s.* Frey, "US Will Become 'Minority White'"; and William H. Frey, "Modeling the Future of Religion in America: If Recent Trends in Religious Switching Continue, Christians Could Make Up Less Than Half of the US Population Within a Few Decades," Pew Research Center Web Page, September 13, 2022, retrieved from https://www.pewresearch.org/religion /2022/09/13/modeling-the-future-of-religion-in-america/.

252 *An example of . . . associated anti-immigrant fervor.* Caroline Kitchener, "Covert Network Provides Pills for Thousands of Abortions in US Post Roe," *Washington Post*, October 18, 2022, retrieved from https://www.washingtonpost.com /politics/2022/10/18/illegal-abortion-pill-network/.

253 *Specific to Catholicism: . . . top global spots.* Wikipedia, "Catholic Church by Country."

Nobody Does It Better: These United States as Globalization in Miniature (Thread 39)

255 *Building our Empire . . . American-style market economics.* Barnett, *Great Powers*, 81–85; and Robert Kagan, *Dangerous Nation: America's Place in the World from Its Earliest Days to the Dawn of the Twentieth Century* (New York: Alfred A. Knopf, 2006), 76.

256 *George Washington's farewell . . . on continental conquest.* "Washington's Farewell Address to the People of the United States," retrieved from www.senate.gov /artandhistory/history/resources/pdf/Washingtons_Farewell_Address.pdf; and Kagan, *Dangerous Nation*, 112–25.

256 *The American System, . . . namely, public infrastructure.* Barnett, *Great Powers*, 85–89.

256 *His goal was . . . European Economic Area.* Ron Chernow, *Alexander Hamilton* (New York: Penguin Press, 2004), 378.

256 *Abraham Lincoln, who . . . the EU's euro.* Barnett, *Great Powers*, 89–98.

257 *Popularly dubbed a . . . inhabiting society's margins.* Heather Cox Richardson, *West from Appomattox: The Reconstruction of America After the Civil War* (New Haven, CT: Yale University Press, 2007), 1.

257 *University of Wisconsin . . . of westward expansion.* Frederick Turner Jackson, "The Significance of the Frontier in American History" (1893), retrieved from http://nationalhumanitiescenter.org/pds/gilded/empire/text1/turner.pdf.

257 *Enter Theodore Roosevelt, . . . by colonizing powers.* Barnett, *Great Powers*, 106–9.

257 *Like TR's promise . . . vulnerable middle class.* Barnett, *Great Powers*, 131–33.

258 *America was considered . . . Cold War eras.* Doron S. Ben-Atar, *Trade Secrets: Intellectual Piracy and the Origins of American Industrial Power* (New Haven, CT: Yale University Press, 2004); and Peter Andreas, *Smuggler Nation: How Illicit Trade Made America* (New York: Oxford University Press, 2014).

Winning the Twenty-First Century: Citizenship Is About Identity, and Identity Is About to Change (Thread 40)

262 *In the former . . . certain income thresholds and are willing to relocate.* Chris Dwyer, "'Digital Nomads' Can Now Live in Spain with Their Families—if They Earn Enough," CNBC Web Page, February 19 2023, retrieved from https://www.cnbc.com/2023/02/19/spains-digital-nomad-visa-lets-remote-workers-bring-their-families.html.

262 *Vladimir Putin has . . . of this dynamic.* David Leonhardt, "The G.O.P.'s 'Putin Wing': In Republicans' Own Words," *New York Times*, April 7, 2022, retrieved from https://www.nytimes.com/2022/04/07/briefing/republican-party-putin-wing.html.

The Climate Redemption: Get Busy Adding Stars or Get Busy Losing Them (Thread 41)

267 *As the American . . . within the US."* Juan Enriquez, *The Untied States of America: Polarization, Fracturing, and Our Future* (New York: Crown Publishers, 2005), 57. .

267 *The United States . . . claimed sovereign status.* Sam Jacobs, "America's Sovereign States: The Obscure History of How 10 Independent States Joined the US," Ammo.com Web Page, retrieved February 22, 2023, from ammo.com/articles/sovereign-states-america-history-independent-states-joined-us-union.

268 *Per Enriquez, "Countries . . . up or die."* Enriquez, *Untied States*, 3.

268 *A nation's origin . . . beliefs and ideals.* Enriquez, *Untied States*, 21 and 252.

268 *Channeling Charles Darwin . . . responsive to change."* Quoted in Enriquez, *Untied States*, 239.

269 *Again Enriquez: "Grandchildren . . . and even sacrifice.* Enriquez, *Untied States*, 42–45.

269 *Therein lies the . . . removed from maps."* Enriquez, *Untied States*, 42.

269 *As true globalization . . . hope of earth."* Abraham Lincoln, "Annual Message to Congress—Concluding Remarks," December 1, 1862, retrieved from https://www.abrahamlincolnonline.org/lincoln/speeches/congress.htm.

269 *As Enriquez observes, . . . rapidly homogenizing world.* Enriquez, *Untied States*, 28.

We're Still the One: The Durability of America's Superpower Brand Appeal (Thread 42)

275 Hollywood–*70 percent . . . films are American.* Tom Brook, "How the Global Box Office Is Changing Hollywood," BBC Web Page, October 21, 2014, retrieved from www.bbc.com/culture/article/20130620-is-china-hollywoods-future; and "All Time Worldwide Box Office," The Numbers Web Page, retrieved February 22, 2023, from www.the-numbers.com/box-office-records/worldwide/all-movies/cumulative/all-time.

The Americanist Manifesto: Summoning the Vision and Courage to Remap Our Hemisphere's Indivisible Future (Throughline Seven)

279 *A spectre is . . . progressive hemispheric integration.* The opening here is modeled on the original by Karl Marx and Frederick Engels entitled *Manifesto of the Communist Party–and Its Genesis,* published in 1848 and retrieved from www.marxists.org/admin/books/manifesto/Manifesto.pdf.

Thesis: American Acceptionalism (Thread 43)

283 *If America does . . . bulk themselves up.* Adapted from Thomas P.M. Barnett, "The 51st, 52nd, 53rd, 54th, and 55th State," *Esquire,* October 2007, retrieved from classic.esquire.com/article/2007/10/1/the-51st-52nd-53rd-54th-and-55th-state.

283 *Visionaries like Alexander . . . and true Americans."* Maurice G. Baxter, *Henry Clay and the American System* (Lexington, KY: University Press of Kentucky, 2004), 57.

285 *Ditto for Beijing's . . . across Latin America.* Christoph Nedopil, "Countries of the Belt and Road Initiative"; Green Finance & Development Center, FISF Fudan University, 2022, retrieved from https://greenfdc.org/countries-of-the-belt-and-road-initiative-bri/.

285 *Russia props up . . . underwrite Ukraine's resistance.* Ishaan Tharoor, "Biden's Hemispheric Summit May End Up a Dud," *Washington Post,* June 10, 2022, retrieved from https://www.washingtonpost.com/world/2022/06/10/biden-summit-of -americas-south-dud/.

286 *Immigrants, overwhelmingly Latino, . . . over this century.* Abby Budiman, "Key Findings About US Immigrants," Pew Research Center Web Page, August 20, 2020, retrieved from www.pewresearch.org/fact-tank/2020/08/20/key-findings -about-u-s-immigrants/.

286 *With it, we . . . to our economy.* Budiman et al., "Facts on US Immigrants, 2018."

286 *Immigration is a . . . simple as that.* Adi Gaskill, "Immigrants Create More Jobs Than They Take," *Forbes,* November 11, 2020, retrieved from www.forbes.com /sites/adigaskell/2020/11/11/immigrants-create-more-jobs-than-they-take/; and Miller, "Long-Term Jobs Killer."

286 *This is the . . . globalization's nefarious elites.* Simon Foy, "Don't Turn London into 'Singapore-on-Thames,' MPs Tell Rishi Sunak: Treasury Must Not Water Down Square Mile Regulation, Committee Warns," *The Telegraph,* June 16, 2022, retrieved from https://www.telegraph.co.uk/business/2022/06/16/dont -turn-london-singapore-on-thames-mps-tell-rishi-sunak/; and John Heathershaw et al., "The UK's Kleptocracy Problem: How Servicing Post-Soviet Elites Weakens the Rule of Law," Chatham House Research Paper, December 2021, retrieved from https://www.chathamhouse.org/sites/default/files/2022-10/2021 -12-08-uk-kleptocracy-problem-heathershaw-mayne-et-al.pdf.

286 *America can either . . . "main character energy."* Per the Urban Dictionary, "A person who unintentionally lives, breathes, and is like the protagonist in a story or series," retrieved on February 22, 2023, from https://www.urbandictionary.com /define.php?term=Main%20Character%20Energy.

Antithesis: American Apartheid (Thread 44)

289 *US journalist Bill . . . news and entertainment."* Bill Bishop, *The Big Sort: Why the Clustering of Like-Minded America Is Tearing Us Apart* (Boston: Houghton Mifflin, 2008), 39.

289 *As Bishop noted, . . . can smell it."* Bishop, *Big Sort,* 23.

289 *Far from "replacing" . . . shaped by, migration.* Bishop, *Big Sort,* 41.

290 *The Right's ethno-nationalism . . . size in population.* Bryan Metzger, "Sen. Josh Hawley Predicts the Overturning of Roe v. Wade Will Cause a 'Major Sorting Out Across the Country,' and Allow the GOP to 'Extend Their Strength in the Electoral College,'" MSN Web Page, June 24, 2022, retrieved from www .msn.com/en-us/news/politics/sen-josh-hawley-predicts-the-overturning-of-roe -v-wade-will-cause-a-major-sorting-out-across-the-country-and-allow-the-gop -to-extend-their-strength-in-the-electoral-college/ar-AAYQ6n2.

291 *With the Senate . . . wield that veto.* Adding up forty current Republican senators from the least-populated states yields WY 2 (2), AK 2 (4), ND 2 (6), SD 2 (8), MT 1 (9), ME 1 (10), WV 1 (11), ID 2 (13), NE 2 (15), KS 2 (17), MS 2 (19), AR 2 (21), IA 2 (23), UT 2 (25), OK 2 (27), KY 2 (29), LA 2 (31), AL 2 (33), SC 2 (35), WI 1 (36), MO 2 (38), and IN 2 (40). Adding up those state populations (and dividing by half for states with only one GOP senator) yields a sum (63M) equal to 19 percent of the total US population (331M).

291 *During South Africa's . . . to enforce order.* "White South Africans," Wikipedia (citing Statistics South Africa), retrieved February 22, 2023, from en.wikipedia .org/wiki/White_South_Africans.

291 *America currently displays . . . Congress's legislative activity.* Jesse M. Crosson et al., "Partisan Competition and the Decline in Legislative Capacity Among Congressional Offices," *Legislative Studies Quarterly* 46, no. 3 (2021), retrieved from https://onlinelibrary.wiley.com/doi/abs/10.1111/lsq.12301; and Jonathan Lewallen, *Committees and the Decline of Lawmaking in Congress* (Ann Arbor, MI: University of Michigan Press, 2020).

292 *Such political stalemating . . . Christian) American civilization.* Cassie Miller, "'There Is No Political Solution': Accelerationism in the White Power Movement," Southern Poverty Law Center Web Page, June 23, 2020, retrieved from https://www.splcenter.org/hatewatch/2020/06/23/there-no-political-solution -accelerationism-white-power-movement.

292 *Fortunately, history shows . . . than homogenous ones.* Paul Collier and Anke Hoeffler, "On Economic Causes of Civil War," *Oxford Economic Papers* 50 (1998), retrieved from   http://web.worldbank.org/archive/website01241/WEB/IMAGES/ON _ECONO.PDF.

292 *Given Latin America's . . . nor natural Republicans.* Geraldo Cadava, *The Hispanic Republican: The Shaping of an American Political Identity, from Nixon to Trump* (New York: Ecco, 2020), 323–39.

293 *Per American poet . . . is always through."* Robert Frost, "A Servant to Servants" in *North of Boston* (New York: Henry Holt and Company, 1914), retrieved from https://en.wikisource.org/wiki/North_of_Boston/A_Servant_to_Servants.

Synthesis: Mil Millones de Americanos (Thread 45)

297 *In his 2020 . . . equal in territory.* Matthew Yglesias, *One Billion Americans: The Case for Thinking Bigger* (New York: Portfolio Penguin, 2020).

298 *This is essentially . . . lower-income partner states.* Shengnan Ma, "Growth Effects of Economic Integration: New Evidence from the Belt and Road Initiative," *Economic Analysis and Policy* 73 (2022), retrieved from https://doi.org/10.1016/j.eap .2022.01.004.

300 *Channeling the fictional . . . be the truth.* The original line is "How often have I said to you that when you have eliminated the impossible, whatever remains, however improbably, must be the truth?" Drawn from Arthur Conan Doyle, *The Sign of the Four*, 1890, chapter six, page 111, as recorded in "Sherlock Holmes," Wikiquote, retrieved February 22, 2023, from https://en.wikiquote.org/wiki /Sherlock_Holmes.

300 *The baseline economic . . . as a whole.* Press Release, "Trade Integration Even More Important for Latin America and the Caribbean as Growth Slows," World Bank Web Page, October 10, 2019, retrieved from https://www.worldbank.org /en/news/press-release/2019/10/10/trade-integration-even-more-important-for -latin-america-and-the-caribbean-as-growth-slows; Andrew Mold and Samiha Chowdhury, "Why the Extent of Intra-African Trade Is Much Higher Than Commonly Believed—And What This Means for the AfCFTA," Brookings Web Page, May 19, 2021, retrieved from https://www.brookings.edu/blog/africa -in-focus/2021/05/19/why-the-extent-of-intra-african-trade-is-much-higher -than-commonly-believed-and-what-this-means-for-the-afcfta/; and O'Neil, *Globalization Myth*, 8–13.

301 *As the editorial . . . to democratic stability."* Editorial Board, "The US Can't Get the Hemisphere Together Because It's Coming Apart," *Washington Post*, June 5, 2022, retrieved from www.washingtonpost.com/opinions/2022/06/05/us-cant -get-hemisphere-together-because-its-coming-apart/.

301 *If your country . . . or political structure.* Jonathan Palma, "China and the US Offer Competing Visions for Ecuador's Debt," *Dialogo Chino*, August 23, 2021, retrieved from dialogochino.net/en/trade-investment/45451-china-and-the-us -offer-competing-visions-for-ecuadors-debt/; and Alberto Araujo, "China, Ecuador to Renegotiate 'Harmful' Loan Terms," Argus Media Web Page, February 9, 2022, retrieved from www.argusmedia.com/en/news/2300419-china-ecuador -to-renegotiate-harmful-loan-terms.

301 *A good example . . . South Pacific archipelago."* Ralph Jennings, "Solomon Islands Pact Clears Lane for China to Sail into South Pacific," Voice of America Web Page, April 26, 2022, retrieved from www.voanews.com/a/solomon-islands -pact-clears-lane-for-china-to-sail-into-south-pacific-/6545723.html.

Coda—An Americas-First Grand Strategy: Crowdsourcing the Right Story, Choosing the Right Paths

305 *Slouching toward Armageddon, . . . human neck—forever.* George Orwell's original line, uttered by Inner Party member O'Brien, was, "If you want a picture of the future, imagine a boot stamping on a human face—forever"; see Orwell's novel *Nineteen Eighty-Four* (New York: Harcourt, Brace and Company, 1949), 271.

306 *The Pentagon recently . . . diversity and pluralism.* Michael J. Mazarr, "The Societal Foundations of National Competitiveness," RAND Corporation Research Report, 2022, retrieved from https://www.rand.org/pubs/research_reports/RRA499-1.html.

306 *As Michael J. Mazarr, . . . spiraling into decline."* Michael J. Mazarr, "What Makes a Power Great: The Real Drivers of Rise and Fall," *Foreign Affairs*, July/August 2022, retrieved from www.foreignaffairs.com/articles/united-states/2022-06-21/what-makes-a-power-great.

307 *In his autobiography, . . . impossible, has happened."* Winston S. Churchill, *My Early Life: A Rolling Commission* (London: Thornton Butterworth, 1930), in "Chapter Five: The Fourth Hussars," retrieved from www.fadedpage.com/showbook.php?pid=20160543.

Fig. 1

19 Our World in Data, "World GDP over the Last Two Millennia," https://ourworldindata.org/grapher/world-gdp-over-the-last-two-millennia.

19 Our World in Data, "Globalization over 5 Centuries: KM," https://ourworldindata.org/grapher/globalization-over-5-centuries-km.

19 Our World in Data, "Distribution of Bilateral and Unilateral Trade Partnerships," https://ourworldindata.org/grapher/distribution-of-bilateral-and-unilateral-trade-partnerships.

Fig. 2

36 Federation of American Scientists, "Status of World Nuclear Forces," last modified 2021, https://fas.org/issues/nuclear-weapons/status-world-nuclear-forces/.

36 Noah Shachtman, "Nations That Gave Up Nuclear Bombs," *Newsweek*, October 12, 2009, https://www.newsweek.com/nations-gave-nuclear-bombs-78661.

36 Hannah Ritchie and Max Roser, "Nuclear Weapons," Our World in Data, September 2019, https://ourworldindata.org/nuclear-weapons.

36 Bryce Vennard, "Nuclear Warheads by Country: From 1945 to 2022," Visual Capitalist Web Page, last modified January 12, 2022, https://www.visualcapitalist.com/cp/nuclear-warheads-by-country-1945-2022/.

Fig. 3

43 Our World in Data, "The Number of Active State-Based Conflicts," https://ourworldindata.org/grapher/the-number-of-active-state-based-conflicts?country=~OWID_WRL.

Fig. 4

67 Viviane Clement et al., "Groundswell Part 2: Acting on Internal Climate Migration," World Bank, Washington, DC, 2021, https://openknowledge.worldbank

.org/entities/publication/2c9150df-52c3-58ed-9075-d78ea56c3267 License: CC BY 3.0 IGO.

67   Economics & Peace, "Global Terrorism Index 2021: Measuring the Impact of Terrorism," 2021, https://www.economicsandpeace.org/wp-content/uploads /2021/10/ETR-2021-web.pdf.

Fig. 5

72   "Alarming new report finds entire global warming scenarios are now 'within the realm of possibility'," Phys.org, January 16, 2023, https://phys.org/news/2023 -01-alarming-entire-global.html.

72   Elizabeth Kolbert, "Redrawing the Map: How the World's Climate Zones Are Shifting," Yale Environment 360, January 9, 2023, https://e360.yale.edu/features /redrawing-the-map-how-the-worlds-climate-zones-are-shifting?fbclid=I wAR2ayhTxcaIgyoroAot3Gs6X-mtKs1nDjNRDSU4WPDR0XULrHr _4RDmzmVQ.

72   Timothy Andrews et al., "Emergent risks from Arctic Ocean warming," *Nature Climate Change* 8 (2018): 713-718, https://www.nature.com/articles/s41558 -018-0161-6.epdf.

Fig. 6

80   M. Baker, "Seattle will be home port for new class of icebreakers," *The Seattle Times*, March 22, 2022, https://www.seattletimes.com/seattle-news/seattle -will-be-home-port-for-new-class-of-icebreakers/.

80   Visual Capitalist, "Breaking the ice: Mapping Changing Arctic," https://www .visualcapitalist.com/breaking-the-ice-mapping-changing-arctic/.

Fig. 7

91   United Nations, Department of Economic and Social Affairs, Population Division, "World Population Prospects 2022: Demographic Indicators," https://population.un.org/wpp/Download/Files/1_Indicators%20(Standard) /EXCEL_FILES/1_General/WPP2022_GEN_F01_DEMOGRAPHIC _INDICATORS_REV1.xlsx.

Fig. 8

104   OECD, "GDP Long-Term Forecast (Indicator)," OECD Data, doi: 10.1787 /d927bc18-en.

104   FOECD, "The World Economy, 1–2001 AD," in The World Economy: Volume 1: A Millennial Perspective and Volume 2: Historical Statistics (Paris: OECD Publishing, 2006), https://doi.org/10.1787/9789264022621-21-en.

Fig. 9

111   Our World in Data, "Median Age," https://ourworldindata.org/grapher/median-age.

Fig. 10

144   Homi Kharas and Kristofer Hamel, "Global Middle Class: How Will They Spend Their Money?" Brookings Institution, February 28, 2017, https://www.brookings.edu/wp-content/uploads/2017/02/global_20170228_global-middle-class.pdf.

Fig. 11

156   C. K. Chan, "China's Belt and Road Initiative Opens Up Unprecedented Opportunities," *Forbes*, September 4, 2018, https://www.forbes.com/sites/great speculations/2018/09/04/chinas-belt-and-road-initiative-opens-up-unprecedented-opportunities/?sh=7903c9653e9a.

156   Daniel Gros, "The EU's Peripheral Role in China's Global Vision," WIIW Research Report, No. 269, 2018, https://wiiw.ac.at/the-eu-s-peripheral-role-in-china-s-global-vision-n-269.html.

156   OECD, "China's Belt and Road Initiative in the Global Trade, Investment and Finance Landscape," OECD Publishing, 2018, https://www.oecd.org/finance/Chinas-Belt-and-Road-Initiative-in-the-global-trade-investment-and-finance-landscape.pdf.

Fig. 12

163   "What is India's Necklace of Diamonds Strategy? India to Counter China's String of Pearls." Streamed live on YouTube, Jul 21, 2020, https://www.youtube.com/live/y9qjo5ewGaY?feature=share.

163   "7th January 2021 Editorials, Opinions, Analyses," Legacy IAS Academy, https://www.legacyias.com/7th-january-2021-editorials-opinions-analyses/.

Fig. 13

168   Sheena Chestnut Greitens and Rogier Creemers, "Dealing with Demand for China's Global Surveillance Exports," Brookings Institution, April 28, 2020, https://www.brookings.edu/wp-content/uploads/2020/04/FP_20200428_china_surveillance_greitens_v3.pdf.

Fig. 15

180   "Here are the countries that allowed Huawei to build 5G," HuaweiCentral, https://www.huaweicentral.com/here-are-the-countries-that-allowed-huawei-to-build-5g-list/.

Fig. 16

215   U.S. Department of Homeland Security, "2019 Yearbook of Immigration Statistics: Lawful Permanent Residents," https://www.dhs.gov/sites/default/files/publications/immigration-statistics/yearbook/2019/yrbk_2019_lpr_excel_final.zip.

Fig. 17

221   European Commission, Directorate-General for Neighbourhood and Enlargement Negotiations, EU accession process, Publications Office, 2020, https://data.europa.eu/doi/10.2876/8416.

Fig. 18

232   U.S. Energy Information Administration, "Annual Refined Petroleum Products Consumption," https://www.eia.gov/international/data/world/petroleum-and-other-liquids/annual-refined-petroleum-products-consumption.

Fig. 19

239   Max Roser, Hannah Ritchie, Esteban Ortiz-Ospina, and Lucas Rodés-Guirao, "World Population Growth," Our World in Data, https://ourworldindata.org/world-population-growth.

239   Food and Agriculture Organization of the United Nations, "Review of World Water Resources by Country," https://www.fao.org/3/y4473e/y4473e00.htm#Contents.

Fig. 20

245   "FAO. Crops and livestock products," License: CC BY-NC-SA 3.0 IGO, extracted from: www.fao.org/faostat/en/#data/TC.

Fig. 21

259   Bureau of Economic Analysis, "Gross Domestic Product by State, First Quarter 2022," https://www.bea.gov/data/gdp/gdp-state.

259   U.S. Census Bureau, "Population Estimates, Population Division," https://www.census.gov/data/tables/time-series/demo/popest/2020s-state-total.html.

259   Organisation for Economic Co-operation and Development, "Gross Domestic Product (GDP)," https://data.oecd.org/gdp/gross-domestic-product-gdp.htm.

259   The World Bank, "Population, Total," https://data.worldbank.org/indicator/SP.POP.TOTL.

Fig. 22

271   National Museum of American History, "Flag Facts," Smithsonian Institution, https://www.si.edu/spotlight/flag-day/flag-facts.

Fig. 23

287 American Community Survey 5-Year Data (2009-2021), https://www.census
.gov/data/developers/data-sets/acs-5year.2019.html#list-tab-1036221584.

Fig. 24

294 Encyclopedia Britannica, "Members of the U.S. Senate," https://www.britannica
.com/topic/Members-of-the-U-S-Senate-1935165.

294 Stats America, "Population by State: 2023," https://www.statsamerica.org/sip
/rank_list.aspx?rank_label=pop1&ct=S18.

INDEX

conflict, civil (*continued*)
    middle class and, 123
    number of, 40, 43 (fig)
conflict, East-West, 89–90
conflict, international, 147, 148. *See also* wars,
    state-on-state
Confucianism, 131
connectivity, 49. *See also* globalization; integration
    vs. control, 9–10
    empowerment by, 50
    offered by China, 178. *see also* Belt and Road
        Initiative (BRI)
    rules and, 17
conspiracy theories, 116, 124
consumption, 2, 85. *See also* demand
    by China, 22, 190, 202
    climate change and, 54–55, 207
    global, 21, 22
    growth of, 10
    infrastructure for, 190
    middle-class, 95
    popular, 9
    US, 21, 22, 23
containment, 155, 284
contraception, 84. *See also* reproductive rights
control, 185. *See also* social control; surveillance
    vs. connectivity, 9–10
    cyber sovereignty and, 192
corn, 242
counterinsurgency strategies, 165, 166
COVID-19, 71, 95, 123, 184, 248
crime prevention, 31. *See also* social control;
    surveillance
crises, global, 2. *See also* climate change
crisis, perceptions of, 25
cultural heritage, of US, 251–252, 267
cultural identity, 252, 269
cultural imperialism, 217
culture wars, 5, 121, 143, 178, 252, 268, 269, 275
cyber sovereignty, 185, 189, 191–192
cybersecurity, 263
cyberspace. *See also* digital globalization
    control of, 185

D

data flows, 189–190, 191
debt, 301
    BRI and, 153, 154, 155
    Millennials/Gen Z and, 142
defense, 29. *See also* military; security
    repurposing assets of to security, 125
    vs. security, 30–31, 47, 126
defense spending, 159
de-globalization, 190
demand, 4, 22, 23, 190, 201–204. *See also*
    consumption
democracy, 1
    income and, 10
    middle class and, 141, 298
    potential failure of, 11
    race and, 115
    recession of, 30, 165, 173, 291
    survival of, 124
    threats to, 94, 117

democratization, 95
demographic dividend, 87
    in Africa, 94, 100
    in Arab world, 100
    in China, 94, 247
    education and, 88
    in India, 94, 100, 102
    in Japan, 94
    in Middle East, 94
    in US, 286
demographic transitions, 2–3, 84, 91 (fig), 154. *See*
    also age; aging, demographic; Asia
demographics, 61, 120
Deng Xiaoping, 9
Denmark, 76, 77
dependency ratio, 87
Diamond, Jared, 59–61
dictatorship, 132. *See also* authoritarianism
digital flows, 1–2, 9
digital globalization, 30, 148, 184–185, 189,
    190–191, 192, 261. *See also* surveillance;
    technology
    cyber sovereignty and, 191–192
    establishing structure and rules for, 191
    5G networks, 177, 178, 180 (fig), 263
    lack of understanding of, 190
    social credit scores, 173
    US and, 225–226
diplomacy, debt-financed, 155. *See also* Belt and
    Road Initiative (BRI)
diplomatic unilateralism, 183
disconnectedness, 49, 101. *See also* integration
District of Columbia, 285
diversity, 117. *See also* race
droughts, 65–66, 237, 238, 243

E

East-West relations
    conflict dynamics, 89–90
    heartland theory, 160
East-West world, 59, 61
economic determinism, 61
economic growth, 17, 141
economic interdependency, 203
economic models, 93, 95–96. *See also* capitalism;
    communism
economic nationalism, 10, 120, 247
economies, developing/rising, 1, 17. *See also* China;
    India
economy, global, 16, 22
education, demographic dividend and, 88
elder share, 107–108. *See also* aging, demographic
elections, US, 262–263, 290, 291
electric vehicles (EVs), 202, 231
enemy, peer, 29–31, 46
enemy archetypes, 23
energy crisis, 201
energy resources, 76, 80 (fig), 201, 229–231. *See*
    also oil
    BRI and, 152
    hydropower, 238
    Russia and, 41, 230, 231
energy self-sufficiency, 159
Enriquez, Juan, 267, 268, 269

China's, 151, 152
integration with, 85
Latin America and, 248
regionalized, 190, 247–249
vertical integration. *See* North-South integration
Vietnam war, 45
Vince, Gaia, 55, 56, 65
violence, 292. *See also* conflict; wars
virtual reality (VR), 171, 261, 262, 264
viruses, 70–71
voters, Latino, 292

W

Wallace-Wells, David, 54
Waltz, Kenneth, 25–26
War on Drugs, 31, 198, 219, 223, 252, 285
wars. *See also* conflict, civil; Global War on Terror (GWOT)
    definition of, 25
    forms of, 25. *see also* nuclear weapons
    North vs. South in, 59
    superpowers and, 26
wars, proxy, 50
wars, small, 25–26, 29, 45
wars, state-on-state, 26. *See also* conflict, international
    avoiding, 203
    number of, 39, 43 (fig)
    rules of, 39–42
wars, subnational, 26, 39–40, 263. *See also* conflict, civil
wars, system-level, 26
Washington, George, 256
Washington Consensus, 130, 258
Washington Post, 301
water, 235–238, 239 (fig)
    agricultural flows and, 244
    climate change and, 237
    rights to, 238
    strategic importance of, 235
    in Western Hemisphere, 238
water shortages/insecurity, 65, 66, 161, 237, 238
"way of life," 289
wealth inequality, 11, 88
wealth transfer, climate change and, 69–70
weapons of mass destruction (WMD), 34. *See also* nuclear weapons
Western Hemisphere. *See also* Latin America; North-South integration; South America; *individual countries*
    capacity for hemispheric integration, 280–281
    energy self-sufficiency of, 232 (fig)

integrating, 299–300
lack of regional economic integration, 300
oil production in, 229
population of, 297
racial heritage in, 251, 253
religion in, 252–253
supply chains in, 248
US expansionism in, 256
water in, 236–237, 238
wheat, 242–243
White Christian nationalism, 120, 292, 293
White majority-minority status, 120
White minority rule, in US, 289
White privilege, fear of loss of, 121
winning, definition of, 138
WMD (weapons of mass destruction), 34. *See also* nuclear weapons
women. *See also* fertility rate
    education and, 88
    empowerment of, 50, 89
    in traditional societies, 89
workforce
    climate change and, 64
    India's, 162
    labor surplus, 85, 88, 94
World Bank, 16, 209
World Food Programme, 65
World Trade Organization (WTO), 17, 18
World War II, 9, 94, 160
    causes of, 11, 143
    deaths in, 25
WTO (World Trade Organization), 17, 18

X

xenophobia, 5, 84, 90, 123, 165, 198, 276, 279
Xi Jinping, 3, 96, 132, 202. *See also* China
    goals of, 152
    irredentist impulses, 135
    national rejuvenation plan, 100
    in superpower brand wars, 126

Y

Yan Xuetong, 131–132
Yglesias, Matthew, 297
youth
    America's brand and, 269
    control of, 173
youth bulge. *See also* aging, demographic
    India's, 94
    instability and, 2, 84
    in Middle Earth, 89

ABOUT THE AUTHOR

 **Thomas P.M. Barnett** has worked in US national security circles since the end of the Cold War, starting with the Department of Navy's premier think tank, the Center for Naval Analyses. He then served as professor at the U.S. Naval War College, where he assisted Vice Admiral Arthur Cebrowski—the father of "network-centric warfare." After 9/11, Barnett joined Cebrowski's new Office of Force Transformation in the Office of the Secretary of Defense as his Assistant for Strategic Futures. In that capacity, he developed an influential PowerPoint brief on globalization and international security (see his 2005 TED Talk), which later morphed into a *New York Times*–bestselling book, *The Pentagon's New Map* (2004). Barnett extended his "Pentagon's New Map" series with the volumes *Blueprint for Action* (2005) and *Great Powers* (2009).

Upon leaving government service in 2005, Dr. Barnett worked for a series of technology start-ups exploring cognitive artificial intelligence, crowdsourced wargaming, and enterprise resilience. He worked for years as a journalist, both as a contributing editor at *Esquire* and a Scripps News syndicated columnist. Barnett was likewise a visiting strategist at the Oak Ridge National Laboratory and later a senior research fellow at the Beijing-based Knowfar Institute for Strategic & Defence Studies.

Thomas presently serves as principal business strategist at Throughline, a Washington, DC–based enterprise design and strategy firm that serves the US national security community, major US government agencies, multinational corporations, and nonprofits. Dr. Barnett's 2023 book, *America's New Map*, is a unique product of the author's deep collaboration with the firm's senior leadership, graphic artists, and content designers.

Over his career, Thomas has generated more than five hundred publications and has delivered more than one thousand speeches across all fifty US states and approximately fifty countries. Dr. Barnett holds both a PhD in political science from Harvard University and season tickets from the Green Bay Packers.